THE COMING OF THE *COMET*

THE COMING OF THE *COMET*

The Rise and Fall of the Paddle Steamer

Nick Robins

Seaforth
PUBLISHING

TITLE PAGE: *Medway Queen* (1924) off Southend Pier Head, August 1962. (AUTHOR)

FRONT ENDPAPERS: The Detroit & Cleveland Navigation Company's majestic Great Lakes steamer *City of Cleveland* (1907).

REAR ENDPAPERS: *Royal Eagle* (1932) on wartime duties as an ack-ack ship.

Copyright © Nick Robins 2012

First published in Great Britain in 2012 by
Seaforth Publishing,
Pen & Sword Books Ltd,
47 Church Street,
Barnsley S70 2AS

www.seaforthpublishing.com

British Library Cataloguing in Publication Data
A catalogue record for this book is available from the British Library

ISBN 978 1 84832 134 2

Designed by Neil Sayer
Printed in China through Printworks Int.Ltd.

CONTENTS

Preface   VI

1   *Comet* to Cunard: early days of steam   1

2   Wooden paddle steamers on the High Seas   15

3   The challenge of the Pacific Ocean: 28
    more wooden ships

4   Technical evolution: engineers and architects   42

5   Mostly iron ships   56

6   The fast, the curious and the furious   70

7   Inland waters: some specialist roles   85

8   Passage west: on the Great Lakes   101

9   The saloon steamer and *Princess Alice*   117

10 Of tugs, tenders and trawlers   131

11 Military duties for brave little ships   145

12 The excursion role   157

13 In the wake of *Comet* and *Clermont*   171

    References   183

    Index   184

PREFACE

Robert Fulton commissioned his *Steam Boat* on the Hudson River at New York in the USA in September 1807, and Henry Bell had *Comet* running on the Clyde in Scotland in August 1812. Now, 200 years on, the paddle steamer is a maritime curiosity with enthusiast groups keen on preserving those few steamers that remain. Fulton and Bell led the world towards steam navigation, as wooden-hulled paddle steamers soon crossed the Atlantic and in due course also the Pacific. They finally stood down from transpacific duties in 1877. The paddle steamer supported coastal services for passengers and goods in the early days when the stagecoach was the only alternative. Paddlers provided trade routes far and wide, depending at first on sailing colliers to supply coaling stations along the journey. The paddle steamer provided the opportunity for commerce and trade following the Industrial Revolution, but in those early days it was generally the merchants who took the profit, not the shipowner. Paddle steamers and sternwheel river steamers were also critical to the development of the western states of the USA, and developing the cotton exports from the Mississippi and Ohio catchments. Paddle steamers provided the vehicle for trade on the Irrawaddy in Burma and on the Rhine in Europe, in fact everywhere that a river or lake provided a highway for a shallow-draft paddler to navigate.

Paddle steamer development peaked with the mighty 22-knot Great Lakes steamers and the fast day steamers on the Dover Strait and elsewhere. Gradually overtaken by the screw-propelled steamer, it fell to the paddler to pursue specialist roles in which manoeuvrability and shallow draft were key. Paddle tugs and the excursion trade occupied many paddle steamers for the first 60 years of the twentieth century, while tourist roles were adopted on lakes and rivers once rail, road and eventually air connections had otherwise put the waterway traffic out of business.

This is the story of the evolution of the paddle steamer, merchant and military, the naval architects who designed the steamers, the men who operated them, the machinery with which they had to cope, the social aspects of the paddle steamer and even the economics of its operation. The book draws on historical records and writings of the day; the graphic description by author Charles Dickens of 'Winter-North-Atlantic' aboard PS *Britannia*, for example, is inspirational.

The text has benefited greatly from critical review by Ian Ramsay and Donald Meek. Ian also contributed significantly to Chapter 4. The helpful guidance given throughout by Seaforth Publishing is much appreciated. As always, I am grateful for help from a number of diverse sources, particularly the Alpena State Library, Missouri, that has greatly improved the breadth of this book.

Dr Nick Robins
Crowmarsh, Oxfordshire

1 *COMET* TO CUNARD: EARLY DAYS OF STEAM

… It has been quite correctly stated that the wealth of Britain in the nineteenth century was due to the exploitation of the British Empire. But a major contributory factor was the ease of communication provided by steam during the aptly named Industrial Revolution, and it was both the short- and long-distance paddle steamers that provided the main form of transportation during this period.

From *Paddle Steamers* by Bernard Cox

Chalk boards inscribed 'Round the bay and back for tea – weather and other circumstances permitting' were once part of the seaside scene. They are less familiar nowadays, when the attractions of overseas sunshine holidays take people farther and farther from home, but the steamer trip was once the annual highlight for mum, dad and the kids. Although trips are still on offer from a variety of seaside towns, the once ubiquitous and smoky paddle steamer has long been displaced by motor launches, catamarans and other energy-efficient vessels. The concept, however, remains the same; to put to sea to view the coast and perhaps its resident wildlife, to enjoy the excitement of the journey and to sample the

delights of shipboard food, drink and entertainment – should the weather remain kind. In the good old days the steamer returned the family to the pier in time for supper at the boarding house, whereas the modern family disembarks and returns to the car to make the journey home.

One seagoing paddle steamer still graces the British coast in summer time. *Waverley*, operated by Waverley Excursions, offers a variety of long and short day cruises from a disparate catalogue of departure points. During the season the steamer's base drifts from Scotland through west coast England and Wales to the south coast and the Thames. Built in 1947 to operate from the London and North Eastern Railway's shal-

'Weather and other circumstances permitting'. An early Edwardian view of Bournemouth Pier with *Majestic* (1901) and *Brodick Castle* (1878) preparing for 'trips round the bay'.

One of the more successful preservation projects is *Waverley* (1947), which still graces Britain's coasts each summer. (AUTHOR)

Medway Queen (1924) in the Medway before the Second World War.

low water base at Craigendoran for the Lochs Long, Goil and Lomond Tour, *Waverley* has been considerably modified, with many structural and engineering components now replaced to satisfy both modern-day regulations at sea and to upgrade equipment before it should fail. A programme of rebuilding *Medway Queen*, one of the former Thames favourites, is also under way, but whether it will emerge from the process as *Medway Queen* 1920s-style or become *Medway Queen* of 2013 or when-

ever remains to be seen.

Although it is easy to visualise the paddle steamer as the excursion steamer of old, this role was actually a niche adopted as other roles fell away. Of course, all early steamers were single-cylinder wooden-hulled paddle steamers, and their initial development was a strangely Scottish and American affair. The paddle steamer developed rapidly from Henry Bell's deployment of his novel steamship *Comet* on the Clyde in 1812 (named after the appearance of Hal-

ley's Comet that year), with its inaugural trial trip from Glasgow to Greenock in August 1812, to the first paddle steamship crossing of the Atlantic and the eventual formation of the Cunard Steamship Company. In the journal *Yesteryear Transport*, 1979, R K Davies wrote:

> When in 1812 Henry Bell brought together a steam engine and a small wooden ship's hull he not only revolutionised transport but changed the course of history. To realise what an impact this seemingly obvious application of the new steam engine had to a boat, it must be remembered that at the beginning of the nineteenth century there were no railways, and very few usable roads. Anywhere that was not near navigable water was severely inhibited in the development of almost all forms of real trade.

Bell had been a builder and engineer before he became proprietor of the Baths Hotel at Helensburgh. The initial role of *Comet* was to bring the punters to the Baths. He was a man full of ideas, although few actually came to fruition, but he never abandoned the vision of the steamship. He was aboard *Comet* when it was wrecked in 1820, but he survived and died at Helensburgh ten years later, aged 63.

While Henry Bell is widely credited as the force behind the first commercially successful steamship, that accolade rightly belongs to Americans Robert Fulton and John Stevens. Fulton used the earlier designs of American John Fitch, working with a triple screw propeller, and later work by James Rumsey of Virginia to design the 133ft-long paddle driven *Steam Boat* (never officially named *Clermont* but often referred to as such). He supervised its construction on the East River at New York. It received a British-built Boulton & Watt engine that drove its side paddles to give the ship a speed of about 4 knots. *Steam Boat* was commissioned in 1807 and was sent along the Hudson River to Albany and back. It was found to be so unstable that modifications delayed

A replica of Henry Bell's *Comet* (1962) at Port Glasgow. (JIM MACINTOSH)

its next voyage to Albany until 1809, when she was renamed *North River Steam Boat*. Still et al, in *History of the Ship*, describe Fulton thus:

> In 1803 Robert Fulton, who had gone to Great Britain originally to study painting, became extremely interested in mechanical and engineering innovations, including steamboats. Although Fulton was not an inventor and certainly should not be put in the same category as Fitch, Rumsey and other experimenters, he nevertheless deserves recognition for convincing various individuals that they could assemble a successful steam vessel.

John Stevens was watching and learning while Fulton's steamer was being put to the test. Stevens developed the steam paddler further with *Phoenix*, which was launched in 1808 and was vastly superior. It was a real pioneer, as it sailed from New York to Philadelphia in gale-force conditions and was then deployed as a passenger carrier on the Delaware River over the subsequent six years.

The first deployment of a paddle steamer in a military role took place even before Henry Bell's *Comet* had taken to the water. This first military paddle steamer was commissioned in 1812 to defend New York

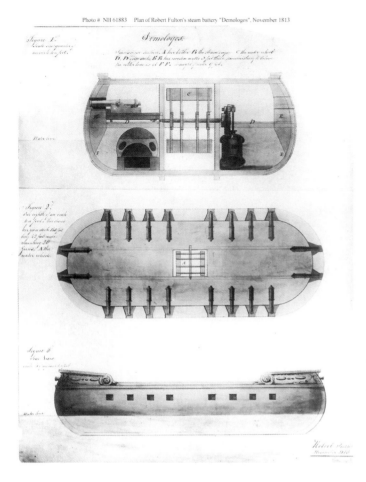

Photo # NH 61883 Plan of Robert Fulton's steam battery "Demologos", November 1813

Plans signed by Robert Fulton, in November 1813, of the armed battery *Demologos* (1812).

Bell and Fulton. In due course John Robertson supplied Bell with an engine and shipbuilder John Wood a hull. Indeed, the role adopted by Bell was similar to that of Fulton, as both inspired others to create their vision. Bell announced at the launch of *Comet*:

> Wherever there is a river four feet of depth of water through the world, there will speedily be a steamboat. They will go over the seas to Egypt, to India, to China, to America, Canada, Australia, everywhere, and they will never be forgotten among the nations.

Unhappily, at that stage Symington sued Bell for breach of his patent for steam navigation that he had filed in 1801. Bell counterclaimed with a libel suit and the matter was dropped. Indeed, Symington had been involved with steam navigation even earlier than 1801, as Craig Osborne explains in his book on Henry Bell:

> There is a tombstone in Old Cumnock Churchyard bearing the following inscription: 'In memory of James Taylor, the inventor of steam navigation, who died at Cumnock, 18 September 1825, and was interred'. James Taylor … was involved in drawing up plans for a steam engine to drive a vessel, and William Symington was employed to put the plans into effect. On 14 October 1788, a vessel was fitted with a steam engine upon the deck which moved the vessel at the rate of five miles an hour across Dalswinton Loch … Taylor's first engine, in the Science Museum, is labelled 'The parent engine of steam navigation'.

against attack by the English during the two-year Anglo-American war. Robert Fulton was asked about the feasibility of a steam-powered battery that could be deployed in the harbour. The result was the steam paddle-driven armoured battery *Fulton I*, later renamed *Demologos*, which had a single-cylinder engine and a single paddle wheel concealed from enemy guns in a tunnel along the centreline. Alas, it arrived on station too late to fire in anger.

Robert Fulton had earlier visited Scotland to see William Symington's prototype paddle steamer *Charlotte Dundas*, developed with James Taylor, who designed the engine. Converted from a horse-drawn barge in 1801, this vessel had various engine configurations and was successful as a steam tug, although vested interests prevented it from being used in that role. The engineering skills of Symington and Taylor inspired both

But if Bell, Symington, Taylor, Fulton and Stevens were the key founders of commercial steam navigation, men such as Robert Napier and his older cousin, David Napier, were the founders of marine engineering. Born in Dumbarton in 1791, Robert Napier was the son of a blacksmith and in due course was apprenticed to his father.

When he was 24 he set up in business making land engines and put David Elder in charge of his engine works. David's son, John Elder, was to become the pioneer in compound expansion engines and founder of what later became the Fairfield shipbuilding works on the Clyde.

The early development of steam navigation in the UK was driven by a small group of Scottish business and engineering entrepreneurs whose names, like Napier and Elder, are inextricably linked. George Burns, for example, a famous pioneer steamship owner, witnessed the inaugural departure of Henry Bell's *Comet* from Glasgow and was at once converted to the way of the steamship. Other converts were brought into the steamship circle, and, as new and larger steamers quickly emerged on the Clyde, Bell turned his back on the competition and pioneered *Comet* on the west-coast route up to Fort William via the Crinan Canal in August 1819. Thus he needed an agent to look after his affairs in Glasgow. The man Bell appointed was Lewis MacLellan. MacLellan was hugely impressed by the new steamer, and had persuaded diverse interests in the Irish trade to merge as the Glasgow, Dublin & Londonderry Steam Packet Company. Among those interests were some familiar ship-owning names: Alex A Laird & Sons, Thos Cameron & Company and McConnell & Laird. The first steamers for the merged company were delivered in 1816; *Britannia*, almost twice the length of *Comet*, and the slightly shorter *Waterloo*.

The first steamship on the Thames, *Richmond*, started in service in 1814. It plied slowly between Hammersmith and Richmond and was seen off within a year by a combination of the Great Frost, when the river froze over, and a defiant stand by the Thames Watermen, fearful that the 'dangerous and generally unreliable' paddle boat would ultimately undermine their livelihood. *Richmond* was followed in 1815 by a down-river steamer called *Marjory* which had been built on the Clyde and sailed to London via the Forth and Clyde Canal. It operated for Captain Cortis between Wapping Old Stairs and Milton, just below Gravesend, so as not to offend the Watermen's right to operate the Long Ferry, with their traditional sails and oars, to Gravesend itself. *Marjory* was scheduled for three two-day return trips per week, carrying passengers for eight shillings in the main cabin and four shillings in the fore cabin. *Marjory* missed numerous trips while its engineer tinkered with valves and adjusted levers and rods, but the travelling public was more than prepared to excuse the steamer's wayward temperament.

But sights were already set on long-distance voyaging. The first transatlantic crossing by a steamship took place in 1819, when Captain Moses Rogers, who had earlier sailed the *Phoenix* to Philadelphia, took the American-built and -owned *Savannah* from New York to Liverpool and via various north European ports to St Petersburg in Russia and back. Built as a sailing ship, it was bought before completion by the Savannah Steam Ship Company, formed by a group of entrepreneurs in Savannah shortly after the steamer *Charleston* had sailed into town in 1817. Space for the machinery was made by removing the second deck forward of the main mast. *Savannah* had an inclined crosshead engine driving 16ft-diameter collapsible paddle wheels. The tiny 350-tons burthen auxiliary steamer took 25 days to cross the Atlantic but used its engines for only eight of them. For the rest of the voy-

Savannah (1819), converted from a sailing ship to prove the concept of the deep-water paddle steamer, left Savannah for Liverpool on 22 May 1819, a day still celebrated in the USA as National Maritime Day.

age better speed could be made under sail, with the paddles shipped in board. The engine was direct-acting and had a massive 40in-diameter low-pressure cylinder. On return to America the ship was converted to a sailing packet, having nevertheless proved the concept of long-distance voyaging under steam.

A second long-distance experiment followed in 1825, when the Honourable East India Company commissioned *Enterprise* for an experimental sailing from Falmouth on 16 August 1821, which eventually arrived at Calcutta on 7 December. But the idea of steam was rejected, as the passage time of 103 days was no better than that of the company's wooden-walled sailing ships, and, like *Savannah*, only about half the days at sea were spent under steam. The East India Company reaffirmed its view on steam when the paddle steamer *Hugh Lindsay*, actually an auxiliary steam sailing ship, was constructed in Bombay in 1829 with a view to running between its home port and Suez. This little vessel was barely adequate, but did usually manage a single voyage across the Indian Ocean each year until the steam frigates *Atalanta* and *Berenice* were delivered to maintain the service in 1836.

The early steamers are, at best, described as fiery and erratic. They had overcomplicated engines and unreliable boilers operating at modest pressures, but they did provide an element of consistent timetabling which no sailing ship could ever maintain. As boiler design improved and engine construction became better founded, so more powerful engines allowed larger hulls and better resistance to being overwhelmed in a cross sea. As with any new technology, progress was rapid, and in only a few short decades the paddle steamer had became the mainstay of much of Britain's trade, both at home and overseas.

One other piece of new technology was tested and proven in these early days: the iron hull. Iron hulls were not set to replace wood in general use until the 1840s and 1850s in the UK, and later still in North America, where wood was plentiful and iron was expensive. Nevertheless, the little iron-hulled paddle steamer *Aaron Manby*, equipped with a Bell engine, was taken overland in sections from the Aaron Manby ironworks near Stafford, Staffordshire, and assembled at Rotherhithe in London. By 1822 it was ready to begin a service between the Thames and up the Seine to Paris – until Parisian merchants bought it for local excursion duties. *Aaron Manby* was 120ft long, flat bottomed and devoid of any

Earl of Liverpool (1824) was one of the original fleet members of the GSN fleet. (DP WORLD P&O HERITAGE COLLECTION)

Leith (1837), complete with gun ports, crossing the bows of tradition. (OIL PAINTING BY J SPURLING)

sheer, a configuration better suited to the sheltered waters of the Seine rather than La Manche. *Aaron Manby* clearly enjoyed success on the Seine, remaining in service until 1855.

In 1824 the General Steam Navigation Company of London (GSN) was incorporated with a modest fleet of mostly second-hand steamers. By the late 1830s steamers such as *Leith* were typical, still ready for trouble with an array of gun ports, and occupied on the crack London to Leith coastal service. Other similar steamers ran to a variety of European destinations.

George Burns, perhaps Henry Bell's very first convert, was also an active shipowner at this time. The foundation of the Burns Line is described by Ernest Reader in an article first published in *Sea Breezes* in August 1949:

In 1824 the [Glasgow] produce firm of James and George Burns became sufficiently interested in shipping to lay the foundation of the Burns Line. At this period the Glasgow and Liverpool trade was largely in the hands of three companies each operating six rantapikes [fast sailing packets]. When the Glasgow agency of one of the operating companies, Mathie and Theakstone, fell vacant,

the Burns brothers took over the agency . . . They soon came to the conclusion that they must adopt steam propulsion or be driven out of the field. The actual date of the first association of the Burns brothers with steam is not definite, but it is believed that their first steamship service was operated by a chartered vessel, the then new 76-ton packet *Ayr*, built by Wood of Port Glasgow. She operated between Glasgow and ports in Ayrshire and Galloway.

It was not until 1829 that the Burns brothers put steamers on to the Liverpool route in place of sailing smacks. This was not without difficulty, as Reader recounts:

Unexpected difficulties arose and had to be overcome. Friday was the most suitable sailing day from an economic viewpoint but not from that of superstitious sailors. To sail on a day other than Friday would mean the breaking of the Sabbath, to which George Burns was equally averse. Further Mr Mathie, at Liverpool, pointed out that the Friday sailing would not synchronise with the local canal traffic. In desperation he wrote that it would be better to sail on a Saturday and provide chaplains, in which case every objection would be satisfied. Burns took the suggestion seriously and went as far as to say that he and his brother would share the whole expense of the experiment. The wits of Broomielaw jeered at Captain Hepburn and his 'steam chapel', but the custom became firmly established and remained until in 1843 the secession of the Free Church from the Established Church of Scotland created such a dearth of ministers that ship's chaplains could no longer be obtained.

The year 1838 was a momentous one for the paddle steamer. Two steamers raced across the Atlantic to New York, where they arrived within two hours of each other to a tremendous welcome. *Sirius* sailed from Queenstown (Cobh) for the British & American Steam Navigation Company on 5 April, and Brunel's *Great Western* left the Bristol Channel three days later. The New York *Evening Post* (25 April 1838) excitedly reported:

> The arrival yesterday of the steam packets *Sirius* and *Great Western* caused in this city that stir of eager curiosity and speculation which every new enterprise of any magnitude awakens in this excitable community. The battery was thronged yesterday morning with thousands of persons to look on the *Sirius*, which had crossed the Atlantic by the power of steam, as she lay anchored near at hand, gracefully shaped, painted black all over, the water around her covered with boats filled with people passing and repassing, some conveying and some bringing back those who desired to go aboard.
>
> When the *Great Western*, at a later hour was seen ploughing her way through the waters towards the city, the crowd became more numerous, and the whole bay to a distance was dotted with boats, as if everything that could be manned by oars had left its place at the wharves. It would seem, in fact, a kind of triumphal entry.

While *Sirius*, built for North Sea and Irish Sea ferry duties, had been chartered from the Saint George Steam Packet Company (Dublin) for the single voyage, *Great Western* remained on the Atlantic for the next six years, successfully completing some 70 return voyages. It was joined in this early trade by vessels such as *Royal William*, *British Queen*, *President*, *Liverpool* and *Great Britain*.

Meanwhile, George Burns met David McIver, a Scot who had set up business in Liverpool, while Burns was buying the new steamer *Enterprise* in the late 1830s. McIver had paid a deposit on the ship, which was to inaugurate sailings for him between Liverpool and Glasgow, when Burns marched in, cash in hand, and took the ship from under McIver's nose. But from this introductory spat was spawned a much greater venture, the establishment of the prestigious Liverpool-based North American Royal Mail Steam Packet Company. Contracted to carry the mails fortnightly between Liverpool, Halifax and Boston, the new company was soon rebranded as none other than the Cunard Line.

As stated in the author's history of British cruise ships (see references):

> Although Samuel Cunard is generally credited with the foundation of the Cunard Line in 1839, his acknowledgement might not have been so widely given but for the distinctiveness of his name. The idea of a fortnightly steam sailing to and from North America was certainly that of Cunard. However, co-signatories of the contract with the British Government that established the original British and North American Royal Mail Steam Packet Company were the Scottish ship-owners David McIver and George Burns. McIver and Burns were also responsible for much of the initial capital outlay that created the company. A third Scot was instrumental in the success of the company by recognising the physical difficulties of maintaining a twice monthly service and in specifying ships that were capable of the

job, both in size and power and in number. This was the famous Clyde engineer Robert Napier:

At the age of 52, having developed various shipping threads, including mail services to Bermuda and Quebec, he [Cunard] followed a vision to London in which he foresaw three small paddle steamers maintaining a fortnightly mail service between England and Halifax. Although Robert Napier agreed to build the three ships for £30,000 each at a meeting at his house, Napier soon realised that larger and more powerful vessels would be needed and that a four-ship service would be required. Cunard was devastated at this news, for now he already held the Admiralty mail contract with a start date scheduled for summer 1840. But worse still, Cunard had no more funds to expand the capital required to set the company up.

Introductions to both George Burns and David McIver soon guaranteed 50 per cent of the capital outlay for the four larger ships under a contract signed in May 1839. Glasgow businessmen were offered £100 shares in units of £5,000, the first taker being Mr William Connal, who was persuaded by George Burns and responded simply by saying: 'I know nothing of steam navigation, but if you think well of it I'll join you'. Eventually there were 29 Glasgow businessmen who invested alongside McIver and Burns to form The Glasgow Proprietory in the British and North American Steam Packets. Samuel Cunard was now in a position to confirm his orders with Robert Napier, who in turn instructed four shipbuilders to start work on the vessels: the yard of Robert Duncan to build *Britannia*, John Wood, who had earlier built the hull of *Comet* for Henry Bell, to build *Acadia*, Charles Wood *Caledonia* and Robert Steele *Columbia*.

The launch of the first ship, *Britannia*, was described in a glowing accolade of both the ship and the intended transatlantic service in the *Glasgow Herald*:

She is to be propelled by two engines, each of 220 horse power and when put to sea will be succeeded by three other ships ... to carry the mails and passengers between Liverpool and North America, a scheme, it will be remembered which was originated by the Hon S Cunard, of Halifax, Nova Scotia, who with a small party of influential gentlemen in Glasgow, is associated with this undertaking.

The vessel's hull and machinery are constructed under the direction and superintendence of Robert Napier, of the Vulcan Foundry, Glasgow, and as we mention this gentleman's name as being connected with such a work, we give a guarantee that when completed nothing better will be found in the United Kingdom.

Samuel Cunard 1787–1865

Samuel Cunard was born to a large family on 21 November 1971. His father Abraham was a carpenter at the Halifax Naval Dockyard. Samuel became a lively, intelligent child who attended Halifax Grammar School with his brother William. His mother, Margaret, did all she could to stimulate and encourage the boys' learning. Samuel was fascinated by ships and the sea, and the highlight of each month, between April and November, was the arrival at King's Wharf of the English mail ship. Samuel started work as a clerk but soon moved to Boston to take up a job in a shipbroker's office. When he was just 20 years old he returned home to persuade his father to join him in founding Abraham Cunard & Son. They purchased the brig *Margaret* and with a capital of just £200 established a coastal cargo service from Halifax. The

Anglo-American war of 1812 allowed Cunard to fly the neutral flag of Canada. Business was clearly good because they soon bought the captured American sailing ship *White Oak* and advertised its sailing for London with 'good accommodation for passengers'.

Memorial to Samuel Cunard at Halifax, Nova Scotia. (DR HUGH DAN MACLENNAN)

At the age of 25 Samuel Cunard won the English mail contract for the 'conveyance by sailing vessel of HM mails between Halifax and Newfoundland, Boston and Bermuda'. At 27 he married Susan Duffus, the daughter of a respected merchant in Halifax. When his father died in 1823 A Cunard & Son was rebranded S Cunard & Company. He now had interests in merchant banking, timber and a tea agency as well as shipping. His business commitments often took him away from home and it was left to Susan to maintain the home and bring up their children. Rex Norfolk in an article in *Sea Breezes*, November 1987, writes:

She insisted on daily prayers, daily Bible readings and regular attendance at church. Her ninth child, Elizabeth, was born in January 1828, but she herself died ten days later. Samuel, with his children, became a regular attendee at St George's Church, Brunswick Street.

In 1830 Samuel and two of his brothers established the Quebec & Halifax Steam Navigation Company to trade between these same two ports. Not content with bringing steam to the Canadian domestic trade, in 1833 his brand new paddle steamer *Royal William* became only the third steamer to cross the Atlantic. This introduction to the transatlantic trade made Samuel Cunard appreciate the massive potential that America now offered as it picked itself up and enjoyed demographic growth accompanied by the development of wealth-creating industry and commerce. It was with this background that Samuel sailed to England to meet Charles Wood, the Secretary of the Admiralty, and to befriend the successful marine engineer Robert Napier. In due course the Cunard Line was born in collaboration with George Burns and David McIver under the technical guidance of Napier.

The success of the Cunard service connecting Liverpool with Halifax and Boston ultimately made Cunard a household name. The Cunard brand is still in use today by the Carnival Group of cruise ship companies and is still synonymous with good, solid and reliable ideals.

Rex Norfolk wrote of Samuel Cunard:

Samuel Cunard was governed by principle of caution, care, good service and plain food. He was a sound and able man and the company he pioneered established a fine reputation for reliability, its motto being 'Speed, Comfort and Safety'. . .

In 1859 Samuel Cunard, whose ships had been used in the Crimean War . . . and in the Indian Mutiny of 1857, was made a Baronet. He died in London on 28 April 1865 at the age of 77.

Fortunately both for Glasgow and the Clyde, the ships were indeed the focus of excellence the *Glasgow Herald* promised. Samuel Cunard had written to David Napier earlier, stating:

You have no idea the prejudice of some of our English [ship] builders. I have had several offers from Liverpool and this place [London] and when I have replied that I have contracted in Scotland they invariably say 'You will neither have substantial work nor completed on time'. The Admiralty has assured me that the boats will be as good as if completed in this country and have assured me that you will keep to time.

The faith displayed in Glasgow and its men both by Samuel Cunard and his client, the Admiralty, was, of course, well repaid by a reliable four-ship service to Halifax and Boston. The Cunard association with the Clyde remained until the end, with nearly all its mainline steamers built on the Clyde and calls by its secondary steamers maintained in competition with local Scottish passenger companies, notably the Allan Line, Anchor Line and the Donaldson Line. Indeed, all Cunard ships were registered at Glasgow until 1878, when it adopted Liverpool, then its centre of operations, as its base.

The four Cunarders were state of the art but were hugely inefficient. Fitted with side-lever engines of 740 indicated horsepower, they each had a speed of about 10 knots, but consumed 38 tons of coal per day or nearly 5lb of coal per indicated horsepower per hour. The bunkers were correspondingly large and allowed the ships to leave port with 640 tons of coal on board. Frank Bowen in *A Century of Atlantic Travel: 1830-1930*, commented:

They were two-decked ships, the upper deck having the officer's cabins, galley, bakery and cow house, while on the main deck were two dining saloons, the accommodation for one hundred and fifteen cabin passengers and all the other

necessary fittings for a passenger ship. Only cabin passengers were carried, the emigrants of that day having no alternative to the sailing ships. In addition the *Britannia* and her sisters carried two hundred and twenty-five tons of cargo, all at special rates.

Author Charles Dickens, after a night in the Adelphi Hotel ashore in Liverpool, begged to differ with the Cunard agents' spin on the new ships, in his book *American Notes,* 1842:

I shall never forget the one-fourth serious and three-fourths comical astonishment, with which, on the morning of 3 January 1842, I opened the door of, and put my head into, a 'state-room' on board the *Britannia* steam-packet, 1,200 tons burthen per register, bound for Halifax and Boston, and carrying Her Majesty's mails.

That this state-room had been specially engaged for 'Charles Dickens, Esquire, and Lady,' was rendered sufficiently clear even to my scarred intellect by a very small manuscript, announcing the fact, which was pinned on a very flat quilt, covering a very thin mattress, spread like a surgical plaster on a most inaccessible shelf. But that this was the state-room concerning which Charles Dickens, Esquire, and Lady, had held daily and nightly conferences for at least four months preceding: that this

Britannia (1840) leaving Boston on 1 February 1844 after it had been ice-bound in the harbour and a channel had been cut in the ice for its departure. (*THE ILLUSTRATED LONDON NEWS*)

could by any possibility be that small snug chamber of the imagination, which Charles Dickens, Esquire, with the spirit of prophecy strong upon him, had always foretold would contain at least one little sofa, and which his lady, with a modest yet most magnificent sense of its limited dimensions, had from the first opined would not hold more than two enormous portmanteaus in some odd corner out of sight (portmanteaus which could now no more be got in at the door, not to say stowed away, than a giraffe could be persuaded or forced into a flower-pot): that this utterly impracticable, thoroughly hopeless, and profoundly preposterous box, had the remotest reference to, or connection with, those chaste and pretty, not to say gorgeous little bowers, sketched by a masterly hand, in the highly varnished lithographic plan hanging up in the agent's counting-house in the city of London: that this room of state, in short, could be anything but a pleasant fiction and cheerful jest of the Captain's, invented and put in practice for the better relish and enjoyment of the real state-room presently to be disclosed; these were truths which I really could not, for the moment, bring my mind at all to bear upon or comprehend. And I sat down upon a kind of horsehair slab, or perch, of which there were two within; and looked, without any expression of countenance whatever, at some friends who had come on board with us, and who were crushing their faces into all manner of shapes by endeavouring to squeeze them through the small doorway.

The 30-year-old Dickens was more impressed by the culinary arrangements for the voyage:

and one party of men were 'taking in the milk,' or, in other words, getting the cow on board; and another were filling the icehouses to the very throat with fresh provisions; with butchers'-meat and garden-stuff, pale suckling-pigs, calves' heads in scores, beef, veal, and pork, and poultry out of all proportion . . .

And Dickens at sea:

The labouring of the ship in the troubled sea on this night I shall never forget. 'Will it ever be worse than this?' was a question I had often heard asked, when everything was sliding and bumping about, and when it certainly did seem difficult to comprehend the possibility of anything afloat being more disturbed, without toppling over and going down. But what the agitation of a steam-vessel is, on a bad winter's night in the wild Atlantic, it is impossible for the most vivid imagination to conceive. To say that she is flung down on her side in the waves, with her masts dipping into them, and that, springing up again, she rolls over on the other side, until a heavy sea strikes her with the noise of a hundred great guns, and hurls her back – that she stops, and staggers, and shivers, as though stunned, and then, with a violent throbbing at her heart, darts onward like a monster goaded into madness, to be beaten down, and battered, and crushed, and leaped on by the angry sea – that thunder, lightning, hail, and rain, and wind, are all in fierce contention for the mastery – that every plank has its groan, every nail its shriek, and every drop of water in the great ocean its howling voice – is nothing. To say that all is grand, and all appalling and horrible in the last degree, is nothing. Words cannot express it. Thoughts cannot convey it. Only a dream can call it up again, in all its fury, rage, and passion.

But despite Dickens's passion, the wooden-hulled paddle steamer had really come a long way since Henry Bell's pioneering efforts, although even the new Cunard quartet were heavy, cumbersome and difficult to handle in heavy weather. There were various incidents. *Britannia* was ice-bound at Halifax in January 1844 until the residents of the town cut a channel through the ice for its escape. Three years later it was aground in fog at Cape Race in southern Newfoundland. Sails were clewed, forward boilers emptied and passengers and all moveable items moved right aft so that engines at full astern shifted the vessel off the rocks into deep water. Captain Harrison considered his position and in the belief that the pumps could cope with the water 'making at about 14 inches per hour', set sail for St John's. A report in the *New York Commercial Advertiser* stated:

> St John's was some 50 miles north of us, but as the fog still continued there was no probability of getting into that port, and having full confidence of Captain Harrison's statement, that the ordinary pumps would keep the ship free . . . we arrived at Halifax on Friday morning where a survey was held, and the report was made . . . that the forefoot had been knocked off, her keel injured . . .

It was later found that the forward part of the keel was entirely gone, the bows were damaged and much of the copper sheathing needed to be replaced. But these little wooden steamers had conquered the Atlantic with a typical passage time to Halifax of just 10 days.

The paddle steamer had also brought with it a new era of seamanship, as R K Davies surmised in his article in *Yesteryear Transport, 1979:*

> For instance, a ship's bridge got its name from the bridge-like structure that straddled the paddle boxes of the early steamers so that the master could move easily from one side of the vessel to the other when manoeuvring in confined waters. Its elevated position also gave the best all-round view, making the old practice of controlling the ship from the stern where

all the sails could be seen, outdated. Another sailing ship practice that was soon to go was steering from the stern where the linkage from the wheel or tiller to the rudder was shortest. Mechanical and power connection from the newly found vantage on the bridge to the rudder at the stern soon became possible.

By 1840, just 28 years after the diminutive *Comet* first sailed across the Clyde to Helensburgh, the wooden-hulled paddle steamer had become a key part of both trade and defence. In many trades sail remained supreme. The famous Aberdeen Clippers were yet to be conceived, with ships such as *Cutty Sark* still to come off the drawing boards. Coastal traffic remained the province of sailing smacks, ketches and schooners well into the nineteenth century, with paddle steamers operating only in the summer months until boilers and engines could propel bigger and safer hulls to promote passenger confidence. The early steamers were expensive to operate and required regular replacement boilers, due to the requirement to use salt water feed when on passage, which resulted in a build-up of damaging scale, and persistent maintenance of engines and paddle floats alike. But confidence did build and passengers soon preferred the regularity of the steamer voyage rather than the vagaries of sail. By 1833, for example, 400,000 passengers were carried between London and Margate, and ten years later 18,000 used the steamer between Edinburgh and London while a million Londoners journeyed down the 'long ferry' to Gravesend each year.

But if the steamer was a success in Britain and Europe, it was becoming an even greater success in America. By 1848 America had 427,000 tons of steamboats compared with the 168,000 tons in Britain. In 1850 the Americans were building wooden paddle boats 420ft long. Although many were destroyed by fire, others lasted in service for over 50 years. At the pinnacle of seagoing paddle power and design were the

The largest of them all. Detroit & Cleveland Navigation Company's *Greater Buffalo* (1924) alongside at Detroit.

large and fast American coastal steamers exemplified by the Fall River Line's ships, such as the famous pair *Priscilla* and *Commonwealth* which operated in Long Island Sound. *Priscilla*, a massive 5,292 tons gross, was built in 1894, and the even larger *Commonwealth* was built in 1908. The ships carried 1,500 passengers on four passenger decks and had a service speed of 20 knots. Both ships lasted until the closure of the Long Island Sound service in 1937. The even larger and more luxurious paddle steamers *Greater Detroit* and *Greater Buffalo* were later built for use out of Detroit on Lake Erie (see Chapter 8). Indeed, these magnificent steamers made the contemporary crack British paddlers on the Dover Strait look like toys on a boating lake!

TABLE 1 Some record passages across the North Atlantic up to 1869, when screw propulsion finally outpaced the paddle wheel

Year	Steamer		Gross tons	Owners	From	To	Passage Days and hours	Average speed knots
1838	*Great Western*	Paddle	1,340	Great Western S N Co.	Bristol	New York	15 12	8.7
1840	*Acadia*	Paddle	1,154	Cunard	Liverpool	Halifax NS	11 4	9.3
1840	*Britannia*	Paddle	1,154	Cunard	Halifax NS	Liverpool	9 28	11.0
1845	*Cambria*	Paddle	1,422	Cunard	Liverpool	Halifax NS	9 21	10.7
1848	*America*	Paddle	1,825	Cunard	Liverpool	Halifax NS	9 0	11.7
1851	*Pacific*	Paddle	2,860	Collins (American)	New York	Liverpool	9 20	13.0
1851	*Baltic*	Paddle	2,860	Collins	Liverpool	New York	9 20	12.9
1852	*Arctic*	Paddle	2,860	Collins	New York	Liverpool	9 17	13.1
1856	*Persia*	Paddle	3,300	Cunard	New York	Queenstown	9 2	13.1
1863	*Scotia*	Paddle	3,871	Cunard	New York	Queenstown	8 1	14.2
1864	*Scotia*	Paddle	3,871	Cunard	Queenstown	New York	8 3	14.5
1869	*City of Brussels*	Screw	3,747	Inman	New York	Queenstown	7 20	14.7

2 WOODEN PADDLE STEAMERS ON THE HIGH SEAS

In 1850 Samuel Cunard's company found itself in direct competition with the American Collins Line, established by Israel Collins originally for the export of cotton from the southern states. At the behest of the Federal Government it won a mail subsidy out of five competing American-owned companies to try to break the British transatlantic monopoly. Collins was later to lose this favoured position to the American owned Ocean Steam Navigation Company, which had earlier won the north European US mail contract in 1847, with a nominal stop at Cowes, Isle of Wight, en route to Bremen in Germany. Ocean later lost its mail contract because it had provided only two steamers, not four as stipulated in the US mail contract (see Chapter 5). It deployed the wooden paddlers *Washington* and *Hermann*, built in 1847 and 1848 respec-

tively, but they were not a success and there were persistent complaints about poor on-board service. They were described in the media as 'the most ugly ships ever designed' as they had little sheer and blunt bows.

The withdrawal of the Ocean Steam Navigation Company provided an opportunity for Mortimer Livingston, a partner in a packet company serving both New York and Le Havre, to establish the New York & Havre Steam Packet Company. Offering alternative sailings to Bremen and Le Havre, this company commissioned the *Franklin* and *Humbolt* in 1850 and 1851 respectively. During 1853 and 1854 both steamers were wrecked, and they were later replaced by *Arago* in 1855 and *Fulton*, the latter then building for the Pacific Mail Steamship Company, although it had an almost identical hull configuration to *Arago*. Still et al de-

The *Arago* (1855), built at New York for the New York & Havre Steam Navigation Company, shown in 1864 in service with the Navy Department during the American Civil War.

The Collins Line steamer *Arctic* (1850) was built and owned at New York as one of four fast ships designed to break the British monopoly on the North Atlantic.

scribed *Arago* in *History of the Ship*:

> To improve safety further in heavy weather almost all of the *Arago's* accommodation had been placed below the spar deck. The main deck contained the first and second class cabins and dining saloon, and the berth deck contained quarters for the crew, additional cabins for passengers and space amidships designated for the vessel's machinery.

The two-ship service was popular with passengers and shippers alike. The company held its head high as Cunard and other companies' ships returned from the Crimean War to resume competitive business on the Atlantic. The end of the New York & Havre Steam Packet Company was hastened by the Civil War, when *Arago* and *Fulton* were taken up for service, one in the Navy Department, the other in the Quartermasters Corps in 1862.

But what of the Collins Line? Four wooden paddle steamers were built in 1849 at New York for the Collins Line: *Atlantic*, *Arctic*, *Baltic* and *Pacific*. They each had two side-lever engines, also built at New York, placed abreast of each other. The side-lever engine was unusual for an American-built ship, but the preferred walking-beam engine had a high centre of gravity, and two side-by-side could have been an unwarranted hazard in the North Atlantic. The engine cylinders were of 95in diameter and the stroke was 9ft. Each vessel was about 3,000 tons gross, and not only were they larger, but they were also

a little faster than any of the Cunarders of the day. They were designed with luxury in mind for their 200 first-class passengers, according to one contemporary report:

> marble topped tables, mirrors, paintings, thick carpets, carved and upholstered furniture, and not a few startling innovations – automatic signals from bridge to engine room and from state rooms to stewards quarters, a French maître de cuisine, steam heating in the passenger areas, wide 'wedding berths' for honeymooners, and a glorious barbers shop with the patent reclining chair.

They also reputedly had the largest wine cellars afloat. There was also accommodation for 80 second-class passengers. *Atlantic* took the first sailing from New York to Liverpool and beat the best time of Cunard by over twelve hours. But they were expensive to maintain and burnt fuel at an excessive rate.

To answer the Collins challenge Cunard ordered two majestic wooden paddle steamers from Robert Steele & Son at Greenock. These were *Arabia* and *Persia*, and they were intended to outpace the Collins Line steamers and at the same time offer superior 'luxury' accommodation. They were designed around powerful machinery in wooden hulls with very fine lines. This combination meant that the vessels were demanding on fuel, and as the fine hull forms had inadequate buoyancy forward the ships tended to plunge into heavy seas. Besides, the engines were of such intense power that they would inevitably destroy the wooden structure of the vessels even though they had to reduce speed in anything approaching rough weather. But before the first vessel was completed the Royal Mail Steam Packet, which had just lost *Amazon* by fire with the loss of 108 lives, made a generous offer for *Arabia*, which was still on the stocks. Cunard could not resist, and the vessel was completed as *La Plata*, while its erstwhile companion was completed in June 1852 as the new *Arabia*.

John Isherwood writes in *Sea Breezes* for August 1958:

Very strongly built, with round bilges and a flattish bottom, her oak frames were closely spaced and tied together by diagonally crossed iron braces. All fastenings below the waterline were copper and the outer wooden planking was sheathed for the whole submerged part of the hull by first a layer of hair felt, then rock elm planking and finally overall copper sheathing. She was a beautiful looking ship, with a fine clipper stem and an Arab chief for a figurehead. Contrary to previous Cunard practice she was rigged as a brig and she also had two funnels – the first Cunarder so fitted.

Her accommodation, nominally for 180 passengers (all presumably first class), is stated to have equalled that of the Collins ships. The main saloon aft, unobstructed by the foot of a mizzenmast, was said to be a magnificent apartment, with a low dome of stained glass, and she boasted two small libraries, a small but much appreciated smoke room and a children's nursery. Biggest boon of all probably was the fitting of a steam heating system throughout. Her fittings and general equipment in fact were well ahead of all her contemporaries.

Instead of the normal single-cylinder side-lever condensing engine there were twin-cylinder units, but still arranged on the side-lever principle. The engines were the most powerful afloat at that time, but they were fuel hungry and devoured 120 tons of coal a day, so that the bunkers were huge compared with the capacity of the cargo holds. The ship rose out of the water by as much as 5ft during an average ten-day voyage across the Atlantic as the bunkers were consumed. Isherwood describes the engines:

In this type of engine the cylinders were at the bottom of the bedplate and each piston rod worked upwards. It carried a short yoke, the ends of which were attached by connecting rods to the ends of two heavy rocking beams, one each side of the cylinder. The other ends of the beams were coupled by a connecting rod to one of the cranks of the paddle-shaft. … In effect, side-lever engines were similar to the American walking beam type but the beam was at the base of the engine and working upwards instead of high up in the ship and working downwards … This type of machinery [in the *Arabia*] was heavy and took up a lot of space. But it kept weight low in the ship and it proved well balanced and reliable.

The foundation of that other great company, the Peninsular Steam Navigation Company, later P&O, also illustrates the evolution of the ocean-going paddler (Table 2). The 206-ton *William Fawcett* was chartered for early runs across the Bay of Biscay to Spain and Portugal. Owned by the Dublin & London Steam Packet, it was one of a number of small steamers chartered through Richard Bourne to help the Peninsular company's founders, Brodie Willcox and Arthur Anderson, achieve a weekly departure for the Iberian Peninsula. In 1837 they managed to obtain the mail contract and their first mail ship, the paddler *Don Juan*, sailed in September with Arthur Anderson on board. Sadly, while returning from Gibraltar, the maiden mail service was wrecked on the rocks off Tarifa lighthouse in thick fog. But everybody got safely ashore along with the mailbags and a large consignment of cash. Anderson was shocked at the physical loss and also hurt by loss of pride,

Above: Cunard's *Arabia* (1852), originally to be named *Persia*, was built as a direct challenge to the Collins Line.
Right: An etching showing how the engines of the *Arabia* (1852) were packed in amidships. (*THE NATIONAL ENCYCLOPEDIA, A DICTIONARY OF UNIVERSAL KNOWLEDGE*, 1868)

ship is more sickening under power than under sail because sails steady her and give more rhythm to her motion. Paddles were never really suited to the open sea. When a paddle steamer pitched, both paddles came out of the water at once, and let the engine race, then plunged in too deep and almost brought the engine to a stop. When she rolled one paddle was too shallow and the other was too deep, and she proceeded like a corkscrew. Paddlers always rolled excessively because the paddle shaft had to be above the water line and, therefore, the centre of gravity of the machinery was very high. Whatever happened, throughout it all was the slow endless thud of the engine, which in the early days had a single cylinder and ran at about 16 revolutions per minute: a thud every four seconds and a rhythmic series of clunks and hisses in between.

Nevertheless several of the former Dublin boats survived on the Peninsular service for a number of years; *William Fawcett* and *City of Londonderry* until 1845 and *Royal Tar* until 1847.

Anderson and Willcox were given an opportunity to extend their service through the Mediterranean to Alexandria when they won the mail contract (express via Gibraltar and Malta). They quickly realised that they needed larger hulls with more powerful engines. They even tried to buy Brunel's *Great Eastern* from its ailing one-ship transatlantic service (see Chapter 5). Again Richard Bourne came to the rescue and offered Anderson and Willcox the relatively new wooden paddle steamers *Liverpool* and *United States*. They had been built for the new Transatlantic Steamship Company which aimed to challenge the North Atlantic with a two-ship service. This company was an offshoot of the City of Dublin Steam Packet Company. Alas, with only one ship in service throughout 1838 and 1839, pending delivery of *United States*, the service was failing and losing money. A quick sale of the assets to the Peninsular Steam Navigation

but he showed no loss of confidence; after all, the mail contract was still in his pocket.

David and Stephen Howarth in their history of P&O describe the problems of deep-sea paddling in such small ships from the passenger's perspective:

Nobody at the time wrote anything of the discomforts of crossing the Bay of Biscay, notoriously stormy, in a [small] paddle steamer . . . they expected it but it must have been formidable. Any small

The Transatlantic Steamship Company's *Liverpool* (1837) became *Great Liverpool* in 1840 when it was acquired by the Peninsular Steam Navigation Company.

Company was clearly a win–win deal for both parties.

United States was renamed *Oriental* shortly after its launch in 1840 and was joined by its near relation, now renamed *Great Liverpool*, which had been partly re-built for its new trade. While *Great Liverpool* had a gross tonnage of 1,150, *Oriental* was of larger capacity at 1,673 tons gross. Their engines provided over 430hp, giving the paddlers a service speed of about 9 knots. On the main deck, each cabin had a port-hole and the cabin door opened on to the dining saloon with its traditional long table. On the lower deck, cabins were inboard with so-called lounging rooms and a ladies' saloon surrounding the cabins. This was state of the art indeed.

It did not take long for Arthur Anderson to realise the potential of an overland route from the Mediterranean to Suez and a steamer service on to India. However, he had the Honourable East India Company to deal with, as it still held the monopoly on the India service round the Cape and on the direct service from Suez to Bombay. On the Suez route the steam paddle frigates *Atalanta* and *Berenice* were commissioned in 1836 by the East India Company to maintain the Suez to Bombay service. The frigates suc-ceeded the auxiliary steam sailing ship *Hugh*

Lindsay. The East India Company did even-tually concede that Anderson could try his luck on the longer Suez route, but to the east coast of India via Aden and Colombo to Madras and Calcutta, very much a longer and secondary route than the mail service direct to Bombay. But so it was that the em-bryonic Peninsular & Oriental Steam Nav-igation Company challenged the might of the long established and empowered East India Company.

With the promise of up to £20,000 a year from the East India Company, P&O or-dered two new ships for the service. These were the magnificent *Hindostan* and *Bentinck*, purchased against soft loans from a variety of sources, several of which had a secondary agenda which was set upon re-form of the East India Company. David and Stephen Howarth write:

P&O ordered the biggest ships it had ever considered, wooden paddlers 240 feet long, one just under and the other just over 2,000 tons. They had iron wa-tertight bulkheads for safety and 60 cab-ins and 150 berths, but both had engines of conservative design, because reliability in these distant seas was reckoned more important than fuel economy. The first they named *Hindostan*, and the second

Bentinck, after Lord William Bentinck, a governor of India, who had encouraged the company in its early days.

They were elegant ships, clipper bows, long bowsprits and stern windows like early warships. Newspapers were full of praise for their luxury – genteel, superb, magnificent, commodious – and were especially impressed by their warm and cold shower baths; indeed it was something new to be offered such comforts at sea.

The ships were also innovative in that the cabin spaces were divided into three parts by two passages, portside, amidships and starboard. No longer did the cabins open on to the long table of the main saloon, the idea being that the inboard cabins might be sheltered a little from the tropical heat and that passenger comfort amidships would be enhanced if the ship should roll. The maiden outward voyage of *Hindostan* was a huge success, leaving Southampton on 24 September 1842. It called en route to rendezvous with coaling ships that had been

Hindostan (1842) opened the new P&O service between Suez and Calcutta. (DP WORLD P&O HERITAGE COLLECTION)

dispatched earlier, firstly at Gibraltar, then Cape Verde Islands, Ascension, Cape Town, Mauritius, Colombo and Calcutta, quite a logistical undertaking. In the Indian Ocean a simple route could be taken, as neither the ocean currents nor the doldrums had to be avoided, precautions which took the old East Indiamen almost across to the South American coast. The new ships quickly settled to their routine: Calcutta, Madras, Colombo, Aden and Suez, regardless of the state of the monsoon. The Howarths again:

As a regular route the Cape could not compete with Suez because it was so much longer, but P&O could now take the mails and passengers from England to India by the short route all the way, in the *Great Liverpool* and *Oriental* from England to Egypt, and the *Hindostan* or the *Bentinck* from Egypt to Calcutta. This speed and comfort transformed the lives of men who served in India, and their wives and families.

But P&O was not only up against the power

The Eastern Steam Navigation Company's *Precursor* (1841) was purchased by P&O in 1844.

of the East India Company in the Indian Ocean. It also found the efforts of the Eastern Steam Navigation Company particularly irksome, and considered its activities a threat. This company operated *India*, built on the Clyde for the India Steam Company which went bust on the ship's delivery in 1837 and immediately had to sell it, and *Precursor*, an altogether more modern and larger vessel built for the Eastern Steam company in 1841. *India* was the first properly commercial steamship to reach India. It also had one notable design feature as a wooden ship; iron bulkheads at either end of her machinery space – an early deployment of the firewall.

The Eastern Steam Navigation Company was keen to get its Suez–Colombo–Madras and Calcutta service up and running before P&O could get *Hindostan* and *Bentinck* into service, and had bought *India* from a consortium of Greenock merchants who had been running it into the Mediterranean. *Precursor* was still being completed and not likely to be on station until late in 1842. The *India*'s first voyage from Suez started in April 1842. Once the purpose-built *Precursor* arrived at Suez it is likely that it adopted the longer Suez to Colombo link, while *India* then maintained the onward connection to the Indian ports. The competition ended when P&O purchased both *India* and *Precursor* at Calcutta in 1844.

During 1846 and 1847 P&O enjoyed expansion. No fewer than nine new

Euxine (1847) was one of nine ships delivered to P&O in 1846 and 1847.

One of the first batch of steamers for the new Royal Mail fleet was *Forth* (1841). (*THE ILLUSRATED LONDON NEWS*)

year twelve ships were afloat, all wooden paddlers and all except two bearing the names of British rivers.

This was achieved without a naval architect or marine superintendent employed by Royal Mail company, so that each builder could interpret his instructions as he preferred. The importance of such a post was realised only late in 1840, when Captain Edward Chappell, RN, was appointed Marine Superintendent. John Scott Russell spotted a major design fault in that the paddle shaft could be at or slightly above the main deck, and suggested this could best be overcome by raising the height of the deck by 2ft. Robert Menzies, building *Forth* at Leith, had also spotted the error, and left the upright timbers high, awaiting an instruction to increase the height of the deck. But when he received confirmation from Royal Mail that 21ft depth rather than 23ft was adequate, he had his men saw off the tops of the timbers. The counter-instruction from Scott Russell came too late, and Menzies, like several other builders, entered into a round of protracted claims with its client.

The first part of McQueen's vision came to pass on 3 January 1842, when the steamers *Tay* and *Thames* shipped the mails out of Falmouth, bound for the West Indies. The steamer *Forth* had already been dispatched westwards to provide the branch connection to New York while the smaller sailing ships were waiting to provide a web of connections throughout the Caribbean. The crossing to Barbados with coaling stops at Corunna and Madeira averaged 19 days. Each steamer was then deployed on one of the branch services in turn, returning to Falmouth only after a period of between four to six months. It was quickly found that the new company had overstretched itself, and it returned to the Admiralty for a contract variation that suspended the New York and Halifax branch service. This link was not reinstated. The Admiralty also agreed that the home port could be Southampton rather than Falmouth.

At this stage the management of the business was slowly eased away from Mc-

wooden paddle steamers were delivered, ranging from the smaller 700-tonners to *Euxine* and its various counterparts and the slightly larger *Haddington*, each designed to suit one of the company's various services.

Another great champion of the seagoing paddle steamer was James McQueen, who at the age of 60 prepared a 'General Plan for mail communication between Great Britain and the Eastern and Western parts of the world; also to Canton and Sydney westward by the Pacific'. Having sought commercial backing, McQueen obtained a Royal Charter for a fortnightly service to the West Indies starting on 1 December 1841, with branch services to the Spanish Main, New York and Halifax. Fourteen large steamers and three small sailing ships were ordered for the newly created Royal Mail Steam Packet Company to initiate this ambitious duty. Kilner Berry described the building programme in an article which first appeared in *Sea Breezes* for February 1956:

> Sufficient capital having been subscribed, no time was lost and the orders for building the ships were spread as widely as possible, with separate contracts for their machinery in some cases. In February 1841, less than a year after placing the contracts, the first of the fleet, the *Clyde*, was launched by Caird & Company at Greenock. Others followed in quick succession and by November of the same

Queen, who was seemingly a great deal better as a visionary than as a day-to-day operations manager. During 1842 marine superintendent Edward Chappell was put in charge. But any company with lesser backing would not have survived, as these reports of woe to the London company office during the first four months of operation describe:

Actæon: On her return the ship passed Puerto Cabello against instructions; the purser accordingly wants to know how to charge fares.

Clyde: At Nassau, having left the Jamaica mails behind. Running nine days behind schedule.

Forth: Havana authorities complaining of crew's rowdyism.

Solway: A strong 'norther' forced her to omit Tampico. Delayed off Mississippi awaiting a tug.

Tay: Coal trimmers up before the magistrate in Belize.

City of Glasgow: Labour strike in Demerara which made coaling difficult. Did not call at Surinam or Tobago, though ordered to do so. The surgeon was sent home because he was insane. Ship's crew described by Captain Boxer as 'absolutely very little short of savages'. Third engineer imprisoned at Barbados for attacking the saloon cook.

Tweed: Badly strained during heavy weather en route for Chagres, deck seams wide open.

Forth and *Tay*: Both at Nassau at the same time and the naval mail agents could not agree which should carry the homeward mails to Britain – both ships were ordered home.

Despite all its teething problems and despite losing numerous ships in its first few years (Table 3), the Royal Mail company eventually prospered. Its first loss was *Medina*, which grounded on a coral reef off Turks island in the Bahamas on 12 May 1842 during only its second voyage. Its passengers included the Earl of Elgin, who was then Governor of Jamaica; no lives were lost in the incident. An article in *The Illustrated London News* of 3 March 1849 takes up the sorry tale while reporting the loss of *Forth*:

the *Isis* on 8 October 1842, which sunk off Bermuda, having previously struck on a reef; the *Solway* off Corunna, coast of Spain, on 8 April 1843; and the *Tweed* on 12 February 1847, on the Alecranes rocks, Gulf of Mexico, the same reef upon which the unfortunate *Forth* was last seen . . . The company also lost its inter-colonial steamer *Actæon*, on the Nigrellos, near Carthagena, in 1844; and the schooner *Lee*, near Belize, Honduras in 1848. The wrecks of the *Solway* and the *Tweed* were attended with peculiarly distressing circumstances, involving the loss of 120 lives; and in the case of the *Tweed*, with an amount of hardship and suffering to the survivors which has rarely found a parallel in the records of shipwrecks.

The cause of this succession of disasters is that the West Indies steamers, besides their long Atlantic voyages, have to call at a number of ports and islands, the navigation of which is especially dangerous and intricate . . . . These disasters cannot be attributed to the inefficiency of the vessels or their captains and officers, it being generally conceded that the working management of the company is most able, the ships of the best description, both as regards hulls and machinery, and suitable by their mode of construction and equipment for the particular service in which they are employed . . .

It appears that *Forth* was to be reboilered and overhauled on return to England, for which a sum of £15,000 had been set aside by the company. *The Illustrated London News* article concludes with reassurances to the shareholders:

The company has been its own insurers for some years; and to provide for con-

Fire in a wooden ship; the loss of *Amazon*

The largest wooden steamer yet built in England, *Amazon*, was launched on 29 June 1851 by Green of Blackwall. Built for the Royal Mail Steam Packet Company service to Panama with overland transhipment to the PSNC steamer for Valparaiso (see Chapter 3), it sailed from Southampton on its maiden voyage on 2 January 1852. Aboard were Captain Symons and his 109 crew, 50 passengers and the Mail Agent and his servant; 162 people in all. When the ship was off Dorset it was stopped so that sea water could be poured on to the paddle shaft bearings to cool them down – not that an unusual a problem in a new ship.

In the early hours of the second morning at sea, *Amazon* was making about 13 knots and was just entering the Bay of Biscay when smoke was seen emerging from the forward stoke hold. Within three minutes this had become a wall of flame dividing the ship into two separate havens. Chaos reigned as the ship ploughed on with its engineers dead or fleeing from the engine compartment. Any chance of getting the lifeboats safely dispatched as the ship ploughed on at speed was out of the question, and many people jumped into the sea, while one couple, hand-in-hand, stepped into the conflagration down a blazing hatchway. The problem was compounded by the stowage of the lifeboats, which had to be lifted out of deck brackets before they could be swung outboard, no mean feat as people scrambled into the boats while they were still firmly cradled to the deck. There were just 54 survivors.

Big wooden steamers were a serious fire risk. It was customary to keep tallow and other inflammable materials in the midships store forward of the engine room. In the case of *Amazon* the store was situated over the wooden casing around the steam chest of the forward set of boilers. There was also a report that the engineers had put a large drum of grease for use on the bearings at the entrance to the store. As the fire broke out the duty engineer saw flames coming from one of the boiler casings but could not reach the engine controls to shut it down because of the immediate severity of the flames. The cause of the fire was never properly established. That the fire should spread so violently and so disastrously in a steamer heading into the wind at 13 knots was predictable, and the tragedy was recorded as just another fire aboard another wooden steamer. On a brighter note, the Admiralty at last withdrew its insistence on wooden hulls for mail steamers, so encouraging the development of the iron hull.

tingencies and casualties, has a reserve fund, which at the present time, without writing off the *Forth*'s loss, amounts to no less a sum than £125,000 invested in Government securities. The actual value of the *Forth* at the time of her wreck may be estimated at £60,000.

Royal Mail acquired a new mail contract in 1850 to provide a monthly direct service to Rio de Janeiro with a connecting branch south to the River Plate. The inaugural sailing to Rio was taken by *Teviot*. A series of new ships was launched for the company in 1851, including the ill-fated *Amazon*, lost by fire in 1852, and *Demerara*, which stranded and was so severely damaged before it even got to the fitting-out yard that it was sold. The last wooden paddle steamer built for the fleet was *Tamar*, launched at Northfleet in January 1854. From then on, iron-hulled steamers were the order of the day, the last wooden hulls, *La Plata* and *Tamar*, being withdrawn from service in 1868.

But the real achievement of Royal Mail, P&O and Cunard was that they had obtained mail contracts from government which all sped up the transport of the mails and which all provided a scheduled service with comfortable, some might say luxurious, accommodation for passengers.

But what had been going on at home, where the paddle tug had become universally adopted for towage duties, and the home passenger and high-value cargo trade was largely operated by paddle steamers, with lower-value and bulk cargoes left to the sailing ships?

General Steam Navigation received a Royal fillip when the newly crowned Queen Victoria turned her back on sail in favour of steam. The young Queen opted to travel aboard one of GSN's newest fleet members, paddle steamer *Trident*, rather than the royal sailing yacht. The company offered to make the steamer available to the monarch for her visit to Scotland in September 1842, *Trident* being a superior vessel to HMY *Royal George*, which was manned by a scratch crew from the Reserve whenever it was in service. Although the Queen and Prince Albert sailed to Leith aboard HMY *Royal George*, they opted to return

with GSN. The royal party was delighted with the accommodation provided and enjoyed a fast 48-hour passage back to London. *Trident*, in company with the GSN steamer *Monarch*, which conveyed the royal baggage, set off from the Forth at the same time as the royal yacht. By the evening only the two GSN vessels were in convoy, the government ships having been left far astern. Obviously GSN played on its royal patronage for many years thereafter, but it was significant that even the young Queen herself recognised the importance of the steamer.

Second-generation paddle steamers had started to be introduced in the late 1830s and 1840s, replacing the early steamers dating from the 1820s. Boiler pressures rose steadily from the three atmospheres of the early paddlers, and boiler integrity and safety was greatly improved in the 1840s with the introduction of the cylindrical boiler. Meanwhile, fears that speed could be gained at the expense of safety were allayed in 1839 by the introduction of recorded inspections of passenger vessels and a requirement that the boiler pressure gauge be visible to passengers. Passengers were also empowered with the right to open a safety valve if they were

Demerara (1851) was launched at Bristol but was stranded and severely damaged in the Avon on the way to the fitting-out yard and rebuilt as a sailing ship.

The GSN steamers *Trident* (1841) and *Monarch* (1833) escort HM Queen Victoria, aboard HMY *Royal George*, to Leith in August 1842.

not satisfied that a safe margin of error was being maintained.

The higher boiler pressures of the second-generation steamers resulted in greater engine power which, in turn, both allowed and required larger hulls. They remained fully rigged, many with a figurehead proudly jutting out beneath the bowsprit. For the most part the coastal steamers offered a saloon, some with a ladies' cabin, but with very few creature comforts other than well prepared meals, with ale or whisky on tap for the needy or the comfort of hymn singing for others. They were to all intents very similar to the early long-haul steamers, generally smaller and only needing to entertain their passengers for one or two nights before the voyage was complete. But given the greater margin of safety over the smaller first-generation ships there were still many accidents. The Dundee & Hull Steam Packet Company's paddle steamer *Forfarshire* was one such, commissioned in 1836 and only two years later driven on to the Farne Islands in an easterly gale. Of the 63 people aboard,

nine were rescued from a raft by a passing sailing ship, while a further five passengers and four crew members were rescued in a coble crewed by the local lighthouse keeper and Grace Darling, his daughter.

Seemingly the wooden-hulled paddle steamer was here to stay, an unstoppable workhorse of the seas both at home in estuarial and coastal waters, in trade with Europe and the Mediterranean and in trade further afield in the Atlantic, Pacific and Indian oceans. But two developments would conspire in the downfall of the wooden paddle steamer. The first was the screw propeller, patented in 1836 by Francis Pettit Smith in Britain and John Ericsson in Norway, each with variations on the same theme. The second was the introduction of composite iron ribbed wooden-planked hulls, which were quickly followed by iron ribbed and plated hulls. The propeller would provide greater propulsive efficiency over the paddle wheel, and iron would allow lighter construction and far greater deadweight capacities.

TABLE 2 The evolution of the deep-sea paddle steamer under P&O ownership (excluding the Canton and Nile river service vessels)

Ship	Year built	Gross tons	Comments
Braganza	1836	688	1844 rebuilt; 1852 scrapped
Iberia	1836	516	1856 scrapped
Don Juan	1837	800	1837 wrecked near Gibraltar
Liverpool	1830	450	1838 bought from owners in Ireland and resold
Montrose	1837	603	1840 bought from Scottish owners;1852 sold
Great Liverpool	1837	1,140	1840 bought from Transatlantic Steamship Co as *Liverpool*; 1846 wrecked off Spain
Oriental	1840	1,787	1840 bought from Transatlantic Steamship Co as *United States*;1852 sold
Royal Tar	1832	308	1841 bought from Dublin & London Steam Packet Co; 1847 sold
Lady Mary Wood	1842	553	1859 sold
Pacha	1842	548	1851 sunk in Strait of Malacca
Hindostan	1842	2,018	1879 wrecked near Madras
Bentinck	1843	1,974	1860 sold
India	1839	871	1844 bought from Eastern Steam Navigation Co; 1849 sold
Precursor	1841	1,817	1844 bought from Eastern Steam Navigation Co; 1858 sold
Madrid	1845	479	1857 wrecked off Vigo
Achilles	1838	992	1846 bought from J&G Burns; 1856 sold
Ariel	1846	709	1848 wrecked at Leghorn
Erin	1846	797	1855 wrecked at Ceylon
Haddington	1846	1,847	1854 converted to sail; 1871 sold
Pottinger	1846	1,401	1867 scrapped
Ripon	1846	1,508	1870 sold and converted to sail
Tiber	1846	763	1847 wrecked near Oporto
Euxine	1847	1,164	1868 sold and converted to sail
Indus	1847	1,386	1863 converted to sail as collier
Pekin	1847	1,182	1866 scrapped
Sultan	1847	1,090	1855 converted to screw propulsion
Jupiter	1835	610	1848 bought from James Hartley, London (ex-Saint George Steam Packet Co); 1852 sold
Malta	1848	1,218	1858 converted to screw propulsion
Ganges	1850	1,187	1871 sold
Singapore	1850	1,190	1867 wrecked at Japan
Vectis	1853	786	1865 sold
Delta	1859	1,618	1874 sold
Marsila	1860	1,640	1877 sold
Syria	1863	1,932	1870 sold
Nyanza	1864	2,082	1873 sold and converted to screw propulsion

3 THE CHALLENGE OF THE PACIFIC OCEAN: MORE WOODEN SHIPS

The last appearance of the paddle wheel steamers on the Pacific Ocean runs was about 1877, when the Pacific Mail Steamship Company's wooden China liners were withdrawn. On that run, and from San Francisco to Sydney, these vessels were spectacular survivors. They rode and thundered across the seas, sometimes with one wheel in the air and the other buried. The seas pounded under their sponsons till the hulls shuddered again, while the wind whipped the smoke from the funnels or howled down them, making the flames flare out in the eyes of the firemen. And all the time the great walking beam swung steadily over the boat deck as the coal was tossed into the quaint old furnaces.

From *Pacific Steamers* by Will Lawson, 1927

The Pacific was a difficult arena to develop, being almost devoid of graving docks and maintenance and repair facilities. Many wrecks had to be abandoned that could easily have been salvaged on a better equipped ocean. Besides, every fuelling stop had to be planned as part of the logistics of the steamship that voyaged to the remoter shores of the Pacific, as there were no coaling stations. Frederick Emmons wrote in 1973:

> The development of the Pacific passenger liners was shaped by conditions far different from those which prevailed in the North Atlantic. The first was, of course, the sheer size of the ocean area with its 68 million square miles of water, and its remoteness from the centres of world power and trade. Its shores to a large extent were sparsely settled by peoples whose civilisations by maritime standards, had not reached a stage of material development comparable to that of western Europe . . .

One of the first steam navigation companies on the Pacific coast, and later attracting a mail contract, was the Pacific Steam Navigation Company (PSNC). It was founded by William Wheelwright from Massachusetts. Voyaging in Chilean waters and later settling locally, Wheelwright took a proposal to the Chilean president to bring steam navigation to the coast. In 1835 President Prieto granted a decree giving Wheelwright exclusive rights to coastal steam navigation for the next ten years, conditional on him having two steamers in service within two years.

Wheelwright travelled to New York to raise the capital, but being unsuccessful there he sailed to London, where he was better received. A share capital of £250,000 was slowly raised and orders placed for two sets of engines. While Wheelwright preferred iron hulls his directors preferred wooden construction, and in due course the steamers *Peru* and *Chile* were constructed (Table 3). Thus an American initiative became a British company and remained so until its demise in the 1980s. John Lingwood, historical archivist for PSNC, wrote in *Sea Breezes* for July 1980:

> The *Peru* had been launched at Limehouse on 18 April [1840] being christened by the Honourable Mrs P Campbell Scarlett, the wife of one of the founders of PSNC, and the *Chile* followed three days later – both from the yard of Carling & Young at Limehouse. They were copper sheathed, wooden steam paddle ships of 700 tons burthen with side-lever engines of 90 horse power each. Each vessel was 190 feet in

length, 29 feet beam and had a draft of 18 feet . . . Each vessel carried on her stern the resplendent arms of the republic after which she was named . . .

The ships were distinctive as they carried patented safety boats set snugly upside down on top of the paddle boxes, each able to carry 100 people. They were equipped with a full set of square sails, and the funnels could be lowered out of the way into chocks on the deck when sail was set and the fire damped down.

Wheelwright had wanted the ships to sail out to the Pacific with their paddle wheels stowed on board to save wear on the machinery. This was vetoed by the commanders of the ships, Captain George Peacock in charge of the *Peru* and Captain William Glover of the *Chile*. Although they sailed from Britain independently, the *Chile* on 27 June from Falmouth and the *Peru* on 4 July, they proceeded on from Rio de Janeiro in company. Seven and a half weeks after the ships sailed from Britain they arrived off Valparaiso, there to be met by a double line of Chilean naval and other vessels including the British flagship HMS *President*. The *Chile* stayed at Valparaiso while the *Peru* sailed north again to take up station at Callao, where a similar reception awaited, complete with a welcome by the President of Peru. Wheelwright's vision of a coastal service was fulfilled.

Wheelwright soon obtained permission to operate in Ecuadorian waters as well, and was able to run a branch line along the coast from the Panamanian Isthmus, connecting overland with the Royal Mail service from Colon to London. He returned to London in 1845 to seek a mail contract, only to find that his directors had dismissed him because of the way he was perceived to have dealt with the substantial difficulties encountered

Chile (1840) was one of a pair of pioneer vessels deployed by William Wheelwright on the west coast of South America. (OIL PAINTING BY AUTHOR, 2011, BASED ON A DRAWING BY HIGGINS OF THE VESSEL APPROACHING LIMA)

in getting the new steam service up and running. Wheelwright countered to his shareholders, highlighting the incompetence of the Board; wooden hulls instead of iron, and purchase of an unseaworthy brig, *Elizabeth*, to tranship coal to the steamers. Wheelwright's next job was to attract the British mail contract, and to do this he finally got his iron-hulled paddle steamers (see Chapter 5).

William Wheelwright with his PSNC of Liverpool was not the only person or company interested in commercial steam navigation on the Pacific. The most famous of the American liner companies on the Pacific was the Pacific Mail Company, formed in New York in 1847. This company relied heavily on its wooden paddle steamers long after it should have looked to iron and screw propulsion. William Henry Aspinwall had been looking for backers to start such a service throughout the 1840s, and was devastated when he learned of Wheelwright's success in attracting British backing for just such a scheme. Although large deposits of gold had not then been found in California, it was known to exist there and this knowledge spurred the need for the east to acknowledge the burgeoning importance of the west of America and ultimately the potential for trade across the Pacific.

Aspinwall was no newcomer to shipping and was a partner in Howland & Aspinwall, owners of a fleet of clippers including the famous *Ann McKim*, described in contemporary reports as the fastest ship afloat. In 1845 the company took delivery of *Rainbow*, which by all accounts was even faster and considered to be the first of the extreme clippers. The next year the company had *Sea Witch* built, which set a speed record from China to New York that was never beaten under sail.

At the end of the Mexican-American War in 1848 the American Pacific coastline stretched from Puget Sound to San Diego. The Mail Steamer Bill was passed by Congress in 1847 to authorise the carriage of mail by sea and across the Isthmus of Panama from east coast to west. Two

steamship lines were required, one along the east coast from New York to Chagres, then part of Colombia and situated on the Panama isthmus, and the second from Panama to Astoria, Oregon, north along the Pacific coast. Aspinwall was able to secure a ten-year government contract for the Pacific sea link in exchange for payment of $199,000 per annum from the American government. With the help of Arnold Harris in the New York Senate, Aspinwall was quickly able to incorporate the newly created Pacific Mail Steamship Company (PMSC) with a capital of $400,000. The main condition to Aspinwall's funding was that any company steamers would be available to the federal government should need arise. Aspinwall was elected company president. Meanwhile, the east coast link to Chagres was awarded to George Law and his US Mail Steamship Company.

Three ships were ordered from the yard of William Henry Webb in January 1848. These were *California*, *Oregon* and *Panama*, each of about 1,000 tons and each equipped with a walking beam engine (Table 4). The first ship, *California*, left New York on 5 October 1848 bound ultimately for San Francisco. While it was on its delivery voyage via Cape Horn, gold was discovered in California and an eager crowd awaited it at Panama for the journey north to San Francisco. By January the Californian gold rush was in full swing, and both *Oregon* and *Panama* were greeted by excited prospectors ready for passage north, having travelled overland from Chagres.

Chagres was then just a village at the mouth of the Chagres river. From there prospectors and other passengers travelled up-river to Las Cruces using small flat bottomed boats locally known as a bongos. The rest of the trip across the Isthmus to Panama City on the Pacific side was made on foot in the company of pack mules. In these early days of the gold rush many were reported 'lost to Chagres Fever or cholera' during the overland trek.

In 1850 the PMSC was sufficiently endowed by profit from the California gold rush to enable it to enter into direct competition with the US Mail Steamship Company between New York and Chagres. Not to be outdone, George Law placed his own steamers, *Antelope*, *Columbus*, *Isthmus* and *Republic*, in the Pacific in competition with William Aspinwall's steamers. Consequent financial losses led, in April 1851, to an agreement between the companies whereby the United States Mail Steamship Company purchased the Pacific Mail steamers on the Atlantic side and George Law sold his Pacific ships to the Pacific Mail Line.

Exploits included *Northerner* arriving in San Francisco with $2.5 million in gold dust, and an epic 22-day voyage by the same ship from Panama to San Francisco after losing a paddle wheel at sea.

The PMSC now maintained a monopoly on the Panama-Oregon trade. It purchased two steamers from the Empire City Line, *Crescent City* and *Empire City*, to help maintain its intensive schedules, while large numbers of prospectors travelling to California had boosted the capital of Pacific Mail to over $2 million by 1850. Pacific Mail opened depots both at Panama City and Benicia in California. Aspinwall also invested heavily in the Panama Railroad Company, which would cut travel time from four days along old and rutted wagon trails to just four hours. George Law went into partnership with Aspinwall in 1852 and developed the eastern railroad terminal next to the wharf at Aspinwall, Columbia, although he sold his interest the following year. The railroad opened in 1855, reducing the steamship-railroad-steamship journey between San Francisco and New York to just 21 days.

The Pacific coastal service became even more important when the Fraser River gold rush took off in 1856, and voyages were soon extended to Vancouver and Portland. Not surprisingly, the company continued to flourish. Aspinwall retired from the position of president, and former company secretary William Davidge took on the presidency in 1856. Under his control the company's capital increased, but it was Davidge who had

to face the 1858 deadline when Pacific Mail's contract with the government expired; as did that of the United States Mail Steamship Company. Contracts were nevertheless successfully renegotiated when, in 1859, the United States Mail Steamship Company filed for bankruptcy and ceased trading. A through service was essential, and the Pacific Mail Line was quickly able to buy ships from the ailing Collins Line. Competition from other steamship companies in the Atlantic was fierce, and within a few years the Pacific Mail Company withdrew again to the west coast. But all was not lost, and between 1860 and 1875 the company built or bought 60 steamers, many of which were wooden paddlers.

During the American Civil War Pacific Mail used its steamers to carry gold to the east coast to support the Federal cause. The finely appointed *Colorado* was delivered by William Webb at New York in 1864, the same shipyard that had built the first ship in the fleet, *California*. *Colorado* was the ultimate in wooden-hulled transpacific paddle steamer design, and one of the largest paddle steamers built for Pacific duties. When the war ended in 1865 Pacific Mail was able to buy out its competitor on the New York west coast service, the Atlantic Mail Steamship Company. Pacific Mail at last was able to provide the service from New York to the West Coast via the Isthmus as a monopoly, unhindered by competitors.

During the Civil War, shipbuilder William Webb of New York built three fast paddle steamers for charter to the Federal Government. Webb hoped that Government would purchase his speculative builds, but at the end of the war they were returned to him to find alternative employment. Temporary employment was found in the West Indies, after which Webb sent them round to San Francisco, where he formed the California, New Zealand & Australian Steam Navigation Company in collaboration with local entrepreneur Ben Holliday. The ships, *Dakota*, *Nebraska* and *Nevada*, were wooden-hulled paddlers built at New York to a very high standard. *Dakota* and *Nebraska* were delivered in 1865 and *Nevada* followed two years later.

The San Francisco *News of the World* enthusiastically reported on the arrival of *Nevada* and *Nebraska* on the transpacific routes:

Running along the centre of the deck are 20 state rooms, each having a close and Venetian door, and a window 32 inches square. These state rooms are all double, with doors on each side and ventilators on top. Right aft is the ladies' sitting room, well fitted up, private and well ventilated. Forward of this is the smoke room, fitted up with a degree of comfort seldom seen on board ship. On the main deck is the grand saloon, 90 feet long, 28 feet wide and 8 feet high. On each side of this saloon is a row of state rooms, opening on the deck and accommodating 80 passengers, with two bridal chambers in the forward part of the saloon. The berth deck is occupied by the third class passengers and will accommodate 620 of this class. Abaft of this are 40 well ventilated state rooms for second class passengers.

For extinguishing fire, an iron pipe

Colorado (1864) and the coastal paddle steamer *Senator* at the Pacific Mail Line dock at San Francisco c.1880.

leading the whole length of the ship has some 15 branches of hose always connected, and water and steam are available. There are lifebuoys in each berth and boats capable of carrying 830 passengers.

They each had the standard walking-beam engine, *Nebraska* and *Nevada* operating at a humble 25 pounds per square inch (psi) and *Dakota* upgraded to 65psi. However, the higher-pressure system was problematical because the cylinders and glands tended to leak and the high pressure caused problems in the condenser, which did not have the capacity to condense the steam quickly enough. However, the service speed for the ships was about 10 knots and lower steam pressures were acceptable.

In 1866 Pacific Mail bid for and won the US Government's $500,000 per annum contract to carry the mails between San Francisco and the Far East. This required the company to operate a transpacific service to Hong Kong via Japan and the Sandwich Islands (later renamed Hawaii). *Colorado*, wooden hull and all, was selected for the inaugural sailing and was withdrawn from the

New York-San Francisco route to be made ready. *Colorado* was fitted with a mizzen mast and its coal bunkers were enlarged ready for the voyage, which in 1867 took it across the Pacific Ocean from San Francisco to Yokohama, Japan, and onward to Hong Kong. Meanwhile, Pacific Mail ordered four new ships for its new transpacific service, *China*, *Japan*, *Great Republic* and *America*, all wooden-hulled steamers with walking-beam engines. These ships were ordered at a cost of $1 million, and the capital of the company was increased to $20 million to cover this cost.

The Pacific Mail had four different branches by 1867, complete with an onward link to Shanghai:

1. The Atlantic Line, between New York and Aspinwall, Panama, offering three round trips per month.
2. The Pacific Line, which linked with the Atlantic Line, and which ran between Panama and San Francisco, stopping at Acapulco and Manzanillo. This route also offered three services per month, except for the latter, which was monthly.
3. The China Line, operating monthly between San Francisco and Hong Kong, stopping at Yokohama and linking with the Pacific Line.
4. The Shanghai Line, which ran between Yokohama and Shanghai, via Nagasaki, also monthly, linking with the China Line.

The opening of the Transcontinental Railroad across the North American continent in 1869 provided the key to the success of the new transpacific service. *Colorado*, a large steamer of 3,728 tons, was scheduled to run between San Francisco and Yokohama and on to Hong Kong in just 29 days. The purpose-built *Great Republic*, *China*, *Japan* and *America* were among the largest wooden-hulled seagoing paddlers. Their hulls were built of white oak and chestnut and the ships were about 4,500 tons gross. The massive vertical walking-beam engines operated at 20psi and had a 105in-diameter cylinder with a stroke of 12ft!

Cargo and passengers could now be moved from New York to Yokohama in 42 days, to Shanghai in 47 days and Hong Kong in 50 days, inclusive of all transfers, ship-to-ship and railroad-to-ship. By 1867 the company owned 25 ships with an aggregate tonnage of 61,474, most of which comprised wooden-hulled paddlers with walking-beam engines.

One of the most respected steamers was *Golden Age*, known as the 'luck ship'. The 'luck ship' not only rode out a typhoon but managed to ram a wharf at full speed, and on neither occasion suffered the slightest injury. It was bought from the New York & Australia Steamship Company. That company planned a fleet of five transpacific liners. However, high running costs and the earlier lack of a connecting railroad across

Japan (1867) was one of the Pacific Mail Steamship Company's big wooden steamers powered by a walking-beam engine.

Golden City (1863), from a lithograph by Charles Parsons, depicting the ship after the New York & Australian Steam Navigation Company had sold it to the Pacific Mail Steamship Company.

The burning of the steamship *Golden Gate* (1851) on passage from San Francisco to Panama, 27 July 1862.

the Panama isthmus inhibited the viability of the service and the vessel was quickly sold on to the ever-demanding Pacific Mail Company. Its lower frames were made of live oak and the top frames of cedar, and the entire hull was diagonally braced with iron straps. Its walking-beam engine had a diameter of 85in. The saloons were panelled in rose, satin and 'zebra' woods, and the furnishings were crimson and gold or white and gold, with much use of mirrors to give a sense of spaciousness. There was accommodation for 200 first-class, 200 second-class and 800 third-class passengers, and it could carry 500 tons of cargo in addition to

1,500 tons of coal for its furnaces.

Pacific Mail began its own service to Australia and New Zealand. *Golden Age* pioneered the Australian service from San Francisco in 1854. It was not a financial success because of the high price of coal at Tahiti, but it was certainly proof of concept. *Golden Age* was later joined by *Golden City*, also originally owned by the New York & Australian Steam Navigation Company.

On 27 July 1862 *Golden Gate*, built for Pacific Mail in 1851, caught fire amidships off the Mexican coast on passage from San Francisco to Panama. The ship was run towards the coast so that passengers and crew could attempt to row or swim through the surf on to the desert shore, but there were only 80 survivors out of a total complement of 338. The master was last off the ship, plunging into the sea as the rope he held burnt through.

Completion of the Transcontinental Railroad meant that the passenger traffic on the Panama route declined, but the US government doubled the subsidy on mail transported by Pacific Mail in 1869 to secure this strategic service. The new contract required doubling the frequency of sailings and modernisation of the fleet. This was

partly in response to Congressional Commission that put pressure on shipowners to commission iron and screw steamers to compete with the British. Although America was blessed with abundant resources of timber and a plethora of skilled carpenters, it had just one shipyard capable of building iron ships. But in 1875 the Union Pacific Railroad underwrote the new (British registered) Occidental & Oriental Steamship Company to compete with Pacific Mail, which clearly needed new ships to survive such an onslaught. It was almost with reluctance that the Pacific Mail Company, now with a large part of its stock held by the Southern Pacific Railroad, approached John Roach & Sons with orders for two big and modern ships. The engines for these were built at New York at the company's Etna Ironworks, and the ships themselves were built on the Delaware River. These were the famous iron screw steamers *City of Tokio* and *City of Pekin*, which were delivered in 1874. More competition arose, this time from Canadian Pacific Railway with a new screw steamer service to the Far East out of Vancouver. But the big wooden paddle steamers had done their job in opening up an important trade route, and in 1879 the iron-hulled *China* took the final paddle, sailing to the far East before standing down.

By 1873 Webb was tiring of his loss-making California, New Zealand & Australian Steam Navigation Company sailing between San Francisco and Australasia, and he sold his ships to the Pacific Mail Steamship Company. Within a few months all three ships, *Dakota*, *Nebraska* and *Nevada*, had been demoted from transpacific to coastal duties. In 1878, towards the end of its career, *Dakota* actually made the 920-mile trip to Victoria in British Columbia in 66 hours, averaging a respectable speed of nearly 15 knots. William Henry Aspinwall died in January 1875, aged 68.

The transpacific services provided the ideal route for Chinese immigrants to get to America. This influx of cheap labour eventually raised the hackles of American labour-ers, who found themselves out-priced and out of work. In July 1877, following three days of rioting by the unemployed in San Francisco, the famous 'Pick Handle Brigade' fought off the rioters to prevent them from setting fire to the South Beach dockyard of the Pacific Mail Line in an attempt to prevent more workers arriving from China.

The ultimate efficiency of screw over paddle rapidly saw the demise of the old wooden-hulled steamers on the deep-sea routes, the last, *Alaska*, being withdrawn in 1877, just two years before the iron-hulled paddlers were also withdrawn. The new transpacific fleet comprised both American- and British-built screw steamers, and now served 47 ports in the Pacific, including several in Australia. But the wooden paddlers were not done yet. The *Alaska*, like the *Nebraska*, spent another decade on the Alaskan coastal service. In his book *Pacific Steamers* Lawson wrote:

> She had double beam engines, enabling each paddle to be worked independently. Pilot Swanston of San Francisco, tells of a day when the *Alaska*, approached the Golden Gate with one wheel crippled. The Captain decided that he was due at the pier at a certain time, and nothing would stop him coming in with his helm hard over against his full-power paddle; and he barely missed Lime Point as his high-sided ship barged her way into the port.

The Southern Pacific Company acquired control of Pacific Mail in 1893. In 1902 Pacific Mail commissioned its first steel-hulled screw propelled ships, *Korea* and *Siberia*, and two years later *Manchuria* and *Mongolia*. These were the largest and fastest passenger-freight ships in the Pacific, and larger than any other ships the company had previously owned.

The Pacific coastal routes had spawned their own steamers over the years following the introduction of the British-built steamer *Beaver* on the British Columbian coast in 1836. In due course competition became intense between the various operators that soon appeared on the scene. These included the Pacific Coast Steamship Company in 1874, which operated the paddle steamers *Mohongo*, *Orizaba*, *Senator* and the all-time favourite *Ancon*, along with a fleet of screw steamers. There was also the Oregon Steamship Company with the big paddle steamers *Oriflamme* and *John L Stephens*, which plied between San Francisco and the Columbia River along with the smaller iron-hulled *Alaskan*. *Alaskan* was wrecked in May 1889 with the loss of four crew, including its captain.

The Hudson Bay Company also operated steamers. *Labouchere* was built in 1858 by Green at Blackwall, and sailed round Cape Horn to San Francisco. It was unique on the west coast, having oscillating engines driving her paddles. It was lost in 1866. The Californian Steam Navigation Company

bought *Orizaba* from the Pacific Mail Company for $60,000 in 1865 when the vessel was ten years old. It ran alongside *Brother Jonathan*, but was wrecked shortly after being sold to Pacific Mail. *Orizaba* had earlier operated as *Commodore* for the Vanderbilt Nicaragua Line, although it was originally built for the New York to Long Island ferry. But little by little the old beam engined paddlers were displaced from the west coast and replaced by modern screw steamers, eventually leading to the turbine flyers operated largely by the railway companies.

The beam engined paddlers were eventually reassigned to cross-harbour duties, which they performed admirably, and, along with their cousins the stern wheelers, remained the mainstay of North American inland water transport well into the twentieth century (see Chapter 7).

Australian coastal service had been ini-

Plan and section of the steamship *Sea Horse* (1837) constructed by T Adamson and P Borrie of Dundee. *Sea Horse* served owners in Dublin until 1845, then sailed for Australia, where it became one of many British and American expatriate steamers on the Australian coastal services. It was out of register by 1855.

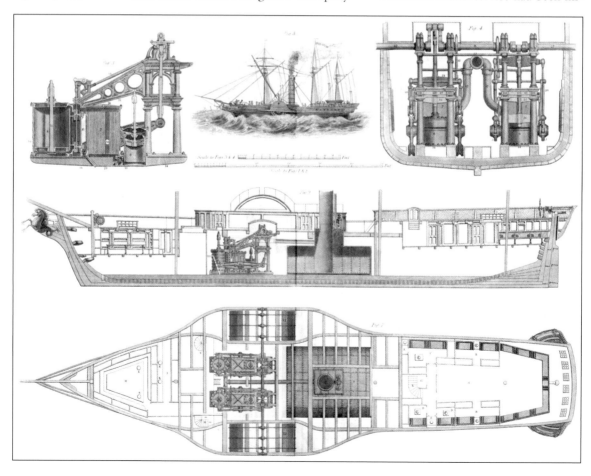

tiated once *Sophia Jane* arrived from England in 1831. But Australian enterprise had not been slow, and shortly after *Sophia Jane*'s arrival *William IV* was launched on the Williams River, complete with engines built by Fawcett & Company in Liverpool. Thereafter the Australian coastal services received new ships from local builders and a succession of new and secondhand vessels that came out from Britain. One of these was the little steamer *Sea Horse*, of just 439 tons gross and built at Dundee for Dublin owners in 1837. It was re-registered at London in 1845, when it sailed for Australia to try its luck on the coast. It was bought by B Boyd in 1849 in readiness for the profit-taking of the Australian Gold Rush, but was out of register by 1855. That was quite an adventurous career for a small wooden-hulled vessel with twin single-cylinder engines and a length of just under 150ft.

Australian coastal services were boosted by American paddle steamers crossing the Pacific to investigate the Australian Gold Rush in the early 1850s. While the Australasian Steam Navigation Company took delivery of three fast new British built paddlers, *Telegraph*, *Brisbane* and *Illalong*, American reinforcements were not far behind. In 1853 *Monumental City* arrived from America for the Sydney to Melbourne route, only to be wrecked shortly afterwards. The wooden-hulled *New Orleans* followed, to be renamed *Governor General*, a favourite on the Australian coast under subsequent ownership of the newly formed Melbourne Steam Packet Company and later the Australasian Steam Navigation Company. Another American paddle steamer to cross the Pacific from San Francisco in search of gold was *Ben Bolt*, renamed *General Urbistende* on purchase by Australasian Steam Navigation in 1854.

The walking-beam engine

The original Newcomen engine required cold water to be sprayed on the cylinder to condense the steam inside, thereby creating a partial vacuum. James Watt modified this rather inefficient system, in which premature condensation could occur on the cold cylinder walls, so that condensation was effected in a separate cold water injection condenser. It was this engine that was the mainstay of the water pump that helped dewater the mine workings of Britain. It was this same land engine which first took to water, the up-and-down action of the overhead beam translated into a circular motion by a crank of half the engine stroke, connected directly to the paddle shaft. This effectively was the American walking-beam engine. The land engine took to the water in Britain in a modified form, whereby the beam was placed adjacent to the cylinder to maintain a low centre of gravity. This was the side-lever engine. In both the walking-beam and side-lever engines the fulcrum for the beam or lever was at or near its centre point. A modified version of the side-lever engine was the grasshopper engine, in which the side-lever fulcrum was at the end of the lever and the connecting rod to the paddle shaft eccentric was taken off the middle of the lever.

But it was the American walking-beam engine that was the direct descendant of the land engine. Its operation, particularly in the early days, was something of an art and depended on the engineer getting to know his particular engine. Many a mishap occurred when the engineer transferred to another vessel and the starting handle operated in the reverse direction of the one to which he was accustomed! Bob Whittier, in his book on American steamboat engines, describes the worst sin of all:

> The most often mentioned walking-beam bungle was allowing the engine to stop with its single piston, and therefore, the massive paddle crank, stuck on top

or bottom dead centre. This locked the engine into immobility and left the boat adrift without power . . . Waterfront people could tell at a glance when a boat was in this predicament – she would obviously be drifting, and her walking beam would be motionless, cocked up at its maximum angle of tilt . . . If a boat had any way on at all, water pressure against the paddle-wheel floats would combine with whatever momentum might be present in these heavy wheels, to carry an engine past dead centre.

When an engine did get really locked up, crewmen rushed to one of the paddle boxes and opened one of the access doors that were built into the inner wall. Then they grabbed a long, stout lever kept on a rack for this purpose, inserted one end of it through the opened door, and hooked under any convenient part of the paddle wheel. Then they bore down on it hard, to ease the wheel around a bit and get the piston off dead centre. The job had to be done with as much care as one would use in picking up a rattlesnake. If a leaking steam valve was admitting steam into the cylinder, upon being moved off dead centre this could give the piston a momentary and quite energetic shove . . . So the men used it with respect, standing and holding it so they could let go and get clear if it should kick.

To start the engine, to coax it into motion, the engineer had a starting bar. On instructions from the pilot to start up, the engineer would half-open the steam valve then push down (or up) on the heavy starter bar. As the engine began to move he would push high over his head and down to his waist at an ever faster rate until the automatic valve mechanism could be engaged by 'dropping the hooks' over the eccentrics. Once that was done he needed to make sure that enough cold water was being injected into the condenser to create the appropriate vacuum – the correct amount was given by a ringing noise as the cold water hit the hot steam. The water pump was powered by the walking beam in the early days, but in later years, as steam pressures increased, the pump was driven by an auxiliary steam engine.

Some larger engines had two starter bars. This was useful for training the junior engineer to get used to the vibrations and pressures of the engine as it started up. On short coastal runs the starter bar was left in its socket, while on longer deep-sea journeys it could be removed and placed out of the way until it was needed again. But in the largest of all the walking-beam engines the starter bar was connected to a set of steam rams, each of which had to be delicately worked up to the motion of the engine as it gathered momentum.

The largest engines of all were some of those installed in the big coastal steamers of the Fall River Line connecting New York with Boston. The 176-mile sea trip from New York through Long Island Sound to Fall River took just over eight hours, and there a waiting train took passengers the remainder of the journey to Boston. The steamers were big and luxurious and built to withstand rough weather. The biggest of its day was *Priscilla*, commissioned in 1894, but the biggest walking-beam engine, which also had compound cylinders, was installed aboard *Puritan* in 1889. The upper part of the beam was concealed from view aboard *Puritan* by a protective glass dome that shielded it and the engineers below from the vagaries of the New England weather.

Lubricating the moving parts was as essential to a steam engine as oil is to the modern-day car engine. In the early days animal fat or tallow did the job. In later more sophisticated designs oil was injected into the steam pipe to the cylinder to lubricate the piston and cylinder. Even so, there was still a need for someone to go round greasing all the moving connections. Bob Whittier again:

It is believed that our slang term for a mechanic, 'grease monkey', originated from the antics of walking-beam engine-room men as they clambered about and reached out to do their work. On ferryboats, grease and oil cups could be tended while the engines were idle between crossings, but grease monkeys were kept busy on boats that ran for several hours at a time without stopping. During the early, unsophisticated days of steamboating, a number of careless engine room men slipped and fell to gruesome deaths in the massive crank mechanisms. Later [designs] consequently had generous guard rails and hand holds.

Control platform aboard the Fall River Line's *Puritan* (1889) clearly showing 'the hooks'.

The walking-beam engine did have some drawbacks. It was heavy, so heavy that it had to be placed on a specially strengthened engine bed that was part of the longitudinal strength built into the hull to support this weight. Another issue was its size, which, coupled with the boiler spaces, meant a limitation in available deadweight. The walking-beam engine also had quite a high centre of gravity, not a problem in long flat-bottomed river boats but an important factor in the stability of seagoing vessels. Its visual character, the walking beam itself rocking back and forth above the deck houses, gave the ships an appearance of motion to which side-lever engined vessels, with their concealed moving parts, could never aspire. The European side-lever engine looked not to the English mine dewatering pump engine as the Americans had done, but to the mill engines of the industrial

The sturdily built and powerful *Puritan* (1889), from a contemporary engraving.

revolution. These were the original side-lever engines. The principle was the same, but these engines were more compact and had a much lower centre of gravity, the mass of the engine being below the paddle shaft. Again the cardinal sin of the engineer was stopping his engine with the piston at the extreme ends of its motion, when small puffs of steam might coax it forward, as might the drag of the immersed float of the stalled paddle wheel in the water.

TABLE 3 William Wheelwright's paddle steamers of the embryonic Pacific Steam Navigation Company (British flag) iron-hulled vessels, unless otherwise described. See also Chapter 4

Ship	Year built	Gross tons	Comments
Chile	1840	682	Wooden hull: 1852 sold
Peru	1840	690	Wooden hull: 1852 stranded
Ecuador	1845	323	1850 sold to Pacific Mail; 1851 wrecked
New Granada	1846	649	Lost
Bolivia	1849	773	1870 hulked
Santiago	1851	961	1859 sold
Lima	1851	1,461	Lost
Quito	1852	1,461	1853 wrecked near Huasco
Bogota	1852	1,461	1871 grounded on Tarada Point and hulked
La Perlita	1853	140	Lost on delivery voyage from UK
Osprey	1852	109	Lost on delivery voyage from UK
Inca	1856	1,090	1874 sold, wrecked November 1874
Valparaiso	1856	1,060	1871 lost on Layerto Island
Callao	1858	1,062	1870 hulked
Peruano	1860	639	Wooden hull, built New York: 1874 hulked
Talca	1862	708	1874 hulked
Chile	1863	1,672	1870 sold to Chilean Government
Quito	1863	1,388	1864 sold
Ecuador	1863	500	1870 foundered
Payta	1864	1,344	1870 sold to Chilean Government
Pacific	1865	1,631	1870 hulked
Santiago	1865	1,619	1869 wrecked in Straits of Magellan
Limena	1865	1,622	?
Panama	1866	1,642	1870 hulked
Favorita	1865	837	Wooden hull, built in America: 1871 destroyed by fire in Calloa Bay
Arica	1867	740	1869 foundered off Peru
Quito	1867	743	1882 hulked
Santiago	1871	1,451	1882 sold
Truxillo	1872	1,449	1882 hulked

The ultimate Pacific Steam fleet member on the Liverpool to west coast South America run was *Reina del Pacifico* (1931), a complete contrast in comfort and luxury to the early paddle steamers.

TABLE 4 The key wooden-hulled paddle steamers of the Pacific Mail Steamship Company (American flag)

Ship	Year built	Gross tons	Comments
California	1848	1,058	1866 sold to California, Oregon & Mexican Steamship Co; 1872 bought back; 1874 sold
Oregon	1848	1,099	1861 sold
Panama	1848	1,087	1861 sold
Tennessee	1848		1849 bought; 1853 wrecked near San Francisco
Carolina	1849		1854 sold
Unicorn	1838		1850 bought; 1853 resold to original owners
Columbia	1850	777	1862 sold to Chinese owners
Ecuador	1845	323	1850 bought from PSNC; 1853 wrecked at Coquimbo
Philadelphia			1851 sold to United States Mail Steamship Co
Crescent City	1848		1850 bought from Empire City Line; 1851 sold to United States Mail Steamship Co
Empire City			1850 bought from Empire City Line; 1851 sold to United States Mail Steamship Co
Sarah Sands	1846		1850 bought; 1857 sold
Northerner	1847	1,000	1850 bought from Mr Howard; 1861 wrecked Humboldt Bay
Isthmus	1850		1851 bought from George Law; 1854 sold
Republic	1850		1851 bought from George Law; 1861 sold
Columbus	1850		1851 bought from George Law; 1854 sold
Antelope	1850		1851 bought from George Law; 1851 sold
Golden Gate	1851	2,067	1862 gutted at sea and beached in Mexico
Sonora	1853	1,616	1868 scrapped
St Louis	1854	1,621	1855 sold to United States Mail Steamship Co; 1859 bought back; 1878 scrapped
Golden Age	1853	2,181	1854 bought from New York and Australia Steam Navigation Co; 1875 sold
Orizaba	1854	1,450	1860 bought from New York & California Steamship Co; 1865 sold to Holliday & Brenham; 1872 repurchased; 1875 sold
Uncle Sam	1852	1,433	1860 bought from Atlantic & Pacific Steam Navigation Co; 1866 sold
Constitution	1861	4,100	1879 scrapped
Costa Rica	1864		1865 bought from Cornellius Vanderbilt
Golden City	1863	3,373	1869 wrecked off Baja, California
Colorado	1864	3,728	1878 scrapped
Henry Chaucey	1864	2,656	1871 gutted by fire and rebuilt; 1877 scrapped
New York	1864		1865 bought from Cornellius Vanderbilt; 1875 sold
Arizona	1865		1877 scrapped
Montana	1865	2,676	1877 scrapped
China	1866	3,836	1883 sold to Henry Villard for use as receiving depot for smallpox patients
Great Republic	1867	3,881	1878 sold
Alaska	1867	4,011	1879 hulked
Japan	1867	4,351	1874 lost by fire on voyage Hong Kong to Yokohama
America	1869	4,454	1972 gutted by fire at Yokohama
Dakota	1865	2,135	1865 bought from William Webb; 1886 sold
Nebraska	1865		1865 bought from William Webb
Nevada	1865		1865 bought from William Webb

4 TECHNICAL EVOLUTION: ENGINEERS AND ARCHITECTS

The side-lever engine and the walking-beam, or land engine, were the direct results of matching a boat with an engine. They were variations on a theme, the one being preferred by the Europeans for its lower centre of gravity, the other preferred by the Americans, who were more focussed on inland waters and less concerned with the height of the machinery's centre of gravity. Both types of engines continually evolved to become more thermally efficient with a reduced power-to-weight ratio. Steam pressures were constrained by the inability of the early boilers to generate steam much greater than a few pounds per square inch (psi), and by the poor steam flanges and glands then available, so that the side-lever and the walking-beam principles could not, in those early days, be bettered. Interestingly, the operating pressure of Brunel's *Great Western* was just 5psi and of Cunard's *Britannia* 9psi. The corollary to these low working pressures was the need for large-volume cylinders to get the most energy out of the steam, while the downside of this was, of course, the massive weight of the cylinders and the structure that supported them and the other parts of the engine.

The packing between the piston and the wall of the cylinder was an initial problem, as component parts were not machined with any consistent accuracy. Greasy hemp rope was a popular solution to stop steam escaping from around the piston. In the very early days with the crudely machined components, the periphery around the piston was filled with any old soft material or 'junk', such as cardboard or greasy hemp, just about anything that would seal the gap between the piston and cylinder wall without causing too much friction. The packing material was held captive in a recess in the

piston and, to this day, the recess in the piston that retains the metallic piston rings is called the junk ring.

The ultimate solution was an elastic, spring-loaded metal seal, but that was not to come until much later in the nineteenth century, and only when the science of metallurgy had made considerable advances. It was found much easier to fit spring-loaded metal piston rings if the crown of the piston from the top of the ring recess was made with a removable peripheral part. It was this part that appropriated the name 'junk ring'.

The other parts of the engine that required steamtight packing between their fixed and moving parts were the piston and valve rods. These had a similar packing arrangement to that of the pistons, and this, again, was not improved until the increase in steam pressures of the late nineteenth century gave rise to the spring-loaded metallic gland packing.

A number of innovative developments were, nevertheless, introduced as time went on. The thermal losses of the early engines taxed their developers, and the search was on to increase the efficiency by reducing the quantity of steam consumed. The initial focus was on the condenser, a device in which the spent steam was cooled to condense it back to water and generate a vacuum. This vacuum gave an effective increase in steam pressure by the difference between atmospheric and absolute pressures. The system of mixing cold seawater with the exhaust steam within the condenser was clearly not efficient, although it was effective. This system, in its developed form, was the jet condenser, in which a spray of sea-water was injected into the condenser to condense the steam. As not all of this salt-contaminated condensate was required to be pumped back into the boiler, the remainder had to be discharged overboard. However, vessels on longer deep-sea voyages had to use this contaminated boiler make up, or feed water, and as the voyage continued an ever-increasingly brackish mix was returned to the boiler via the hot well tank to which the warm water was returned from the condenser. This saline feed water resulted in rapid scaling of the inside of the boiler plates, tubes and steam pipework. It is worth noting that in ships operating in fresh water, such as the Swiss Lakes paddlers and the 110-year-old screw steamer *Sir Walter Scott* on Loch Katrine in Scotland, the jet condenser is still used and is quite efficient, as there is no condensate contamination.

Colin Fleetney explains what was needed in an article first published in *Paddle Wheels* in 1969:

On a voyage lasting more than two or three days the boilers became foul, and the feed water increasingly more saline. It then became necessary to shut down, blow down, empty and clean each boiler in turn. I have intentionally omitted 'cool' from this list. Long before the boilers had time to cool, the black gang would be inside, attending to this terrible job. In fair weather, or foul, each boiler demanded the attention of those toiling half-baked men. Neglect of the job could result in burned plates and the very real possibility of an explosion.

By 1834 the surface condenser was introduced as a more efficient means of creating a vacuum and a means of obviating regular cleaning of the boiler while at sea. This condenser comprised an iron vessel containing an array of thin brass tubes through which cool seawater was pumped so that the spent steam condensed on the outside of the tubes. Air and condensate were pumped out and the condensate or feed water returned to the boiler via the hot well. The surface condenser was a huge advance towards better use of the thermal energy of the steam, but its design was poor and it constantly needed attention. Only when screwed brass ferrules and cotton cord replaced the wood packing for the tubes did the surface condenser become universally accepted. As metallurgical advances allowed for differential expansion and metal-to-metal packing, the condenser became almost maintenance free; conditional upon high-quality brass tubes and latterly of aluminium-brass tubes.

Bearing in mind that the ocean-going paddle steamer was at this stage nothing other than an auxiliary powered sailing ship, it is perhaps not surprising that considerable thought was already being given to the design of the paddle wheel and its floats. Using the analogy of the clock face, the simple radial paddle wheel has the disadvantage that the float is only vertical in the water and developing maximum thrust when it is at six o'clock. Its entry to the water at any point before six o'clock results in energy being expended in pushing the float down against the water, and when the float leaves the water after six o'clock it scoops and lifts a substantial amount of water with it. This results in a considerable loss of energy and reduction in propulsive efficiency.

Radial wheels did have one very significant advantage, in that the floats could be reefed and slowly pulled away from the axis of the wheel as a ship rose out of the sea as its bunkers were consumed on a long voyage. Conversely, as a wooden hull ages the timbers absorb water, the ship becomes heavier and settles deeper in the water, but the floats could be reefed in accordingly to allow for this. For ideal propulsion, the top of the float should be just immersed at six o'clock, while at the same point the bottom of the float should not extend below the keel of the ship, as it could be damaged in shallow water. Seagoing vessels tended to allow for deeper immersion than ships operating in sheltered waters, in order to maintain float immersion as the ship rolled. In addition, lake and river steamers in America tended towards having the combined width of the port and starboard floats equal to that of the breadth of the vessel. Seagoing vessels had a narrower float width designed not to stress the wheel hub, paddle shaft and its bearings unduly to a point of breaking in a rough sea. Radial wheels tended to be large. The biggest of all were the 58ft-diameter paddle wheels installed on Brunel's *Great Eastern*, which ran at 11 revolutions per minute (rpm). With very large diameter radial paddle wheels with many floats there was no need for, or advantage from, fitting feathering gear, as the close spacing of the radial floats achieved almost the same entry and exit conditions.

The dangers involved in the process of 'reefing the wheel' on a transatlantic voyage were painted vividly by Colin Fleetney:

> In theory the floats were readily unshipped, and secured only by hook and bolts. It takes little imagination to see the job on a bleak January day in mid-Atlantic, with the Force 6 blowing. Hook bolts some 1½ inches in diameter and 8 inches long. Teak or oak floats say, 12 feet long, 4 feet deep and 3 inches thick, covered in slimy weed. Nothing below but the Atlantic, which incessantly surges up into the box to engulf everyone. All around, and above, the gigantic frame of the wheel, creaking uneasily, and held as near still as possible by steam on the engines.

But the best use of the radial power transmitted to the paddle wheel can only be attained if the floats enter and leave the water as nearly vertical as possible, and this could be achieved with the feathering float. G E Barr explains the principle in an address given in 1951 to the Institution of Engineers and Shipbuilders in Scotland:

> To satisfy the demand for more power and faster running machinery the feathering type of paddle wheel was invented, originally patented by Buchanan and improved by Morgan in 1813. In 1819 Napier also had a vessel, the *Talbot*, running with a feathering paddle wheel. Several novel forms of paddle wheel were invented and tried, and in 1844 Wingate introduced a caterpillar paddle

arrangement in the *Queen of Beauty*. This comprised two shafts with drums and an endless belt with floats running between them, but it did not prove successful . . . and a normal wheel was fitted. In 1838 Field introduced a form of paddle wheel with floats on a cycloidal curve, for which Galloway had obtained a patent in 1835. The cycloidal form of paddle wheel with floats in four parts, one behind the other, was fitted in the *Great Western* in 1838. These wheels were 28 feet 6 inches over the floats with floats 10 feet broad and ran at 15rpm.

The feathering paddle wheel was introduced as early as 1835 to a design by Seaward, in which the eccentric operating gear, 'star centre' or 'Jenny Nettle', was attached to the paddle box structure on the outboard side of the wheel. Linkages comprising a master, or driving, rod and eccentric rods were connected to an arm on each float, and as the wheel revolved the angle of entry and exit of each float was altered such that it entered and left the water at the most efficient angle. The feathering float was by no means as trouble-free or as easily maintained as the radial float, and many river craft persisted with radials to cope with the flotsam and debris that they regularly encountered. Indeed, part of the downfall of the *Queen of the South* (ex-*Jeanie Deans*) on the Thames in 1967 (see Chapter 12) was repeated damage to its feathering floats caused by timber and other solid debris floating on the Thames.

Although the screw propeller had been recognised as a viable means of propelling a vessel through water from the very early days of the steamship, it was also recognised that the paddle wheel had two very distinct advantages over the screw. The first was that paddle steamers were immune from the hazard arising from leaking propeller-shaft stern-tubes located well below the water line, and from the hazard a broken propeller shaft would create. The second was that any part of a damaged paddle wheel could be raised above the water line while the vessel was at anchor and repaired from either within the paddle box or from a small boat. Vibration of the paddle wheel was an early problem that was overcome by carefully stiffening the inboard hull structure in way of the paddle shaft and the outboard structure supporting the paddle shaft/wheel bearings. Another source of vibration was the spacing of the floats, and the optimum spacing of these was largely determined from the feedback from successful ships in service.

Bob Whittier, in his book on paddle steamer engines, describes the importance of the outside bearings in keeping paddle wheel vibration to a minimum:

> The outboard paddle shaft bearings played a critical part in absorbing paddle wheel vibration. They were themselves of heavy construction, and were mounted on very stout timbers able to hold them securely and restrain their tendency to shake. In some of the later paddle wheelers, these mounting blocks were mounted on support pads which were separated from the hull structure proper by heavy springs, placed under substantial compression by batteries of screws.

The old wooden sailing ships were anything but the best hull shape for paddle power. The sailing ships were of deep draft to balance the pressure of wind in the sails and were heavy in construction. The sailing ship hull did, however, offer a sturdy and rigid platform for the heavy and concentrated weight of engine and boilers, and it was this basic issue that inhibited any significant fining of the form of the wooden hull for seagoing craft. But in America the emphasis was on sheltered water vessels that used the numerous navigable rivers as highways in their own right. Lighter hull construction and greater length-to-breadth ratios provided for efficient shallow-draft steamers. The shallow draft was a prerequisite if steamers were to sail over the numerous shoals of the inland waterways. This hull design was limited in size owing to the need to support the engine and boilers amidships

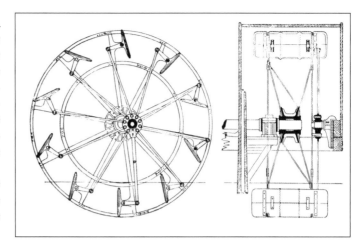

The feathering paddle wheel.

while maintaining hull integrity even if the vessel should go aground.

Lighter construction of narrower hulls promoted observation of the wave patterns generated along the hull when the ship was being driven at its intended service speed. The classic bow wave is followed by a trough and a set of waves and troughs along the length of the hull. In itself, this realisation was not rocket science, but the realisation that the phenomenon was critical to the correct position of the paddle wheel within the length of the hull was an important contributor to propulsive efficiency. Thereafter, naval architects took great care to ensure that the paddle wheel was neither choked within a permanent wave nor continuously lacking immersion over a trough. Optimum immersion of the paddle wheels for the design speed was, therefore, midway between adjacent trough and wave at the design operating speed. At slower speeds the wave creation process is reduced and the position of the wheel is not so critical. The wheel also needs to be somewhere near the mid-length of the hull in order to distribute the weight of the boilers and engines in the area of maximum fullness and buoyancy.

Hull design took two directions from the 1840s onwards. Iron works in Europe were capable of producing rolled wrought-iron plate which promoted the iron-hulled steamer. For some time iron had been used as the framework for ships which were then timber clad, but all-iron construction allowed a lighter hull to be built with sufficient strength to support the heavy machinery and boilers amidships. The huge advantage was that the deadweight capacity, or freight carrying tonnage, was greatly increased, and for the first time there was room for both fare-paying passengers and heavy cargoes. The hull form was streamlined so that the length-to-breadth ratio increased to about 10 to provide a narrow vessel with a tendency to be uncomfortable in a rough sea. In addition the lighter iron construction allowed for a shallower draft than had been customary with the wooden steamers. The shallower draft reduced the volume of water that the ship displaced, and with the ship moving through the water it resulted in a significant reduction in both the frictional and wave-making resistance of the hull.

In America the technology for rolling iron into plate was not then available, although ironwork parts were used for assembling the framework of a hull, which would then be sheathed in timber. The compensation was an abundance of timber with which to build and a plentiful supply of skilled tradesmen able to work the timber. It was for this reason that the Pacific Mail Line maintained wooden-hulled vessels on the transpacific routes even in the years subsequent to the American Civil War. As American shipbuilders stayed faithful to timber they also went to extreme lengths to provide hulls that were engineered to maintain integrity should the hull be stressed by grounding or when encountering head seas. The American solution was the 'inverted suspension' or 'tied arch' bridge principle, in which an arc of timber was built from the keelson in the hull forward to the keelson in the hull aft, and arched amidships above the promenade deck level of the steamer. Called hogging trusses, these arched timbers maintained the longitudinal profile of the hull and supported the weight of machinery at its centre. Hogging trusses also allowed extremely shallow draft vessels to be developed, the longitudinal hull strength coming almost entirely from these trusses.

Both in America, where the long pre-stressed and shallow-draft timber-hulled steamer was popular, and in Europe, where the strength and lightness of the iron hull was preferred, the power of the engine dictated the size of the ship. The walking-beam and side-lever engines were beginning to show their limitations, and something altogether more powerful was required. With the improvement in boiler design, higher steam pressures had been attained and this promoted a radical rethink of the marine engine. By 1848 the state-of-the-art engine was in Cunard's steamer *America*. It had two cylinders, each only slightly larger than the single cylinder of the pioneer Cunarder *Britannia*, but working at double the pressure, a greatly increased 18psi.

Cunard's *Scotia* of 1862 was the high point of the conventional side-lever engine. The engine had twin cylinders with the cranks at right angles to each other and working at 25psi. The boiler furnaces consumed 165 tons of coal per day at a service speed of 14½ knots. Like all side-lever engines, reversing had to be done by hand with slip eccentric gear, and this required the brute force of eight men. The frames of many of the larger engines were quite ornate, with Gothic or Corinthian columns and other styles modelled into them; those aboard *Scotia* were modelled on the nave of Canterbury Cathedral.

The side-lever engine consisted of two vertically mounted cylinders set abaft the paddle shaft and with the top of the cylinders roughly level with the shaft. The piston rods were connected to T-shaped crossheads which were driven upwards and downwards within a rigid slide bolted to each cylinder top. In turn, side rods connected the end of the crossheads to one end of the side-lever beam and a connecting rod linked the other end of the beam to the crankshaft. In the side-lever engine the fulcrum, or pivot, was at the beam centre, whereas in the so-called grasshopper engine it was at the end of the lever furthest from the cylinder. The valve gear for each cylinder was operated by a slip eccentric with its sheave mounted on the crankshaft.

The side-lever engine was specifically a paddle-steamer engine, and in terms of power to weight was poor compared with later engine designs. Nevertheless, it became the standard European paddle-wheel engine and was in wide use through much of the nineteenth century, only falling into disfavour in the twentieth century. One of the last side-lever engines in operational service was that aboard the paddle tug *Reliant*, formally the Manchester Ship Canal Company's *Old Trafford*, which was in use until 1969 and is now partly preserved at Greenwich (see Chapter 10). The last grasshopper engine in operation was probably that in the British tug *Eppleton Hall*, now part of the San Francisco historic ship collection, the tug having made its own way across the Atlantic assisted by auxiliary sail in 1969. It was also the last salt-water steamship to use the old-fashioned jet condenser, and had large-diameter steam pipes installed to prevent scale build-up and consequent blockages, a feature that was perhaps its saving grace on the long sea journey to the USA.

But just as the side-lever engine was the stalwart for paddle propulsion in Britain and Europe, James Watt's walking-beam (originally called a working beam) engine was the main power unit in American steamers. It is easy to forget that the 'American' engine was actually invented and first developed in

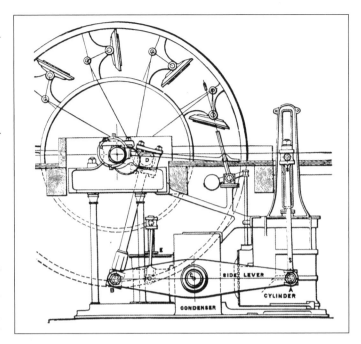

lowland Scotland. Thomas Newcomen's overhead sway beam engine of 1705, based on an earlier design by Thomas Savery of 1702, was later refined by John Smeaton and finally by James Watt. The Watt version incorporated the separate condenser and a valve arrangement to make the piston double-acting, with steam introduced alternately at either end of the cylinder, resulting in a near doubling of power and a 75 per cent increase in thermal efficiency.

Shunned by the local shipbuilders on the

The side-lever engine.

Old Trafford (1907) manoeuvres *Manchester Progress* (1938) into the locks at Manchester on its maiden arrival at its home port. (A R PRINCE)

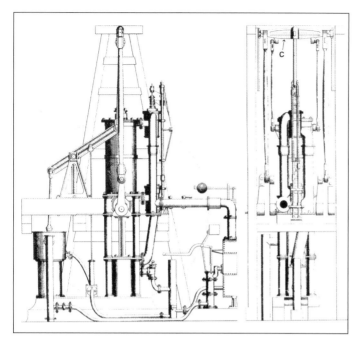

The crosshead engine.

Schematic section of a walking-beam engine, with scale indicated by the silhouette of a man.

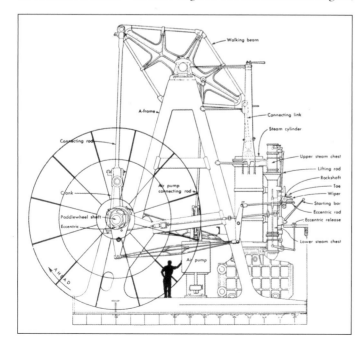

which had a massive lattice A-frame structure and had the cylinder mounted directly above the crankshaft. The crankshaft passed through a gap between the cylinder above and the jet condenser beneath. It was similar to the British steeple engine but differed in that, in the steeple engine, the cylinder was placed below the crankshaft.

Although the crosshead engine remained in favour until the 1850s, it was the introduction of the overhead, or walking-beam, engine from the 1830s onwards that began to displace it. What the walking beam did was to allow for a single, vertical, cylinder of much larger stroke and diameter which could develop the necessary propulsive horsepower. The large cylinder size was necessary due to both the low boiler pressure and minimal engine revolutions. The cylinder was placed vertically to give a positive upward drive to the beam via its connecting rod. This design was a space-saving arrangement that compensated for the weight of the elevated beam and contrasted with the side-lever engine with its beam located beneath the cylinders. The final drive to the crankshaft was by another larger connecting rod from the other end of the beam, which in turn was supported by a double A-frame. In the early days the frame was made of oak to give it a degree of flexibility, but latterly was of cast iron and formed an integral part of the engine. Placing the condenser and other equipment beside the cylinder in the bottom of the ship helped to correct the top-heavy nature of the walking-beam engine.

An early example of the stresses caused by the early walking-beam engines and the need almost for an over-engineered engine support structure occurred in 1857. The New York to Albany 'flyer' *New World* was racing along the Hudson River when a sailing ship was about to cross her bows. Robert Mole takes up the story in an article in *Paddle Wheels* in 1977:

Clyde, the Watt engine did find favour in America, and a small version placed aboard the little wooden hull named *Sea Horse* in 1811 showed the Watt engine to be almost vibration free; a useful attribute in a delicate wooden hull, if perhaps a little top-heavy. One of the early types of Great Lakes' steamer engines was the crosshead engine,

A 76 inch piston having a 15 feet stroke drove 45 feet diameter water wheels and she could make Albany in 8 hours including stops. On this day a schooner crossed ahead of her and the pilot rang down to stop the engine. The engineer 'unhooked' the engine and then, the A frame broke. The walking beam tumbled down, breaking the connecting rod which fell and was pushed through the bottom of the hull by the rotation of the crank and the *New World* went down. There was no loss of life and she was later raised and repaired. The fault was found in the A frame which had rotted.

New World was typical of many American river steamers in that the boilers were placed abaft the paddle wheels on top of the sponsons. Although this was a top-heavy arrangement, it had the advantage of maintaining cool inboard conditions. Should there be an explosion (of which there were many, particularly with the higher-pressure boilers in vogue in the southern states), damage would be limited, especially if the explosion occurred on the outboard side of the boiler.

But common to both the American and European engines was the skill of the engineer and the sheer strength required of his support staff. The engineer would get to know the sounds of his engine and could almost smell when trouble was brewing. It was important to maintain the tallow lubricant on the various bearings and to ensure that steam pressure was maintained for the job in hand. But, above all, the business of starting and stopping the engine, and of reversing it, was all done by a series of manual levers designed to coax the heavy machinery into motion and, most importantly, to coax it to begin to turn the paddle shaft in the desired direction. After all, the instruction 'slow astern' on approaching a pier but which became 'slow ahead' through incorrect manoeuvring on the control platform could have catastrophic consequences. The combination of skill, experience and the quick application of brute strength maintained a reliable engine room and, in turn, gave a vessel its reputation for both speed and safety.

On most of the early seagoing vessels, communication between the captain and the engineer was done by 'knocking', although American river and lake steamers had a system of bell signals audible to the engineer. The Chadburn bridge telegraph was introduced only in the 1870s, when any confusion between bells and knocks was finally overcome. The second and third of David Hutcheson's trio of *Iona*s (see Chapter 6) were some of the first ships to receive the bridge telegraph, and also were among the first to be fitted with steam-assisted steering gear. But in the early days instructions to the engine room were made by a code of knocks with an iron knocker on the grating over the engine room. The grating, of course, was there to allow the all-important air down to the furnaces, as well as to effect some degree of ventilation to the engine and boiler spaces. The grating was replaced in later years by high ventilators with cowls that could be turned into the wind,

Once the largest paddle steamer for fresh-water use, *New World* (1850) was extended in 1855. (*THE ILLUSTRATED LONDON NEWS*)

an altogether better arrangement that avoided seas sweeping over the deck and straight through the grating to flood the compartments below – the cause of the loss of many a fine steamer.

But by far the greatest hazard of the wooden steamer was fire. Indeed, the logic of stacking cords of timber on the sponsons ready to feed the furnaces down below would seem to be entirely flawed. The big American paddle steamers and shallower-draft stern wheelers were all wood fired until well after the Civil War. There are numerous graphic images showing river steamers with extraordinarily tall paired stacks with sparks and even flames spurting from the tops. Many steamers had canvas awnings over the promenade deck aft in order to 'arrest' falling soot and sparks, and buckets of water were strategically positioned on deck to tackle any blaze that might catch in the awning or in the vessel's timber-work.

Coal-fired furnaces were a little kinder to promenading passengers, although blow-backs during gusts of wind invariably ended in a reverse emission of soot and sparks which, given a suitable downdraught, would inevitably land on the after deck. The passenger was not safe even in the days of oil-fired boilers, as long, sooty and greasy strands could descend unannounced on to the unwary. Even the toughest of soaps would not remove oil-based soot stains from clothing. Nevertheless, the funnels of the coal and oil burners were shortened as the efficiency of the boilers improved. On the early steamers the funnels were almost the same height as the masts and, indeed, on Henry Bell's *Comet* and some of its compatriots, the funnel was the mast for the auxiliary square sail. The telescopic funnels of some of the Thames excursion steamers were rarely if ever extended to their full height, *Crested Eagle*, for example, being noted for its short squat (and rather ugly) funnel. *Crested Eagle* was, however, the first pleasure steamer in UK waters to be built with oil-fired boilers.

Boiler design evolved rapidly from the land type installed aboard the *Comet* to the flue boiler. The flue boiler was a cylindrical shell containing a furnace tube and a long grate. Flue boilers were common in the early steamships, including the transatlantic steamers *Royal William*, *British Queen*, *Great Western* and the *Britannia* class of Cunarders. Demand for steam at less than 15psi was easily satisfied by the rectangular, or box, boiler, the Royal Navy preferring the furnace to be entirely contained within the boiler (the wet-bottomed type), as opposed to beneath the boiler (the dry-bottomed type) which was preferred by the Merchant Navy. The rectangular boiler incorporated a series of fire or flue tubes that carried the hot gases through the water chamber, but its square design restricted the maximum steam pressure to no more than 30psi. As a rectangular vessel, its main drawback was that it needed additional staying and bracing, whereas the same combustion principle when applied to a cylindrical shaped boiler did away with much of the bracing. Later in the nineteenth century the cylindrical boiler reached its final development as the workhorse of the seven seas in the form of the Scotch marine boiler.

Variations on the boiler theme included the haystack boiler, a simple watertube boiler that could generate steam up to 120psi. It was of large diameter, much like a haystack, with vertical water tubes mounted above a large furnace bed. The haystack boiler was initially used in conjunction with the steeple engine, which was also designed to be small and compact for the power it developed, but it became very common when it was used in conjunction with the single-cylinder diagonal engine. This combination with both steeple and diagonal engines was found mainly on the Clyde and Scottish west coast passenger services, and is typified by David Hutcheson's (later David MacBrayne's) long-lived, steeple-engined favourite *Glencoe,* built in 1846 as *Mary Jane.* When Hutcheson acquired the steamer in 1857 he had the original jet condenser replaced by a surface condenser, and the original horizontal boiler was replaced in 1883. Then, in 1907, the vessel received its first haystack boiler, secondhand from the pad-

dler *Fusilier* of 1888, which was being re-boilered with a larger one of the same type. This combination served *Glencoe* for a further 21 years until another hand-me-down haystack was installed, this time from the bigger fleet-mate *Grenadier* after its disastrous fire. Three years later, in 1931, the veteran *Glencoe* was withdrawn and broken up, its engines, like the ship, having provided 85 years' service.

Before the *Glencoe* left for the scrapyard it was exhibited alongside the new MacBrayne, state-of-the-art, diesel-electric, twin-screw mail vessel *Lochfyne* at the Broomielaw in Glasgow. Old and new, little and large, alongside each other, but the main difference was that the old steamer had glided and hissed its way to its destinations while the new diesel-electric ship was set to rattle and vibrate across the sea while entertaining its passengers with the din of its engines. The *Glencoe*'s engines were taken to Glasgow's Kelvingrove Art Gallery and put into store for future exhibition. Sadly, in the 1940s, the wartime demand for metals overcame any leanings towards history and the old engines were melted down – a small but no doubt necessary contribution to the war effort.

The final version of the marine boiler was the watertube, in which the steam was raised in many relatively small diameter tubes surrounded by the flames from the fuel combustion. These boilers were initially developed in the 1880s to provide high-pressure steam, 200psi and upwards, for powering the recently introduced fast torpedo-boat destroyers. One of the pioneer boilers was the Yarrow three-drum design. Probably the only watertube boiler ever deployed in raising steam for a paddle engine was of the Yarrow design.

It was found that considerably improved steam generation could be achieved with the use of closed stoke-holds and forced draught, and these were introduced from the late 1880s onwards. The application of forced draught when applied to burning fuel increases the rate of combustion and the release of heat, and provides a much increased quantity of steam from a similar amount of fuel.

But just as boiler design improved, so also did engine design (see diagram outlining the evolution of the paddle steamer engine), the steeple engine being but one relatively minor development of the original crosshead design. Many naval architects and marine engineers preferred to stay with the tried and tested side-lever and walking-beam machinery, and the former remained the preferred power unit for many paddle tugs in Europe until the type was ultimately withdrawn from service.

The engine choices for the larger paddle steamers were many and varied, each type

Fusilier (1888) plied the west coast of Scotland with steam generated by a haystack boiler.

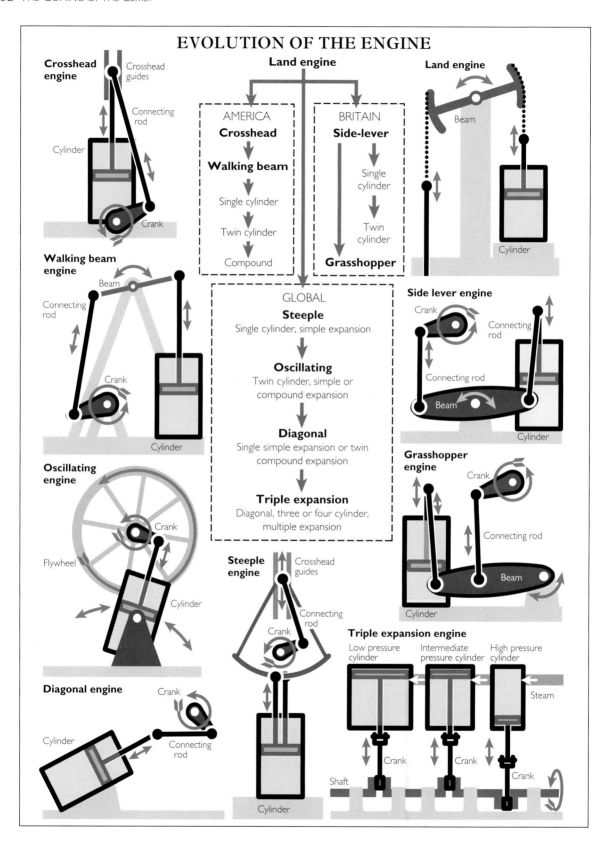

EVOLUTION OF THE ENGINE

being designed successively to be more powerful, more thermally efficient and more compact in space utilisation and weight. The first of the new designs was the oscillating engine, in which the cylinders were mounted on trunnions and situated below the crankshaft. As the piston rod was directly connected to the crank pin without the introduction of a connecting rod, this caused the cylinder block to oscillate back and forth as the pistons rose and fell within the cylinders. This type of engine was very popular because it was compact, relatively light, had a low centre of gravity and was very smooth and vibration-free in operation.

The boiler steam was fed into the engine through a hollow trunnion on one side of the cylinder, and the spent steam was exhausted to the condenser through the hollow trunnion on the opposite side. However, keeping the trunnion joints steamtight was always difficult, and the design eventually fell out of favour with ever increasing steam pressures. Compound oscillating engines were quite common, but twin compound oscillating engines, such as those aboard the Blackpool pleasure steamer *Queen of the North*, were designed with the single purpose of turning the engineer's hair white by the season's end.

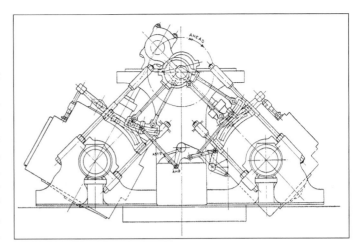

In the pursuit of ever more horsepower, however, the inclined or diagonal engine was the ultimate development of the steam paddle engine, and it became the preferred unit, both in Europe and America, for propelling side paddle wheel vessels. G E Barr outlined the development and benefits of the type:

The diagonal type of engine with roller guides was patented in 1822 by Brunel. The design, although in its original form, was evolved quite early and some examples were fitted in ships as far back as 1844. As its many advantages over all

Schematic section through the simple oscillating engine.

The Blackpool excursion steamer *Queen of the North* (1895) was one of only a few vessels to be powered by twin compound oscillating engines.

other types was realised, it gradually superseded all other forms and became the only type likely to be considered for a modern paddle steamer. Its advantages, such as compactness, low height and weight and the fact that it can be built in almost any size up to about 10,000 horse power, make it the obvious choice. The development of the diagonal engine was comparatively slow and started with the large low-speed single cylinder type. This was fitted in many ships including the now famous [Clyde based steamer, built in 1888] *Lucy Ashton*, on which one could feel the thrust of the huge piston as it moved back and forward to drive the paddle wheels. The difficulties of starting a single cylinder engine and the lack of balance, coupled with the demand for greater economy and smoother running, and the general progress of marine engineering soon led to the introduction of two-crank compound, and three crank triple expansion engines.

Interestingly, when the London & North Western Railway's Holyhead to Dublin overnight paddle steamers *Lily* and *Violet* were re-engined in 1891 the owners stipulated that the new engines must be of the steeple design. The pair had been delivered by Laird Brothers of Birkenhead in 1880 and equipped with two-cylinder oscillating engines to give a speed of 17½ knots. When they came to be upgraded to 19½ knots it was realised that only the steeple engine would be powerful enough while also being able to fit into the existing engine compartment, which was restricted in length because it was situated between two boiler rooms. Six new locomotive-type boilers were installed in each ship to supply steam at 150psi to the new engines. The conversion was hugely successful, did not impact upon the passenger accommodation, and provided both *Lily* and *Violet* with a further 12 years' service.

Owing to the introduction of mild steel of reliable quality in the late 1870s, there was a surge in the improvement of boiler design which led to ever higher steam pressures. It was only then that the benefits to be obtained from the long-established concept of double or compound expansion, and later triple expansion, working were capable of being economically realised. Multiple-expansion working occurs where the boiler steam in the first cylinder performs work, expands and drops in pressure as a consequence. It is then exhausted into an adjacent and larger diameter cylinder, where it again performs a similar amount of work, resulting in a further increase in volume and drop in pressure, after which it is again exhausted, but this time to the condenser. With even higher boiler pressures the expansion can take place in three and sometimes even four separate cylinders.

The triple or multiple expansion engine remained the mainstay of the world's merchant fleet until the advent of the slow-speed diesel engine, but the same multiple expansion type of engine was in use in paddle steamers from the late nineteenth century through to the demise of paddle propulsion that took accelerated hold in the 1960s.

The diesel engine and the paddle wheel – an excerpt from G Barr's paper to the Institution of Engineers and Shipbuilders in Scotland, 1951

The diesel engine has long been a competitor of the steam engine on account of its low fuel consumption. It is not surprising, therefore, that many successful attempts have been made to adapt this form of machinery to drive paddle wheels. At first it was thought that the only satisfactory method would be by diesel-electric propulsion, using a number of small high speed diesel engines to drive electric generators which in turn would supply current to propulsion motors coupled to the paddle wheels. From the first, no trouble was experienced with the electrical part of the equipment; unfortunately the same could not always be said about the diesel engines although these troubles have now been largely overcome [writing in 1951]. The small high-speed diesel engines suffered from having the cylinder jackets cooled by sea water instead of the now almost universal freshwater closed circuit cooling. One of the earliest examples of diesel-electric machinery fitted to a paddle vessel was that fitted to the [Firth of Forth] ferries *Queen Margaret* and *Robert the Bruce*, built in 1934. Two 8 cylinder, 4 cycle diesel engines of 190 brake horse power running at 750rpm each powered a main generator of 130kW at 440 volts, which supplied current to two propulsion motors each of 135 horse power at 270rpm, each of which is coupled to a side paddle wheel by a Renolds Chain reduction gear. The vessels obtained a speed of 9 knots on trials.

Another notable example was the diesel-electric vessel *Talisman*, built in 1935 [see Chapter 12]. This vessel was fitted with four diesel engines of 440 brake horse power driving main generators of 248kW and 295 volts at 600rpm and was notable in having a large low speed electric propulsion motor directly coupled to the paddle wheels, and developing 1,300 shaft horse power at 50rpm. The control of the vessel is directly from the bridge. As the cost of diesel-electric machinery is considerable a successful attempt was made in 1949 to drive a paddle vessel by diesel engines coupled to the wheels through mechanical gearing. This machinery was fitted to the *Mary Queen of Scots*, a sister ship of the *Queen Margaret* and *Robert the Bruce*. The layout of the machinery of this vessel was similar to the two earlier vessels, except that each paddle wheel was mechanically coupled to a 4 cylinder, 2 cycle engine, developing 150 brake horse power at 625rpm through a reverse reduction gear and chain reduction drive. The paddle wheels revolve at 41rpm at full speed.

In order to simplify still further the application of diesel engines driving paddle wheels, the *Richard Lander*, one of two stern wheel vessels for use on the River Niger, was built in 1951. This vessel was fitted with a 4 cylinder, 2 cycle direct reversing diesel engine developing 400 shaft brake horse power at 300rpm and coupled to the stern wheel through a worm reduction gear driving the paddle wheel at 30rpm.

Forth ferry *Mary Queen of Scots* (1949) was powered by a diesel engine coupled to the paddle shaft via a reduction gearbox and reduction chain drive.

5 MOSTLY IRON SHIPS

The Admiralty watched the development of steam closely. It was nervous of the new technology for a variety of reasons, not least a prudish concern that its pristine white sails would get soiled by smoke and soot, and that the introduction of steam would doubtless undermine the art of seamanship. As the Royal Navy was a 'blue water' fleet with a world-wide operational remit, it had to rely on sail power to make long ocean passages, as the warship, if fitted only with steam engines, would not be able to carry sufficient fuel. Coaling stations were almost non-existent then. The Admiralty commissioned four small vessels primarily for towing duties from 1819, but was shy of committing steamers to the battle arena. Indeed, it was only in 1827 that a steamer was allowed to be blessed with the prefix HMS. Essentially armed tugs, these vessels were used to tow the fleet out to sea, after which men were sent alongside the paddle boxes to unhook the paddle floats to allow the 'tugs' to accompany the fleet under sail. The first paddle warships were commissioned in 1828, the same year that formal engineer training commenced. But what rank should those dirty, sweaty men in the stokehold carry? They were simply engineers until well into the 1830s, when they were bestowed the humble rank of Warrant, one junior to Carpenter.

There were, however, two distinct disadvantages to a paddle steamer at war. The conventional paddle wheel was vulnerable to attack, and it also limited the broadside armament, which could be mounted only fore and aft of the wheel assembly. That being so, there are only two recorded incidents of a paddle wheel being damaged in action, and in both instances the vessel carried on steaming at slow speed using the good wheel balanced by the rudder. By the time Cunard's *Acadia* had sailed from Liverpool the Admiralty and a range of other European navies had deployed a number of paddle frigates to a variety of designs. They still built the traditional wooden-walled sailing ships with one deck, or more commonly two decks, lined with cannon. These were the preferred men-of-war, as the paddle steamers were still eyed with suspicion. Besides, it was well known in the navy that the vibration of the steamer's machinery would eventually shake the wooden hulls to pieces without any need for action on the part of the enemy.

But in 1840 the paddler did go to war, and was used in anger on the front line for the first time at the capture of Acre in Syria. John Winton in his history of the Royal Navy wrote:

In November 1840, a fleet which included armed paddle steamers, under Admiral The Honourable Sir Robert Stopford in the *Princess Charlotte*, and Commodore 'Mad Charlie' Napier in the *Powerful*, captured Mehemet Ali's fortress of St Jean d'Acre after a heavy bombardment. Steamships came under enemy fire for the first time and Admiral Stopford shifted his flag to the steam frigate *Phoenix*, commanded by his son, to get closer to the action – the first time a C-in-C had flown his flag in a steamer in action.

The size of the steam frigate grew rapidly in the 1840s, paddle frigates such as *Cyclops*, *Gorgon* and *Geyser* being typical. One oddity was *Penelope*, a former French *Hebe*-class sailing frigate taken from the French along with about 30 similar ships at the end of the Napoleonic Wars. Too small for use in combat, they were laid aside, apart from *Penelope*, which in 1843 was cut in half so that a new 63ft-long middle section could be inserted, complete with two direct-acting engines generating a massive 700hp, boilers and bunkers, and paddle wheels. Although heralded at the time as a success, none of its French counterparts were similarly converted. *Penelope*, with a crew of 300, was capable of taking 1,000 soldiers as far as the Cape of Good Hope on the 600 tons of coal it carried. Its armament sounds formidable: two 10in pivot guns weighing nearly half a ton each, fourteen 32-pounders and eighty-six 8-pounders.

The Honourable East India Company had also commissioned a small number of paddle steamships, but was reluctant to use them on its longer routes. One of the largest of these was the *Moozoffer*, 1,440 tons burthen, which was launched at Limehouse in 1846 and built at a cost of £100,000. It had two engines which provided 500hp. All of the East India Company's steamers were armed defensively. However, a number of these steamers were used aggressively against pirates and during the Opium War to destroy armed junks deployed to prevent British traders bringing opium into China.

The development of the screw propeller inevitably put the paddle wheel under scrutiny. The screw offers better contact with the water as it is totally immersed, whereas the paddle is only partly submerged and sometimes in a rough sea is not submerged at all. But the most significant difference is that the propeller has a tendency to restore a static condition to the turbulence its rotation creates, so reducing frictional losses and greatly enhancing efficiency.

The classic and oft-quoted story of HMS *Rattler* and HMS *Alecto* was the beginning of the end for the paddle wheel, as John Winton reported:

The question of which was the more efficient, paddle wheels or screw propeller, was decisively settled in the famous trials between two frigates of about equal size and engine power, the *Rattler*, fitted with a propeller, and the paddle steamer *Alecto*. In 1845, in a series of races under steam, under sail and under steam and sail, over some 70 miles between the Nore and Yarmouth Roads, the *Rattler* beat the *Alecto* by several miles. In a later trial during March, with the ships tied together at their sterns and both going full speed ahead on their engines, the *Rattler* towed the *Alecto* stern first at a speed of 2.7 knots. It was a convincing result, but in fact the Admiralty were already convinced. They had ordered screw ships for the Navy in the previous year and now ordered more.

Oddly, Their Lordships also commissioned a small steamer for additional tests in an attempt to overcome the accusation that the *Rattler* and *Alecto* trial was not a like-for-like test. The *Bee* had paddle wheels that propelled it one way and a screw that took it the other. Trials with the *Bee* showed clearly that the thrust from the paddles was consistently 12 per cent greater than the early type of screw then in use. The trials were kept hidden from the public and *Rattler* became overall winner despite the uneven playing field.

The Admiralty was less convinced about the viability of iron hulls. While tests were carried out, the first iron-hulled warship, HMS *Alert*, a paddle gunboat, was commissioned in 1840. Several more iron paddle steamers were commissioned over the next five years, after which the Admiralty returned to wooden construction, having uncovered three serious operational difficulties:

1. The resistance of iron to shellfire was untested.
2. Iron hulls tended to foul rapidly compared with the copper bottoms of wooden fighting ships.
3. Magnetic compasses were erratic in an iron hull.

While tests were ongoing, the Admiralty even built a series of wooden-hulled battleships complete with masts and yards but fitted with steam engines coupled to a propeller. It was soon apparent that hulls

built with the much improved quality of iron and sheathed with timber were better suited to resist the impact of missiles. Coincidental with this development was the work done by the eminent physicist Lord Kelvin in developing the mariner's compass, which could be corrected and adjusted to eliminate the magnetic deviation caused by the iron hull, and allowed ships to be more safely navigated. The other drawback of iron hulls, fouling by marine growth, was eventually overcome by Victorian chemists developing anti-fouling paint applications for the submerged areas of the ship's hull. The end of the paddle era was 1861, when the iron screw-propelled battleship *Warrior* joined the fleet to show off its top speed of 13½ knots. (HMS *Warrior* is now preserved at Portsmouth.) The remaining paddle

frigates and gunboats were soon laid up in reserve and gradually released from the fleet.

The Admiralty dislike of the paddle steamer did not stop it deploying paddlers on long deep-sea voyages in later years. For example, in 1882 it received the new survey ship *Triton*, schooner rigged, complete with bowsprit and figurehead and twin funnels. Its first twenty years' service took it mainly to the Pacific. *Triton* became a training ship at Gravesend on eventual retirement from a long and active life, and was broken up only in 1961.

A landmark civilian vessel was *Rainbow*, delivered to GSN by John Laird in 1838. The first iron-hulled vessel in the GSN fleet, it was used by the company to investigate the performance of iron and also caught the attention of the Admiralty, which carried out experiments to validate the magnetic compass aboard an otherwise magnetic ship. *Rainbow* was placed on the Antwerp and Rotterdam services, and the next iron-hulled ship in the fleet, *Magician*, commissioned in 1844, was deployed at Newhaven. Thereafter only iron-hulled vessels were ordered, although a number of wooden-hulled paddlers subsequently joined the company as secondhand purchases.

The viability of larger iron hulls was proved by Isambard Brunel when he designed *Great Britain*, originally as a paddle steamer. Its keel was laid at Bristol in a special dry dock in 1839. It was indeed large,

of nearly 3,000 tons gross and 332ft length overall, complete with six masts and a fiddle bow. Cuthbert Bridgwater wrote in *Sea Breezes* for April 1961:

> Brunel originally meant her to be a paddle steamer like the *Great Western* and she was well advanced when T P Smith's screw boat *Archimedes* arrived at Bristol, and so impressed Brunel with her performance, that, although the *Great Britain*'s paddle box frames were already in place, he had her altered to screw propulsion . . . She took the water on 19 July 1843, Prince Albert coming from Windsor to christen her.

Paddle wheels or not, *Great Britain* was a fine ship built to the traditional hull design of the sailing ship (*Great Britain* is now preserved at Bristol).

Brunel did give the paddle a second chance when he had the massive 18,915-ton *Great Eastern* built by J Scott Russell & Company at Millwall. It was to be managed and part-owned by the Eastern Steam Navigation Company. This company had earlier placed the wooden-hulled *India* and *Precursor* on a Suez to India route to pre-empt the start of the P&O service between India and UK with overland connection between Suez and Alexandria in 1843 (see Chapter 2). The Eastern Steam Navigation Company again created upset when it bid unsuccessfully against P&O for the Australian mail contract; yet here it was again, this time in cahoots with Brunel. Brunel co-opted the outstanding naval architect Scott Russell to help design the ship. *Great Eastern* was launched in 1858, complete with paddle wheels and a screw as well as a full set of sails. The idea was that it should serve the long route to India and with its large bunkers could use the best of paddle, screw or wind, depending on the prevailing conditions, without having to refuel.

The failed launching of the ship and subsequent delays in its completion drained the resources of the Eastern Steam Navigation Company, which was obliged to sell its share in the vessel. Its new owners rather surprisingly put this large-capacity liner on to the North Atlantic, where its extra large bunkers offered no advantage. It was found to be a fit challenge on the Atlantic regarding speed, where a 12-knot service speed and top speed of 14 knots was good for that period. The owners refused to take emigrants from the Continent, and preferred their mighty ship half-loaded. It was soon declared uncompetitive, unable to fill its 4,000 passenger berths, and was chartered out for use as a cable layer. At one stage it was on charter to carry passengers to the World Trade Fair in France, but soon returned to cable laying, later spending 12 years laid up at Milford Haven.

The mighty steamer, which Brunel had often affectionately referred to as his 'Big Babe', ended its days on the Mersey. It had been leased for 12 months as an advertising hoarding to the Bon Marché and Lewis's department stores and as a funfair attraction during the Exhibition of Navigation, Travelling, Commerce and Manufactures held at Liverpool in 1886. It was sold in 1888 for demolition at New Ferry, just up-river from its moorings in the Sloyne Channel. Interestingly, when it sailed from Milford Haven to the Mersey, once the rust had been eased from the long disused moving parts of its engines it was able to make 5½ knots using the screw alone. At that stage in the vessel's career the paddle floats had largely rotted away, and the paddle wheels were removed at Milford Haven before it sailed.

On the Atlantic Cunard had attempted to deal with the Collins Line by introducing an upgraded fleet led by the wooden-hulled *Asia* and *Africa* of 1850 and the improved *Arabia* of 1852. Collins still held supreme. With its ships supporting the Crimean War in 1854, the Cunard New York service was suspended. But it was not all in favour of the Collins Line steamers, larger, more luxurious and faster than the Cunarders though they were. The Collins Line coal bill was so huge that its ships started to run at slower speeds. At each turn-round at New York there were expensive repairs to be made as the ships

Brunel's 'Big Babe' – the *Great Eastern*

Brunel's 'Big Babe' was built at Millwall for a quite staggering cost of £1½ million and known as *Leviathan*. Government had invested heavily in the project, which was seen as an advertisement for British naval engineering. The first keel plate was laid in May 1854, and it took 42 months to get the ship to a state of preparedness fit for launching. The launching was botched because the builders refused to pay extra for Brunel's recommended system of launching rams and because Brunel's system of signalling at the launch was obscured by the crowds of onlookers. The problem was caused by Brunel's usual cleverness/cautiousness in insisting upon a controlled launch with winches and brakes, whereas Scott Russell, the shipbuilder, preferred a dynamic side launch in which the weight of the ship combined with the declivity of the launch-ways would have guaranteed a safe and swift entry into the Thames. The sponsor at the launch named the ship *Leviathan*, and then had to be corrected as that name had been dropped in favour of *Great Eastern*. Although the career of the ship was disappointing it was by no means a failure. The hybrid screw and paddle propulsion could maintain a speed of over 12 knots in a head sea, and it was large enough to ride out the worst of the weather. Had it been able to fill its numerous passenger berths it would have brought the benefit of economy of scale.

The most fascinating part of *Great Eastern* story is the engineering. G M Gaynor wrote in *Sea Breezes*, February 1980:

Brunel's *Great Eastern* (1858), from a lithograph by Whipple & Black, Boston.

The [four-bladed screw was] a single casting in iron weighing 36 tons with a diameter of 24 feet and the paddles were 54 feet in diameter each weighing 90 tons. The length of the vessel was 692 feet with a beam of 83 feet, depth at side 58 feet. The builder's measurement of gross tonnage was 22,927.

There was cargo stowage for 6,000 tons and coal bunkers for 10,000 tons. Draft when loaded was calculated at 30 feet. Another feature was the fact that each separate screw and paddle had its own four-cylinder engine. The normal horse power of the paddle engines was 1,000 and that of the screw engines 1,600.

In the hull there was 6,250 tons of iron and 2,500 tons of woodwork, the anchors and cables weighed a further 253 tons, while about 10,000 tons of iron plates were used in the construction of the hull. As each plate weighed about 1/3 ton and was secured by 100 rivets, there were about 30,000 plates and 3 million rivets employed in the construction.

The tonnage of the vessel meant that it could not be dry-docked, and as its bottom became more and more fouled its speed fell back from the 14 knots achieved in its transatlantic days. Its size also meant that few harbours could accommodate the ship alongside, so Brunel equipped it with 20 anchors at strategic intervals around the ship to ensure its safety. It also carried 20 lifeboats. It was 41 years after its launching before the *Oceanic* exceeded *Great Eastern* in length, and 48 years before it was exceeded in size by the newly completed *Lusitania*. *Great Eastern* was a truly remarkable ship.

continued to tear themselves apart, even when operating at reduced speeds; speeds that were clearly still too fast for the heavy seas the vessels normally encountered on the Atlantic run.

Cunard's comeback was *Persia*, the first iron ship on the transatlantic services. At its launch, attended by 55,000 admiring onlookers, it became the largest merchant ship to date. Completed in 1855, with iron frames and an all-iron hull, *Persia* was 360ft long and 35 ft in breadth, and offered 1,200 tons deadweight, far greater than any of its wooden forebears. On trials it attained 17½ knots, but a more economical speed was about 15½ knots with the paddles turning at about 17rpm. *Persia* accommodated 200 first-class and 50 second-class passengers. The first-class staterooms were on the main deck, and the main saloon was aft of the ladies' saloon and a smoking room for the men, all housed in a long deckhouse on the after deck. It left Liverpool on its maiden voyage on 26 January 1856, some three days after the Collins Line's *Pacific*. *Persia* arrived at New York on 9 February, reporting serious icing on the Grand Banks and having suffered damage to its paddle floats, a third of which were lost in the ice. *Pacific* along with its 240 passengers and crew, was never

heard of again, presumed sunk following a collision with ice.

The earlier loss of the Collins Line's *Arctic*, following a collision at sea in 1854 with the loss of 322 passengers, led to the order for a new paddle steamer to be called *Adriatic*. It was the last wooden-hulled paddle steamer built for the North Atlantic run, but was delayed in building and was not delivered until 1857. With two major losses, the mounting costs of maintaining wooden hulls at fast speeds on the North Atlantic and, finally, the loss of the American mail contract to Cornelius Vanderbilt, the Collins Line was forced, in 1858, to file for bankruptcy. The new *Adriatic* completed only one voyage for its owners before it was laid up and later sold.

New Yorker Cornelius Vanderbilt was an outspoken critic of 'companies profiteering on government subsidies', and tendered a very low offer for the Federal Government mail contract in 1857. He deployed the wooden paddle steamers *Vanderbilt* and *Ariel*, built in 1855 and *North Star*, commissioned in 1853, on the Vanderbilt Line's New York to Bremen service, calling at Cowes with the mails for England. The ships also called at Le Havre between 1855, at the start of the service, and 1857, but that call ceased when

The first iron-hulled steamer in the Cunard fleet was *Persia* (1855).

The American wooden-hulled steamer *Adriatic* (1856) managed only one return crossing of the Atlantic for the Collins Line.

Adriatic, Collins Line, New York

First published in *Frank Leslie's Illustrated Newspaper*, New York, 28 November 1857

The *Adriatic* is the largest steamship ever built in this country, and is, without exception, the largest wooden vessel in the world. She is 354 feet long, 9 feet longer than the United States frigate *Niagara*; 55 broad, and 33 feet 2 inches in depth. She measures 5,900 tons, or 700 tons more than the *Niagara*, 800 more than the *Vanderbilt*, and 2,900 more than the *Atlantic*! So perfect is she in all her proportions – so graceful in every curve, and so exquisitely modelled – that, as she sits upon the water, the spectator at a short distance would hardly give her credit for half the size. She can accommodate over 300 first class, and about 60 second class passengers, and carry some 2,000 tons of cargo.

Her grand dining room on the main deck is 75 feet long by 25 feet wide, and is furnished with three rows of tables. The ceiling is finished in oak, the beams being supported on pilasters with angle trusses, representing heads of different animals, and ornamented with clusters of fruits and flowers. On either side of the apartment are twelve windows, the glass of which is stained with pictures, flowers, fruits, and birds; while the space between the windows is divided into 42 panels, adorned with groups of fruit, flowers, fish, and game, worked in oak dried papier-mâché, but resembling very closely elaborately-carved oak. The seats in the dining room are upholstered in rich crimson velvet, and the curtains are of heavy silk . . .

The smoking room is fitted up in

The 75ft-long grand dining room on the main deck.

exquisite taste and will accommodate 60 persons; it is on the same deck [main deck] together with the store rooms of the stewards and other officers. The second class passenger's dining room is forward on the same deck, and though not equally splendid in decorations with the main saloon, is most comfortable in its appointments, and will accommodate 40 persons. The spar deck has the grand first class saloon, which rivals the dining room in splendour. Its sides are occupied by 130 state rooms, broken at every 12 feet by alcoves; and the ceiling is painted in imitation of fresco, and adorned with gilt diamonded ornaments, through which a constant ventilation is kept up. Paintings, covered with thick glass are let into the panels at regular intervals; while around them inlaid woods, marbles, bronzes, and gold are lavishly bestowed. A soft light streaming through the stained windows gives to the room quite an imposing appearance.

On the same deck [spar deck], and past the forward smoke-stack, are the rooms for the second cabin passengers. In the bow, on the deck below, are store rooms and berths for the waiters and other servants. On this deck the cargo will be stowed. The lowest, or coal deck, is entirely of iron, and the engine and boiler rooms are covered with the same material.

The propelling power of the *Adriatic* is composed of two of the largest oscillating engines ever built, each of 100 inch cylinder, a nominal horse power of 1,500 and an actual horse power of 3,000. The furnaces require from 50 to 60 firemen and coal-passers, and no less than six engineers will be required to attend the engines. The wheels are each 40 feet in diameter . . . Altogether the ponderous mass of the machinery strikes the beholder with awe . . .

The *Adriatic* sailed for Liverpool at the beginning of this week on her first trip across the Atlantic. Her departure was witnessed by admiring thousands, who wished the magnificent vessel a safe trip, a speedy return, and a success such as will meet the expectations of her owners and the American public.

[*Adriatic*, of course, was laid up for sale when it returned to New York from its maiden transatlantic voyage.]

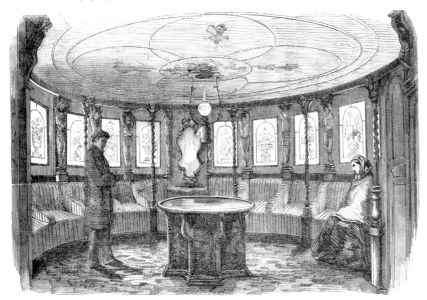

After part of the ladies' saloon.

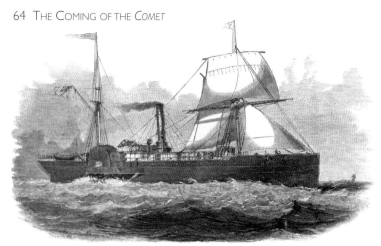

The American owned, wooden hulled *Vanderbilt* (1855) had one of the few walking-beam engines deployed on the North Atlantic.

the French part of the mail contract was revoked. The steamers were well appointed, but they were no match for the innovative iron-hulled screw steamers then being deployed by the Inman Line. The Vanderbilt Line ceased to operate in 1860, and thereafter British companies again reigned supreme on the North Atlantic.

The challenge to Cunard from the Inman Line was significant. The Inman Board had experimentally adopted screw propulsion, initially slower than paddles, but its steamers were giving Cunard a run for its money. It had also introduced steerage accommodation for immigrants in 1852, before which they were obliged to take passage by sailing ship. However, the Admiralty still insisted that its mail contracts be fulfilled by paddle steamers, and the last paddle steamer built for Cunard was the 3,870 ton *Scotia*, completed in 1862 and a fine running mate for the earlier and somewhat similar *Persia*. Cunard went back to Government to ask permission to carry the mails in screw propelled steamers, and with authority now granted it also commissioned the first of its screw steamers, the smaller *China*, also in 1862. The two ships were both built at the same yard by Robert Napier & Sons at Govan on the Clyde. *China* still carried auxiliary sails but it proved the economics of screw propulsion once and for all, although it was quickly superseded and was sold to Spanish owners in 1880.

Scotia was designed very much with safety in mind. There were six transverse watertight bulkheads, just as there were in *Persia*, but *Sco-*

tia also had four flotation 'caisson compartments'. The iron hull was 4in thick to resist ice damage and there were five iron keelsons. The hull was double bottomed for the entire length of the ship. *Scotia* was the last of the side-lever engined liners, with two very large 100in-diameter cylinders with a stroke of 12ft; 2,800 tons of iron was used to construct the ship. It had a gross tonnage of 3,871 and a deadweight of 1,400 tons. The paddle wheels were 40ft in diameter, with 25 fixed floats each 11½ft by 2ft. It could maintain a speed of over 16 knots, and brought the voyage to New York down to just over eight days. *Scotia* held the best eastward and westward records until 1869, beating the Inman liners of the day and ultimately losing to their *City of Brussels* (Table 1). In 1878 *Scotia* was sold and converted for use as a cable layer.

One-time master of *Scotia* was Captain C H E Judkins, greatly respected by his employer but not so popular with his passengers. On choosing a passage, consideration was given in those days both to which ship was available and which master was in charge of it, and Captain Judkins's singular gruffness did little to promote his ship. One of the apocryphal tales about him was that, when the ship was approaching the coast of Newfoundland, a lady passenger asked: 'Oh Captain, do tell me, is it always as foggy and nasty as this off the Banks?' Judkins glanced at the lady and then resumed his vacant stare to reply: 'How the devil do I know, Madam? I don't live here.'

The problem of having to carry enormous quantities of coal across the Atlantic on each voyage was tackled by one company by reducing the distance needed to travel. The Atlantic Royal Mail Steam Navigation Company was established in 1858 with chartered steamers to start a mail service between Boston and Galway on the west coast of Ireland. In due course it commissioned four new steamers, *Connaught* in 1860, which was lost by fire on its second voyage out of Galway, *Columbia* in 1861, and *Anglia* and *Hibernia* in 1863. They were unimpressive paddle steamers with accommodation for about 200 first- and 600 second-class passengers; all were notoriously underpowered. Chartered tonnage also included the 1,470-ton iron paddle steamer *Pacific*, built for the Sydney & Melbourne Steam Packet Company in 1859, with 245 passenger berths, 80 of them in first class. The company even bought the liner *Adriatic* from the bankrupt Collins Line.

The voyage between Boston and Galway had to be carried out in seven days, with complicated overland and sea connections to London and other mainland destinations as well as a sea connection for New York at the other end. Although demands on the bunkers would be reduced by one or two days' sailing, the planned service really went from somewhere nobody wanted to depart from to somewhere many did not want to go to. The new service, dubbed the Galway Line, lost the mail contract in 1861 and suspended its sailings until a new mail contract was awarded in 1863. Speed became the issue, and none of the ships could maintain the schedule demanded by the new mail contract; typical crossing times were 14 days and more. Following repeated penalty payments the company chose in 1864 to opt out of its mail contract and

withdraw from the Boston route. *Pacific* never returned to its Australian owners, and was sold to Confederate Army agents to run the Federal blockade (see Chapter 6).

The Compagnie Générale Transatlantique, or the French Line, as the American travelling public preferred to call it, entered the fray in 1864 when the big 3,200-gross-ton iron-hulled paddle steamer *Washington* sailed from Le Havre for New York. This ship and its companions, *Lafayette* and *Europe*, were built for luxury and elegance rather than sheer speed, but could maintain well over 13 knots. All three were built by Scotts at Greenock. Within a year three more iron paddlers were in service, *Saint Laurent*, *Impératrice Eugénie* and *Napoleon III*, and they were followed in 1866 by the twins *Nouveau-Monde* and *Panama*. Three more ships were laid down as paddle steamers but converted during construction to screw steamers. Trials demonstrated that speeds of a little over 15 knots were feasible with the screw steamers, convincing the owner that the day of the paddle wheel was all but over. The eight paddle steamers were each taken in hand and converted to screw propulsion, *Nouveau-Monde* and *Panama* becoming pioneers in the

Nyanza (1864) was the last paddle steamer to be built for P&O. (DP WORLD P&O HERITAGE COLLECTION)

Atrato (1853) was the first iron-hulled paddle steamer built for the Royal Mail Steam Packet Company.

frozen-meat export trade from the USA, now fitted with refrigerated chambers and duly renamed *Labrador* and *Canada*.

P&O commissioned a number of successful iron-hulled paddle steamers, the last being *Nyanza* in 1864. As with other operators of diverse routes, it was useful to retain paddle steamers in a fleet in which some routes required both speed and a shallow draft. But *Nyanza* lasted in the P&O fleet only until 1873, when it was sold for further service with the Union Steamship Company of Australia.

From 1850 the Royal Mail Steam Packet Company was running two main services from Southampton, to the West Indies and to Rio de Janeiro, with its fleet of wooden-hulled paddle steamers. The last wooden steamer was commissioned in 1854, but Royal Mail had already commissioned its first iron-hulled steamer the year before, the mighty *Atrato*, of 3,467 tons gross and then the largest ship afloat (Table 5). With four decks, accommodation for 224 passengers and fit for a service speed of 14 knots, it instantly became the prestige ship of the fleet.

Royal Mail used pack horses to cross the isthmus at Panama and so provide a connection with the Pacific ports. It later built a highway and contributed to the Panama Railroad, and even provided subsidised transport for West Indian migrant labourers working on the new Isthmus Canal until its eventual opening in 1915. But in the mean-

time Colon was the focus for the company on the Spanish Main. In 1867 the last wooden steamer of the original order of fourteen, *Trent*, was dispatched to be broken up at Woolwich. Little by little, as more and more screw steamers entered the fleet, the iron paddlers were also sold or went to the breakers, the last two, *Arno* and *Eider*, surviving in service until the early 1880s. James McQueen, founder of Royal Mail, died in 1870 at the age of 92 with the satisfaction of having realised his dream and having cemented a vision.

The first iron ship in the Pacific Steam Navigation Company's fleet was *Ecuador*, built by Tod & McGregor at Glasgow in 1845 (Table 3). It was William Wheelwright's response to the award of the British mail contract for a regular service between Panama and Valparaiso, with *Ecuador* looking after the Panama-Callao-Guayaquil link. It was followed in 1846 by *New Granada*, another iron-hulled paddler also built on the Clyde, but this time by Smith & Rodgers at Govan. This vessel was followed by the largest ship in the fleet, the 773-ton *Bolivia*, which left Liverpool in October 1849 with 35 passengers en route for Madeira, Rio de Janeiro and Pacific coast ports. But bigger vessels were needed as the routes developed, as described in an article which first appeared in *Sea Breezes* for August 1956:

In 1850 the *Ecuador*, which had not been as successful as expected was sold, and the

Directors decided to spend about £140,000 on 'four large and powerful steamers'. The four ships were to be named *Santiago*, *Lima*, *Bogota* and *Quito*. The *Santiago* was of 1,000 tons and the other three 1,100 tons, each having horse power of 400. All four ships were built on the Clyde. Two years later (1852) the company suffered its first loss of a mail steamer in the stranding of the [wooden-hulled] *Peru*. In May of that year the *Chile* was sold. An order was placed with the Bank Quay Foundry Company of Warrington for a tiny steamer, *La Perlita* (140 tons) for the service between Buenaventura and Panama. The little ship left the Mersey on 17 June 1853 under Captain Maughan, but never reached the coast, presumably foundering on the way. The same fate befell the steamer *Osprey* (109 tons) purchased for the service between Callao, Pisco and Huacho; she too never reached the coast.

Although the company commissioned its first screw steamer in 1853, it continued to order paddle steamers for its shorter routes. In 1854 the Panama Railroad Company opened for business and Pacific Steam was able to sell through tickets to Europe in collaboration with the Royal Mail Steam Packet Company. Yet another small paddle steamer was lost on its delivery voyage in 1856 when *Panama* was wrecked off Point Tamar. However, two steamers did arrive at their destination, the *Inca* and *Valparaiso*, built by John Elder & Company on the Clyde in 1856. Although only small they were significant in that they were the very first successful applications of the compound engine, which had been introduced by John Elder & Company in 1854. The compound engine had been patented by Jonathon Hornblower in 1781 and unsuccessfully tried in America in 1824, but had to wait nearly 75 years before increase in available steam pressure allowed its successful application. All subsequent steamers built for the company had compound engines, and *Santiago*, *Lima* and *Bogota* were sent home to the UK in 1851 and 1852 to be fitted with the new engines.

Valparaiso was employed on the mail run between Valparaiso and Pueto Montt in southern Chile, as described in the personal diary of Third Officer Joste, March 1872 (later promoted captain and eventually superintendent at Callao):

I was fortunate in getting appointed third officer of the paddle wheel steamer *Valparaiso* of the PSNC. Made a few voyages to Tocopilla when the steamer was placed on the mail run to Port Montt (Pueto Montt), making two trips a month. On the third trip on the way from Port Montt to Ancud, the vessel was steered too near the west side of Lagartija Island. She struck a rocky point and very soon filled up and sank close to the shore. In those days there was no communication by wire south of Valdivia. So the second officer was sent in one of the boats with the few passengers we had on board, to Port Montt, from which place he had to ride to Valdivia, more or less 150 miles, to get in touch by wire to Valparaiso.

It was 8.30 am when the steamer went down, a fine morning and near the beach, so there was no danger to life and all hands were landed before the steamer finally touched on the bottom. I employed myself getting stores from the fore-hold of the vessel which was fairly accessible at low tide. Got cases of candles, soap and butter and occasionally made a dive for the bar… After a stay of about three weeks we were delighted to see the steamer *Peru* heave into sight, and this steamer took us back to Valparaiso.

In 1863 and 1864 *Quito* and *Payta* were commissioned, again products of Elders' yard at Glasgow and designed by Elders' naval architect, Thomas Smith. *The Illustrated London News* of 13 February 1864 reported enthusiastically on the maiden voyage of *Quito*:

This beautiful vessel, which left the Mersey on 12th ultimo with mails and

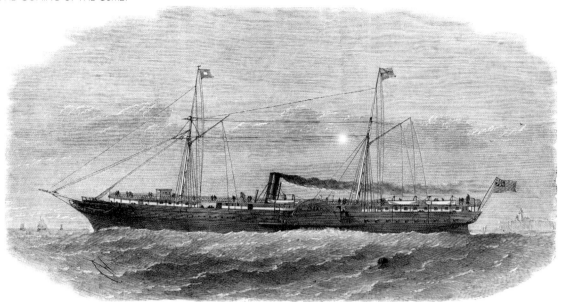

PSNC's *Quito* (1864) left the Mersey on 12 January 1864 to take up station on the Pacific coast. (*THE ILLUSTRATED LONDON NEWS*)

passengers for St Vincent and Monte Video, en route to her station in the South Pacific, measures 71 feet long by 56 feet extreme breadth . . . She is fitted with engines of 1,400 indicated horse power which are the twelfth pair constructed for the company by that firm on their patent double cylinder principle. The *Quito* is fitted with every appliance for the comfort of passengers in warm latitudes and the efficiency of the mail service, which has been suggested by the company's experience since 1840 in Pacific waters. On her trial at Liverpool, a few days before her departure, she attained a mean speed of 13½ knots on the extremely low consumption of 27 cwt [nearly a ton and a half] of Scotch coal per hour, with 25 pounds pressure of steam [psi] and 24 revolutions [per minute] of her engines. She will be a valuable addition to the company's steam fleet, which, commencing with three small vessels, now numbers seventeen first class steamships, and which will be further strengthened by the *Payta*, from the same yard, in July.

Several more paddlers were commissioned for the Pacific company, notably the quintet *Pacific*, *Santiago*, *Limena* and *Panama*. Built in

1865, these were products of John Elder and were paddle steamers with compound engines having boilers exhausting to just one funnel. There was accommodation for nearly 200 passengers. The four ships were intended for the Callao to Valaraiso service but were used instead on a new service. The company had fallen out with the Pacific Railroad Company over fare structures, and decided to inaugurate a direct Valparaiso to Liverpool route. The inaugural sailing for Europe was taken by the paddle steamer *Pacific* in May 1868 carrying 170 passengers, £65,000 in cash, bullion and a full cargo. It arrived at Liverpool 43 days later, and after three weeks in port set off back to Valparaiso.

Sadly, in 1869 *Santiago* was lost after hitting an uncharted rock in the Magellan Strait; two lives were lost. Nevertheless, so successful was the new route to Europe that four purpose-built screw steamers came on line in that year and the paddlers were demoted to Pacific coast duties. The paddlers were later sold out of the company as new screw steamers were commissioned. But the paddle steamers had underpinned the future prosperity of one of the most important British liner companies that would one day host twentieth-century thoroughbreds such as *Reina del Pacifico* and its successor, *Reina del Mar*, on the Liverpool Pacific service via the Panama Canal.

TABLE 5 The paddle steamers of James McQueen's Royal Mail Steam Packet Company

Ship	Year built	Gross tons	Comments
Clyde	1841	1,841	1865 sold
Tweed	1841	1,800	1847 wrecked on Alecranes Reef, Yucatan
Thames	1841	1,889	1865 sold for demolition in West Indies
Forth	1841	1,900	1849 wrecked on Alecranes Reef, Yucatan
Solway	1841	1,700	1843 wrecked on Baldargo Reef, Spain
Tay	1841	1,858	1856 beached near Vera Cruz, Mexico (navigational error)
Medina	1841	1,800	1842 wrecked off Turks Island, Bahamas
Medway	1841	1,895	1861 sold
Dee	1841	1,849	1862 sold
Trent	1841	1,856	1866 sold and scrapped 1867
Teviot	1841	1,744	1864 sold
Isis	1841	1,900	1842 sunk off Bermuda after earlier grounding – escorted at time by *Medway*
Actæon	1837	650	1841 bought from J&G Burns; 1844 wrecked off Carthagena, Columbia
City of Glasgow	1840	1,700	1841 bought from Thomson & McConnell; 1848 sold after two years laid up
Avon	1842	2,069	1862 lost alongside at Colon during storm
Severn	1842	1,886	1856 scrapped
Reindeer	1840	600	1845 bought from G Langtry & Co Liverpool; 1849 sold
Eagle	1846	630	1861 bought from Taylor & Scott, Dublin and resold
Conway	1846	895	1870 sold
Great Western	1838	1,775	1847 bought from Great Western Steamship Co; 1856 broken up after trooping
Derwent	1850	794	1867 wrecked at St Thomas in Great Storm
Orinoco	1851	2,901	1859 scrapped (dry rot)
Amazon	1851	2,256	1852 gutted, maiden voyage, Bay of Biscay
Magdalena	1851	2,943	1866 scrapped after trooping
Parana	1851	2,943	1868 hulked at St Thomas; 1876 scrapped
Demerara	1851	2,318	1851 stranded in Avon before delivery; rebuilt as sailing ship
Prince	1851	398	1862 sold
La Plata	1852	2,404	Built for Cunard, bought on stocks; 1871 sold
Camilla	1853	539	1853 bought from Samuel Cunard, Canada; 1859 sold
Atrato	1853	3,467	First iron RMSPCo ship; 1870 sold
Solent	1853	1,804	1869 scrapped
Tamar	1854	1,850	1871 sold
Tyne	1854	1,603	1875 scrapped
Paramatta	1858	3,439	1859 wrecked on Anegada Island (British Virgin Islands), maiden voyage
Mersey	1858	1,039	1876 sold
Shannon	1859	3,609	1875 converted to screw propulsion and wrecked at Colon on second voyage
Seine	1860	3,440	1871 scrapped
Eider	1864	1,569	1883 sold as Haitian Revolutionary gun boat
Arno	1865	1,038	1882 sold
Danube	1865	2,000	1871 sold

6 THE FAST, THE CURIOUS AND THE FURIOUS

Following the successful trial of the diminutive steamer *Rob Roy* on Belfast to Greenock duties in 1818, the coastal seas of the British Isles were invaded by the humble wooden steamer, as recorded in a Government White Paper published in 1822 (see Chapter 13):

> In the year 1819, the *Talbot*, of 150 tons, built by Messrs Wood, with two 30 horse power engines made by Mr Napier, plied daily between Holyhead and Dublin throughout the whole summer and autumn, and successfully encountered many severe gales. In the year 1820, the *Ivanhoe*, of 170 tons, built by Mr Scott, also with two 30 horse power engines made by Mr Napier, was established on the same station; and in 1821, the Postmasters General introduced steam boats at Holyhead and Dover for the conveyance of the mails. During these three last years, the *Belfast*, *Robert Bruce*, *Waterloo*, *Eclipse*, *Superb*, *Majestic* and *Cambria* were constructed, of large tonnage, and with engines of great power, for conveying passengers between Greenock and Belfast and Liverpool; between Liverpool and Dublin; and between Liverpool and Bagilt in Flintshire. All these vessels, except the *Cambria* and *Belfast*, were constructed on the Clyde. In the year 1821, the *City of Edinburgh* and *Mountaineer* were established to go between London and Leith; and, in the present year [1822], there have already been fitted for the sea the *Saint Patrick* and *Saint George*, at Liverpool; the *James Watt*, for the Leith and London station; the *Swift*, to go between Brighton and Dieppe; the *Sovereign* and *Union*, between Dover and Calais; and the *Lord Melville*, to go regularly between London Bridge and Calais. Twelve more are in hand, and will be completed this summer.

The subsequent progression of the wooden steamer on both sides of the Atlantic allowed larger hulls to be driven by more powerful engines. But apart from the significant advances in maritime engineering, perhaps the biggest breakthrough was the iron hull.

So, while the deep-sea paddlers had been laying down the foundations of international trade, the estuarial and coastal steamers had also been evolving. The shorter journeys they had to make, such as Holyhead to Kingstown or Leith to London, required enough bunkers to sustain required speeds for a relatively short duration. Unlike the long-haul steamer, which rose little by little out of the sea as its coal reserves were used up, the coastal steamer stayed more or less at a constant draft. This meant that the paddles enjoyed a reasonably consistent depth of float immersion. With this in mind the feathering paddle float was introduced in the 1840s for use on short-haul steamers, although it was also introduced to the deep-sea fleet, while efficiency depended on draft and submergence. In due course the curved float was introduced, which further increased the hydraulic efficiency of the couple between the rotary torque of the drive shaft and the water.

But what of the new generation of coastal steamers? New breeds were emerging; the fast day steamer, the slower workhorse and the tug. The cross-Channel steamers competed against the clock, whereas the workhorse was content to take its time on a more fuel-efficient basis accompanied by lower fares and tariffs. The

Orion (1846) sinking off Portpatrick in June 1850, having struck the Barnaugh Rocks. (THE ILLUSTRATED LONDON NEWS)

duty of towing had also been separated from that of passenger steamer, to a large extent, as the steamer had grown in size in keeping with the greater power available as higher steam pressures and greater volumes of steam were generated by improved boilers. It was now possible to differentiate between coasting steamer, fast cross-Channel steamer and coastal passenger liner and the paddle tug, although many of the latter offered passenger excursions in between towing duties.

The increased speed attained by the wooden steamers was won despite accident, injury and loss of life. Numerous boiler explosions and engine failures placed life at risk, but they were not the only causes. When the new crack, iron-hulled steamer *Orion* was commissioned by G & J Burns in December 1846 for the company's Liverpool to Glasgow coastal service, the new ship knocked over an hour off the journey time, reducing the voyage to just 14 hours. Duckworth and Langmuir describe the vessel's ultimate fate:

> On 17 June 1850, the *Orion* left Liverpool with a full complement of passengers, and about half past one the following morning she struck a rock near Portpatrick. Although her hull was divided into four or five reputedly watertight compartments, she sank in seven minutes. Of the two hundred odd passengers who were travelling on her, about 50 lost their lives, among them being Dr Burns, Regius Professor of Surgery at Glasgow University, a brother of the owners of the ship. The night was calm, and the rock which the vessel struck is only 200 yards from the land.

The second mate had been in charge of the bridge. He was accused of manslaughter by cutting the corner around the Mull of Galloway in order to maintain a fast passage time. He was deported. The body of the master, Captain McNeil, was never found. A passenger aboard the ship wrote in *The Illustrated London News* of 29 June 1850:

> Not many minutes after she struck, the bows went down under water, and she heeled over to the starboard side, so much so that no one could stand except by holding by the sides: all was confusion around me; the ladies screaming, and men crying for help from the shore. Some went down to their cabins to save some part of their clothing, and never came up again alive.

By this time the vessel had sunk about half; those that could swim jumped into the water, and others were saved by shore boats which had now come in numbers, and did everything to rescue them from drowning.

Another major cause of trouble was ventilation of the engine spaces and the consequent risk of flooding. When seas were being shipped on deck it was not feasible to cover the ventilation gratings entirely, as air was always needed for the furnace fires. More often than not the sea would wash through the bunkers, carrying with it coal dust and other debris that clogged the bilge pumps. Indeed, a modern-day risk assessment for a wooden steamer carrying a mass of canvas sail with a roaring furnace in the middle of its hull would never be signed off, but in the 1830s and 1840s such risks were willingly accepted, despite the regular loss of ships and people.

Fast paddle steamers were developed on the cross-Channel and island routes, with the power to carry the mails within the times laid down in Post Office contracts.

By the 1850s speeds of 17 knots could be accomplished with ease when the new oscillating engine was introduced. The cylinders were no longer fixed in place but rocked in trunnions to follow the movement of the crank and facilitate the piston rod. However, the system was not suited to the higher steam pressures available later because the steam glands tended to leak as the cylinders rocked back and forth. Oscillating engines also had a huge advantage over the larger side-lever engines as they were easier to operate.

Unless steam engines were fitted with either steam reversing gear or, in the case of the single diagonal paddle engine, a steam starting engine, they were all very difficult to reverse. Until the advent of steam assistance it was very much a case of skill and brawn. Ian Ramsay remembers being told by an old MacBrayne chief engineer some 60 years ago that, when manoeuvring the steeple engine on the paddle steamer *Glencoe,* the engineer had to operate the valve gear manually while the rest of the engine room staff were on hand to restart the engine with a glorified pinch bar, should it stall

An early example of the fast cross-Channel steamer; the South Western Railway Company's *Alliance* (1855). (*THE ILLUSTRATED LONDON NEWS*)

One of the Admiralty packets taken over from the Post Office on cross-Channel duties out of Dover. (WATERCOLOUR BY PAUL SHANNON, DATED 1988)

on top or bottom dead centre. Some of these single-cylinder steeple-engined ships were, like many of the Swiss Lakes paddlers, fitted with balance weights on the paddle wheels to try to prevent stalling with the piston at the top or bottom of the stroke.

One of the early examples of the fast iron-hulled cross-Channel steamer was *Alliance*, built by Messrs C Mare & Company at Blackwall for the New South Western Steam Packet Company's service between Southampton and Le Havre. It had a service speed of just over 13 knots and reduced the twelve-hour passage between the ports to just nine hours. *Alliance* gave 45 years' service on the English Channel, latterly serving the Channel Isles, after passing into the ownership of the London & South Western Railway in 1862. Its entry into service was heralded by *The Illustrated London News* in its issue of 28 July 1855:

This vessel has been named *Alliance* in commemoration of the happy union of the two rival countries, and in placing a boat of her qualities on this station [Southampton-Havre], the management of the South Western [Railway] Com-

pany have proved that they are both ambitious and willing to keep pace with other ports in having vessels of the highest class of speed, for facilitating as far as possible the quickness of transit across the Channel. She is commanded by Captain Smith, late of the *Atalanta*, who is well known on this station, both for his merits as a seaman and gentlemanly attention to the comforts of his passengers.

The Dover Strait cross-Channel services illustrate the development of the fast paddle steamer. Post Office steam packets *Arrow*, *Crusader*, *Ferret*, *Firefly* and *Salamander* operated the Dover to Calais and Dover to Ostend services from the early 1820s. In 1837 they were taken over by the Admiralty but were kept on station into the late 1840s. Three hours was a good crossing to Calais, whereas nearer six was good for Ostend.

A fleet of wooden paddle steamers was maintained on the short sea crossing by the Commercial Steam Packet Company from 1836 onwards, but any idea of service and schedules had not then been encompassed within the business strategy. The South Eastern Railway reached Folkestone in 1843 and continued along the foot of the cliffs to Dover the following year, when the East Kent Railway also arrived to provide a direct link with London. As railway companies were then prevented by law from operating steamer connections, the two companies formed the South Eastern & Continental Steam Packet Company, incorporating what had become the New Commercial Steam Packet Company. Eight fast (12-knot) iron paddle steamers were ordered, four from Ditchburn & Mare on the Thames and four from John Laird at Birkenhead. The Thames ships were powered by twin-cylinder simple expansion engines, while Laird equipped his vessels with the traditional side-lever engines.

The South Eastern Railway was granted rights to own ships in 1853, and in 1861 it ordered the first really fast ship for the crossing. This was *Victoria*, complete with clipper bow, twin funnels with bell tops and an oscillating engine built by John Penn & Sons

of Greenwich. On trials it reached a speed of nearly 17 knots, and later managed 17½ knots with ease. Three similar paddle steamers followed: *Eugénie*, *Albert Edward*, *Alexandra* and *Napoleon III*, all eclipsing the first-generation octet, which was relegated to relief duties and cargo runs.

The next generation of steamers was not needed until 1880, when the landmark steel-hulled paddle steamers *Albert Victor* and *Louise Dagmar* were delivered by Samuda at Poplar, this time with twin-cylinder simple oscillating engines, and again built by John Penn & Sons. The pair was a huge success, each attaining 18½ knots on trials and being among the first paddle steamers to have bow rudders to assist manoeuvring in harbour while going astern. A third, near-identical vessel, *Duchess of Edinburgh*, was built on the Clyde with engines manufactured by her builder, J & G Thompson. These were compound oscillating engines in which the steam was exhausted into a second larger cylinder from the high-pressure cylinder. The ship was disappointing on trials, achieving only 17½ knots, and its engines proved difficult to maintain. *Duchess of Edinburgh* was in service for only one month before it was set aside and later sold. It was replaced in 1882 by another Samuda product, *Mary Beatrice*, which managed just over 19 knots on its trials. The London, Chatham & Dover Railway also upgraded in the 1880s with *Invicta*, delivered by the Thames Ironworks & Shipbuilding Company in 1882. *Invicta* and its younger close relative *Victoria* were both capable of over 18 knots on the Dover to Calais crossing.

The next development of the paddle steamer on the Dover Strait was the South Eastern Railway's fabulous trio *Duchess of York*, *Princess of Wales* and *Mabel Grace*. Each was equipped with compound engines, the high-pressure cylinder exhausting into twin low-pressure cylinders. *Duchess of York* was completed with engines again built by John Penn & Sons, but this new type of engine was problematical at first and the ship was nearly a year settling down until it managed a consistent 18½ knots. The other pair came

Invicta (1882) was the first steamer owned by the London, Chatham & Dover Railway. Capable of 18 knots on the Dover to Calais crossing, it is seen here at Dover in this print from a glass negative exposed about 1885.

from Laird Brothers at Birkenhead and were an immediate success, the second of the two, the magnificent *Mabel Grace*, delivered in 1899, reaching a trials speed of over 20 knots. But speed was at the expense of fuel efficiency, and the three vessels burnt anything up to 20 tons of coal just to cross the Channel. The 21-knot equivalent in the London, Chatham & Dover Railway fleet was the *Empress* of 1887 and *Calais-Douvres*, commissioned in 1889. A further three paddlers, *Dover*, *Calais* and *Lord Warden*, were ordered in the late 1890s to operate at a more economical 18 knots.

Probably the finest fast cross-Channel paddle steamers of all were the French twins *Le Nord* and *Le Pas de Calais*. These were bigger than *Duchess of York*, *Princess of Wales* and *Mabel Grace* at Folkestone as they had a gross tonnage of just over 2,000, and they were vastly superior to the Dover trio, *Dover*, *Calais* and *Lord Warden*, delivered by Denny in 1896. The French twins were built for Chemin de Fer du Nord in 1898 to operate between Dover and Calais. Equipped with state-of-the-art triple-expansion machinery provided with a complex system of forced lubrication, they had a service speed of 21½ knots. Unlike the English paddlers, which were displaced from 1903 onwards by the new turbine triple-screw steamers of

The Queen class, the French pair remained in service until 1923, when *Le Nord* was wrecked off the South Foreland and *Le Pas de Calais* withdrawn and broken up. The story on the Dover Strait was repeated a few months later at Stranraer, when the direct-drive turbine steamer *Princess Maud* arrived on station, displacing the resident paddlers. The fast paddle steamer was at last eclipsed.

There were also a few eccentric paddle steamer designs that were tried on the Dover Strait in the 1870s and operated on behalf of their owners by the London,

South Eastern Railway's *Duchess of York* (1895) leaves Folkestone.

One of the Dover-based steamers delivered in 1896: *Dover*, *Calais* or *Lord Warden*. Once the turbine steamer arrived in the Dover Strait in 1903 the paddlers spent much of their time laid up, and they were sold in 1911.

The turbine steamer totally eclipsed the paddle steamer on the fast daylight services. The cross-Channel turbine steamer *Princess Maud* (1904) was one of the first breed of triple-screw direct-drive cross-Channel steamers. (UNIVERSITY OF GLASGOW)

Chatham & Dover Railway. Dendy Marshall writes in *A History of the Southern Railway*:

The discomforts of the passage in the comparatively small boats experienced by passengers unaccustomed to the sea was so great that in the 1870s inventors began to bring forward schemes by which they hoped to make things more comfortable, and some experimental boats appeared.

The English Channel Steamboat Company was created to experiment with split catamaran-type hulls with the paddles between the hulls. Its first ship was *Castalia*. Each hull had its own boilers and engines which drove a paddle wheel housed against the vertical inner side of each hull. This ship was underpowered and managed 11 knots at best. Confused seas between the hulls greatly reduced the efficiency of the paddles in rough weather, causing the ship to shud-

Chemin de Fer du Nord's crack steamer *Le Pas de Calais* (1898) was one of a pair built in France; perhaps the ultimate in fast cross-Channel design.

der badly. A report in *The Graphic* of 14 August 1875 noted:

> she has been built on the principle of the outrigged canoes or catamarans used by the natives of Ceylon and Southern India. Her designer, Captain Dicey, was for many years Master Attendant at the Port of Calcutta, and has had considerable opportunities for observing the stability and trustworthiness of this form of craft. The *Castalia* is formed of two separate hulls bridged over by one deck, the space between being occupied by the paddle wheels. One hull is expected to act as an outrigger to the other and in some degree to neutralise the rolling action of the waves. In this way the chances of sea sickness would be considerably reduced, and the horrors of the dreaded Channel passage eminently mitigated …

> Shortly after the launch of *Castalia* several trials of various lengths were made but her boilers being found defective, she was taken back into dock, whence a few weeks ago she emerged to stand the test of public criticism. As far as speed goes the trial on Monday week proved her somewhat slow (1 hour and 50 minutes from pier to pier), while as to her steadiness an opinion could scarcely be formed, the sea being smooth and there being little or no wind. Of her steering qualities there can be no doubt, and Captain Pittock … brought her alongside the northern pier at Calais as easily and smoothly as one of the smallest mail boats.

A sister with two hulls in catamaran style with a single large paddle wheel between them was built and named *Express*, then renamed *Calais-Douvres* for its duties with the railway company. In calm weather it was a reliable vessel fit for 13 knots, i.e. it was an ideal ship for night-time services, but was also very expensive to run. Both *Calais-Douvres* and *Castalia* remained serv-

iceable for just nine years, although both were laid up for extensive periods.

One bizarre attempt was made to suspend the main passenger lounge on gimbals in a double-ended ship with widely spaced paddle wheels fore and aft, port and starboard. This was because the central lounge occupied the middle of the ship and engines and paddles had to be fore and aft of this. The ship was the steel magnate Henry Bessemer's brainchild and his attempt to tackle *mal de mer*, of which he was a sufferer. *Bessemer*, as this ugly duckling was named, had a very short life as it was almost totally without steerage at low speeds, making docking well nigh impossible. Besides, the motion of the suspended lounge was even more uncomfortable in a sea than it would

Castalia (1874) leaving Dover for Calais on an inaugural voyage in August 1875 with day-trip passengers for Calais and back. (*THE GRAPHIC*)

have been in a conventional steamer. The double-ended steamer had very low freeboard fore and aft, designed to allow seas to pile up on board in the hope of reducing pitching. Cyril Bracegirdle wrote in *Sea Breezes* for March 1968:

> in 1869 Henry Bessemer floated the Bessemer Saloon Ship Company. Such was his reputation as an engineer that there was no lack of subscribers, and the company started with a capital of £250,000. The ship was built at Hull. She was 350 feet long, and the original estimate of her cost proved far too small, an experience not entirely unknown to the modern business world. Sir Henry had to provide £41,000 of his own money to save the project . . .
>
> What was proved was that Sir Henry was a better engineer on land than on water. His vessel propelled by two sets of paddles; the two after paddles failed to work properly because the water was already travelling at a high speed when it reached them. In fact they had the effect of a drag so that the ship never exceeded 11 knots, a much slower speed than had been expected. Another fault was that her length made steering clumsy, and she was slow to answer the helm.

The suspended saloon was not much use ei-

ther, tending to make sufferers of seasickness queasy while still in harbour. After the first excursion, ramming the harbour at both Calais and on return at Dover, Bessemer installed an hydraulic brake on the hanging lounge to be operated by a brake man aided by a spirit level. Bracegirdle concluded:

> Sometimes when the ship rolled one way the saloon seemed to roll the other. Also not only did the ship crawl through the water like a turtle, but she consumed coal at the rate of a large liner. Finally, when the pier at Dover was rammed for a second time, Sir Henry gave up. The company was liquidated and the ship sold for scrap.

But there were many crack steamers built for the railways elsewhere and for service to the Isle of Man and the Scottish Highlands. One quintet of steamers stands above all others of their time, the City of Dublin Steam Packet Company's *Ulster*, *Munster* and *Connaught* built by Laird Brothers in 1860, and *Leinster*, which came from Samuda on the Thames. Captain Isherwood describes the background to the order for the four 'Provinces' in an article that first appeared in *Sea Breezes* for September 1975:

> By 1830 there were six Post Office steamers on the mail service to Dublin

Ulster (1860) was the first of four crack steamers built for the City of Dublin Steam Packet Company service between Holyhead and Dublin. (*THE ILLUSTRATED LONDON NEWS*)

but in 1837, the Admiralty took over. Both Post Office and Admiralty ships were very unpopular with the travelling public, complaints being that they were poorly maintained, of dubious reliability, and with antiquated and inadequate accommodation. In 1847 four new and rather better steamers were built, later taken over by the City of Dublin Steam Packet Company. The average time for

---

John Laird 1805-1874

Scotsman John Laird was taken to Merseyside from his native Greenock at the age of five, when his father Willam Laird helped open a repair yard at Herculaneum Dock, Liverpool, in 1810. Fourteen years later William bought land adjacent to the Wallasey Pool and established the Birkenhead Ironworks (roughly adjacent to the present site of West Float). John Laird joined his father's company at the age of 23 after training in law. The following year the ironworks started to build three iron barges, leading to an order for an iron steamship for the same company in 1833. This was the 148-ton burthen paddle steamer *Lady Lansdown*, destined for work on the Shannon for the Inland Steam Navigation Company. After trials on the Mersey the vessel was dismantled and reassembled at Killaloe on the Shannon. Later the same year the Laird company sent the disassembled parts of *John Randolph* to America; this was the first American iron steamer, which operated successfully on the Savannah River.

In 1834 the yard delivered the 263-ton paddler *Garryowen* to the City of Dublin Steam Packet Company. Not only was it the largest iron steamer to date, but it was also the first ship to be equipped with watertight bulkheads. The paddles were driven by an 80hp engine built by Fawcett, Preston & Company of Liverpool. This steamer served its owners well for the next 32 years, its lighter construction allowing access to the shallow waters of Limerick for much of the tide while the deeper wooden steamers had to wait offshore. In due course two steamers were built for the East India Company, *Indus* and *Nile*, their names belying their intended service areas. In 1839 a much larger order was fulfilled for the East India Company with the first of a series of gunboats shipped out in pieces to the Persian Gulf and Mesopotamia.

But John Laird could not persuade the Admiralty of the worth of iron ships. In desperation he built his own iron paddle frigate. It was named *Guade-* *loupe*, of 800 burthen tons and, with a 180hp engine the vessel was armed with two 68-pounder guns at bow and stern and a pair of 3-pounders broadside. The Admiralty was impressed, but not sufficiently to buy the ship, which then went to the highest bidder and hoisted the Mexican flag. But Laird did then receive an Admiralty commission and built for them the 1,400-ton iron frigate *Birkenhead*.

Laird also attained a reputation for building shallow-draft river craft. It was this reputation that led him in 1858 to build *Ma Roberts* for David Livingstone's expedition up the Zambezi. Livingstone's specification was very constrained, and Laird resorted to using steel rather than iron for its construction; the vessel needed to be light and portable. Alas, numerous groundings in shallow rivers and corrosion of the thin steel plate led to it sinking after only 18 months' work; nonetheless, Laird had built the world's very first steel ship.

Needing to expand his business, Laird moved to Monks Ferry in 1858 and laid out five dry docks and a wet basin. The first group of ships built at the new yard were the crack cross-Channel paddle steamers *Ulster*, *Munster* and *Connaught*, destined to carry the mails between Holyhead and Kingstown with a fourth vessel, the *Leinster*, built by Samuda.

In 1861 John Laird's interest turned to politics and he was elected Conservative member for the new Borough of Birkenhead. He handed over responsibility for the yard to his sons, and the yard went on to become Cammell Laird & Company, one of the great and innovative shipbuilders of the twentieth century.

In February 1874 John Laird met with a riding accident from which he never recovered. He died eight months later. He was remembered as a good employer who always looked after his workforce, an innovator with a good business sense, and to this day is remembered as the founder of Cammell Laird.

the crossing by the new ships was 4 hours and 16 minutes, and in 1848 the English terminal was transferred from Liverpool to Holyhead. In that year too, the Post Office decided that the service could be run more economically by private contractors than by the Admiralty and the mail contract was offered to private firms.

The City of Dublin company underbid the rival Chester and Holyhead Railway and started running a four-ship service. The ships comprised three of the old packets and the new steamer *Prince Arthur*. The service was little improved and discussions in the latter part of the 1850s led to a new contract which stipulated that the City of Dublin Steam Packet Company maintain enough steamers to operate the twice-daily service at 17½ knots for an annual fee of £85,000. There was to be a service penalty of 34 shillings for each minute delay at the destination port. Marine engineers shook their heads and said it could not be done, but Laird and Samuda in collaboration with engine builders Ravenhill, Salkend & Company showed them otherwise.

Each ship had four funnels venting the four pairs of haystack boilers that were placed in two separate boiler rooms. The steam pressure was 20psi and was supplied to a simple two-cylinder oscillating engine below the paddle shaft. The cylinders were 98in in diameter and the stroke was 78in. Each cylinder weighed a staggering 20 tons. There was a double handwheel rack-and-pinion gear to reverse the engines. Each handwheel was manned by four men, while the engineer was stationed at the stop valve and another man at the cooling water control valve. In all, 18 men were required for engine manoeuvres, presumably assisted by the greasers and fireman as required.

Captain Isherwood again:

The paddle wheels were 32 feet in diameter, each with 14 feathering floats 12 feet long by 5 feet wide. Strong brackets on the hull inside the paddle boxes sup-

ported the main bearing for each paddle wheel and due to the heavy concentration of weight amidships in ships with such long fine lines, together with the tremendous stresses set up by the paddles, especially when rolling, there was heavy longitudinal stiffening amidships, and a strong girder bowed out round the extremity of the sponsons. The two 20 ton cylinders, oscillating 25 times a minute, also called for careful balancing.

Ulster was the first to be completed, and on trials in July 1860 reached a speed of nearly 18 knots with the steam valve held down to give 25psi. *Connaught* was ready a few months later, and managed to top 18 knots, reputedly being the fastest of the four Provinces. The accommodation was superb, both saloons and cabins being described as lofty and well ventilated. Once the full service was up and running in October 1861 it became a byword for efficiency and regularity, and only rarely did the weather, rather than the ships, cost the company against the delayed arrival penalty. Two steamers maintained the two sailings a day each from Kingstown and Holyhead, and a third was in steam as reserve while the fourth was under maintenance. Reboilered and upgraded in the early 1880s, the four steamers were joined by a fifth, *Ireland*, with the quintet set to work now at 25psi, shortening the sea passage again. The paddlers were finally replaced in 1897 by another 'Provinces' quartet, this time equipped with the new triple-expansion machinery and twin screws. The four paddlers were remarkable in that, for the first 15 years of their careers, there was nothing in Europe that could equal them. Indeed, it was the 1880s before 18 knots came even to the prestigious Dover Strait services.

But the fastest steamers were the Belgian Ostend to Dover steamers. Denny built three fast paddle steamers for the Belgian Government, *Princesse Henriette* and *Princesse Joséphine* in 1888, which managed the contract speed of just over 20 knots on trial, and subsequently in 1892, *Leopold III*. It had the

same compound engines but a larger stroke, and was able to work up to 22 knots. Having learnt the skills from Denny with three paddlers which had hull forms honed in the Denny test tank, the Belgian yard Cockerill then built the three final paddle steamers for the fleet between 1893 and 1896. These were *Marie Henriette*, *Rapide* and *Princesse Clementine*, of which the fastest, *Marie Henriette*, could exceed 22 knots, its engines again incorporating an extension of the piston stroke. *Marie Henriette* was lost by stranding in 1914, but the other pair served the company into the 1920s alongside a new breed of 24-knot turbine steamers. Latterly held in reserve, *Princesse Clementine* was sold for scrap at the end of the 1928 season.

Speed was also important on the Isle of Man services. However, the monopoly so long enjoyed by the Isle of Man Steam Packet Company meant that a mere 18 knots had become the standard by the late 1880s. But all this was upset by a bit of hard sell by the Fairfield Shipbuilding & Engineering Company of John Elder pedigree, as Fred Henry describes in his book on the Isle of Man boats:

A competitor to the Steam Packet Company appeared in 1887 when the Manx Line, as the Isle of Man, Liverpool and Manchester Steamship Company was called, commenced a service with the *Queen Victoria* and *Prince of Wales*. These were built on the Clyde by the Fairfield Shipbuilding Company, without the builders having received an order for them, and they were built to excel the *Mona's Isle* and *Mona's Queen*, it being the intention of the shipbuilding firm that the Steam Packet Company should be forced to buy these two ships.... the performance of the *Queen Victoria* was noted on its arrival at Liverpool to commence the Isle of Man service. It arrived on the Mersey on 21 May 1887, from Greenock at 10pm after a run of nine hours and twenty minutes, making an average speed of 22½ knots. A heavy sea was running and half a gale of wind blowing. This was up to that time the fastest run on record between the two ports.

To counter these rivals the Steam Packet Company reduced fares. The Manx Line retaliated ... Because of the competition and the reduced fares both companies lost money in 1887 and 1888, and as had been intended at the end of 1888, the Steam Packet Company bought the two Manx Line ships which became notable additions to their fleet.

The ultimate paddle steamer in the Isle of Man fleet was the 21½-knot *Empress Queen*, completed in 1897, also by Fairfield Shipbuilding & Engineering. Its 32 furnaces re-

Empress Queen (1897) was the ultimate fast and large paddle steamer in the Isle of Man Steam Packet Company's fleet.

The fabulous *Royal Sovereign* (1893) off Southend Pier in 1914. Note the telescopic funnels to allow it to get under London Bridge.

quired the constant attention of 16 firemen, and a total of 95 crew were needed to transport up to 1,994 passengers on the three and a half hour journey between Liverpool and Douglas. Fairfield was also instrumental in placing fast excursion steamers on the Thames. *Koh-i-noor*, *Royal Sovereign* and the larger and slightly faster *La Marguerite* were offered to the Victoria Steamboat Association in the early 1890s at favourable hire-purchase terms (see Chapter 9).

Speed was not only an attraction to cross-Channel, Irish Sea, fast island routes and long-distance excursion services, as it also had a more sinister attraction for which many of the faster steamers gained an element of notoriety. In 1861, at the outbreak of the American Civil War, the greater part of the American Navy had declared for the Union. This superiority enabled the Federal Navy to blockade the Confederate ports and prevent the export of cotton to provide the funds for much-needed arms and other supplies. The Confederates looked to Britain and its plethora of fast steamers, many of which could easily outrun the Federal warships. Various clandestine agents armed with

letters of guarantee from various American banks started to arrive in Britain, and numerous deals were soon agreed. One of the earliest deals was the release of the transatlantic liner *Pacific* from its service between Galway and Boston (see Chapter 5).

Another example was the crack flush-decked steamer *Iona*, delivered to David Hutcheson for the long service to Adrishaig on the Firth of Clyde in 1855. Equipped with oscillating engines, *Iona* was good for 17 knots. Robins and Meek described the action that followed:

The first *Iona* was hugely popular and hugely successful. She was flush decked . . . She could accommodate 1,400 day passengers in luxuriously appointed, wood panelled cabins, complete with bars, shop and the obligatory ship's pipe band . . . After only six summer seasons – she was laid up in the winter – the pride and joy of the fleet was sold to an American agent acting on behalf of the Confederates . . .

Stripping the *Iona* of her panel-work and fine fittings at the end of the 1862 season, the Hutcheson company received an over-generous bounty for their ship as it set sail for her Atlantic crossing. But no ship carrying the name *Iona*, and the sacred connotations that go with it, could ever be part of a war . . . Leaving Glasgow in the early afternoon of 2 October and loaded with coal for the journey, she parted the Clyde for the last time on her way to Nassau to be fitted out for her new role. Five hours later Providence took a hand, when a steamer struck the *Iona* off Gourock, and sank the heavily ballasted ship in just a few minutes. Charitable to the last, the ship with the sacred name allowed all of her crew to leave unharmed.

David Hutcheson took his money back to the shipbuilders and asked for a repeat, incorporating all the finery stripped from the first ship. This, the second *Iona*, was ready for the 1863 season and was upgraded to 18 knots. It was different in that it took advantage of the tonnage concession that had been granted that year, which allowed deck saloons to be tonnage exempt. And a handsome steamer it was too, with canoe-shaped bow and twin funnels. Its first-class saloon featured white and gold fluted pillars and velvet curtains, and there was a post office and a barber shop aboard. Robins and Meek again:

In late September, it was announced that the new *Iona* would be stripped of her fittings and finery, and would attend the Confederates bidding across the Atlantic. Setting out in January 1864 to cross the Atlantic . . . *Iona* safely made the south of Ireland, whereupon she was sunk . . . during severe weather, her light construction having been designed principally for sheltered waters. Again the Confederate money was in the bank, and, yet again, J & G Thompson was contracted to build a new ship. This was the third *Iona*, launched on 10 May in time for the 1864 summer season . . . This was the ship *par excellence*, and it was

this *Iona* which, albeit displaced in 1879 to the Oban station, was to reap rewards for her owners [later David MacBrayne Limited], to the delight of her regular summer clientele, for the next 72 years.

But many fine paddle steamers did make it to the Southern States, several built especially by British shipbuilders eager to please the Confederate agents. Paddlers were preferred because many of the approaches to the southern ports were shallow winding channels requiring considerable manoeuvrability. *Scotia* and *Anglia* on the Holyhead to Kingstown service, for example, were purchased from the London & North Western Railway in 1861. When new, they were good for 14 knots, *Anglia* slightly more than *Scotia*. The funds to buy the ships were generated from the sale of the cotton crop, and the pair duly sailed for a new base in Bermuda. In October 1862 they were captured by the Federal Navy and given new names.

The South Eastern & Continental Steam Packet sold its brand-new crack paddle steamer *Eugénie* to the Confederates in 1863. It too was based at Bermuda, where it was renamed *Cornubia* and was actually set on fire at one stage to avoid capture by the Federal forces. The ship survived the American Civil War and in due course recrossed the Atlantic to become GSN's Thames excursion steamer *Hilda*.

In 1858 Robert Napier delivered the powerful steamer *Douglas* to the Isle of Man Steam Packet Company. Its side-lever engine gave it a trials speed of over 17 knots – probably the fastest steamer afloat at that time. This ship, too, went to the southern states, this time based at Nassau. Renamed *Margaret & Jessie*, it was caught off Eleuthera Island by the Federal warship *Rhode Island*. A direct shot hit the boiler room and the blockade runner had to be run up the beach. But it was not done, and the Confederates later refloated the wreck and repaired it sufficiently to rejoin the other blockade runners. Again it was captured and, as the prize of the warship *Fulton*, was taken

to New York, there to become the Federal steamer *Gettysburg*.

There were several other Confederate purchases, including J & G Burns's Belfast-Glasgow steamer *Stag*, Burns's 18-knot *Giraffe* dating from 1860, and the new steamer *Leopard*. From the rival Laird Line came *Thistle* and *Laurel*, while the Caledonian Railway contributed *Alice* and *Fannie*, the former carrying over $1 million out of Wilmington for Confederate purchases overseas. Other ships included the North Sea steamer *Juno*. *Thomas W Wragg* joined the Confederate fleet, formerly on a New York to Charleston service, its owners clearly preferring the Confederate cause. But the transatlantic trade worked the other way round after the war, with two purpose-built blockade runners later joining the Zeeland Steamship Company and one also the Liverpool & Dublin Steam Navigation Company.

Of the purpose-built blockade runners, James Quiggin & Company of Liverpool had it down to a fine art, building 17 block-ade runners between 1862 and 1865. The first was the famous *Banshee*, 215ft long and built with a light steel hull. It was the first steel ship to cross the Atlantic. Philip Banbury described its role in an article first published in *Sea Breezes* in December 1962:

Her continuous speed was about 11 knots and to achieve this her 12 firemen had to shovel 30 tons of coal per day to produce 140 nominal horse-power. But the vital parts of the voyage were done slowly, at night, when invisibility and silence were the key factors. No gleam of light was allowed to escape from the stoke-holds, and the binnacle was covered with a viewing hood. Steam was blown off under water, and the paddle boxes had canvas skirts to water level to deaden the splash of the floats.

Later in 1865 Quiggin delivered the largest steel ship to date, the 1,800-ton gross Confederate paddle runner *Colonel Lamb*, capable of 17 knots.

7 INLAND WATERS: SOME SPECIALIST ROLES

The paddle train ferry was a particularly early development, and served as a means of crossing lowland or tidal rivers to obviate the need to invest in bridges. By the 1890s this was common practice in America, where numerous double-ended, flat-decked and often wooden-hulled paddle steamers carried trains on twin tracks across the broader lowland rivers. The locomotives shunted the carriages aboard and waited patiently at the bank for the steamer to return with another set of carriages to form the return train.

The largest of the American train ferries was the wooden-hulled paddle steamer *Solano*, built in 1878 for the Central Pacific Railroad. Heralded as the largest train ferry afloat, its job was to provide the link in the coastal railway between Benicia and Port Costa across the Carquinez Strait outside San Francisco, California. It had four tracks

and could carry two goods trains or one passenger train, including the celebrated *Overland Limited*. *Solano* lost its 'biggest' status when running mate *Contra Costa* was delivered to supplement the service in 1914. Both were retired when traffic finally justified investment in a bridge, opened in 1930.

But the train ferry goes back a long way before that. The Edinburgh, Perth & Dundee Railway had two obstacles to cross, the Firths of Forth and Tay. Indeed, its main line ran across the Kingdom of Fife virtually from nowhere to nowhere, from the banks of the Forth at Burntisland via the town of Cupar to the banks of the Tay at Ferryport-on-Craig, later renamed Tayport by the North British Railway Company. The Tay crossing was initially only for passengers and goods, with the paddle steamer *Express* running the ferry across the Tay to Broughty Ferry. But in 1850 and 1851 Robert Napier

A charming contemporary image of 'the world's largest train ferry' *Solano* (1878) taking the Overland Limited from San Francisco across the Carquinez Strait.

designed and built two train ferries, *Leviathan*, which ran from Granton near Leith to Burntisland and *Robert Napier*, which started to carry rail wagons across the Tay and was joined by the slightly larger *Carrier* in 1858. Passengers were not allowed on the wagon boats, which were to all intents and purposes low sheerless double-ended barges with a central set of paddle wheels adjacent to a control platform.

When the mighty North British Railway took over the route in 1861 construction of the Tay Railway Bridge was begun. Seven months after it was opened in 1878 the displaced train ferries were again reinstated following the tragic collapse of the bridge in a storm. The second Tay Bridge was opened in July 1887. *Carrier* went on to a new career in 1884 when it was used as a goods ferry, carrying wheeled vehicles to and from the Isle of Wight for the next nine years.

But rivers are not just an encumbrance to roads and railways; they are also a highway in themselves. The characteristic winding and shoaling nature of rivers lends itself to the paddle steamer with its manoeuvrability and shallow draft. Classic examples of early river steamers were *Boulac*, *Cairo*, *Lotus* and *Delta*, operated on the Nile by P&O to offer the connection for passengers and mail be-

tween the Mediterranean steamers and the onward Indian connection (see Chapter 2). P&O also had paddle steamers on the Canton river in China, notably *Canton*, built in 1848, and *Tartar* of 1853, both substantial ships of over 300 tons gross.

In due course the great travel entrepreneur Thomas Cook was awarded the Egyptian Government contract to carry the mail from Cairo up the Nile to Aswan. Four years later in 1874 the contract was amended to include the upstream section from Aswan to the Sudanese border. By 1884 Cook had attained a monopoly on the river and had built his own hotel at Aswan for the passengers when they changed steamers. His vessels were largely inherited from the Egyptian Government. In 1884 all of his steamers were requisitioned to deal with the Sudanese uprising, and those that did come back were in no state to be reinstated on the mail run. Cook set about rebuilding his fleet over the next thirty years with some orders placed at British shipbuilders for steamers to be assembled in his shipyard at Boulac. There were the 80-passenger steamers *Sudan*, *Arabia*, *Egypt*, *Rosetta* and *Damietta*; the 50-passenger *Delta* and *Thebes*; and the stern-wheelers *Memnon*, *Chonsu*, *Oonas*, *Fostat*, *Seti* and *Scarab*.

Thomas Cook's *Arabia*, built in the late nineteenth century, was one of a fleet of luxury tourist steamers on the Nile.

The British India Line's *Rasmara* (1890) ran on the Rangoon to Moulmein service across the Gulf of Martaban. (Captain J Van Puyvelde)

Cook did have some opposition. In the 1890s the Anglo-American Nile Company arrived on the river with the sternwheelers *Mayflower*, *Indiana* and *Niagara*, merging in 1906 with the Hamburg America Line to become the Hamburg-American Nile Company. This company quickly commissioned five more steamers that went into direct competition with yet another new company, the Express Nile Navigation Company, also American, which introduced *America* and *Virginia*. Thomas Cook's fleet held its own throughout this expansive period, when American and German tourists joined the British to see the wonders of Egypt from the luxuriously appointed fleets of steamers.

Nile steamer services took several years to be reinstated after the First World War, but were maintained throughout the late 1920s and through the 1930s despite Egyptian independence and various subsequent political setbacks. The steamer *Karnak*, of course, was immortalised in Agatha Christie's whodunit, *Death on the Nile*, first published in 1937. The former Thomas Cook paddler *Sudan* deputised in the making of the film which starred Peter Ustinov as Hercule Poirot, released in 1978. But the Second World War brought an end to the

tourist trade, and it was doomed after the war owing to political unrest in Egypt. This indirectly led to the nationalisation of the respective fleets which, by the early 1950s, fell into disarray. Today a number of the old steamers lie in states varying from dereliction to static preservation, while four have been restored to their former glory and put back to use in the luxury tourist trade. These are side-wheeler *Karim*, built in 1917 for King Farouk; King Farouk's former royal steamer, sternwheeler *Misr*, built in 1918 originally for the Royal Navy; paddle steamer *Sudan*, built by Bow, McLachlan at Paisley in 1921 (not in 1896, as often reported); and sternwheeler *Memnon*. The last two were once part of Thomas Cook's fleet.

But perhaps the most ambitious inland steamer service was that developed in collaboration with P Henderson & Company of Glasgow on the Irrawaddy and Chindwin rivers in Burma. The Irrawaddy Flotilla and Burmese Steam Navigation Company of Glasgow was formed in 1865 with a capital of £55,500 by Todd, Findlay & Company which had been awarded the mail contract to the Upper Burma frontier and back at £50 per trip. The company started life with four decrepit steamers and three flats taken over from Government, and ordered two purpose-built paddle steamers to be sent out from the Clyde. There followed considerable debate between the agents and pilots in Rangoon with Scottish shipbuilder William Denny as to the optimum vessel for the various Irrawaddy services.

In the meantime the British India Steam Navigation Company was starting a rival service between Rangoon and Moulmein at the mouth of the Salween River, making life even more difficult for the Irrawaddy Flotilla company. This service crossed the Gulf of Martaban and was run by a motley collection of steamers until, in 1887, the purpose-built paddle steamer *Ramapura* was delivered, followed three years later by *Rasmara*. These were the only coastal paddle steamers ever operated by British India, although it owned a plethora of small vessels and harbour craft which were deployed at ports such as Calcutta. The two paddlers had just eight first-class berths, slightly less in second class, and space for no fewer than 1,600 deck passengers. They maintained the route until *Ramapura* was sold for scrap in 1919, its running mate going two years later, first as a hulk at Singapore and then in 1926 to the scrapyard.

But despite competition and political hindrance the Irrawaddy Flotilla did succeed, and the Henderson house flag, adopted also for the Irrawaddy Flotilla Company, was seen the length and breadth of the Irrawaddy and its tributaries. The first vessel, designed and built by William Denny, was the paddler *Taiping*, the result of a visit to Burma by Denny in 1875 to see the conditions at first hand. A new development was the arrival of Scottish-built sternwheelers, which better suited the narrower confines of the Chindwin river from 1875 onwards, most of the new ships arriving at the dockyard in Rangoon in pieces aboard Henderson's cargo liners.

In 1885 the French signed a treaty with the King of Upper Burma and the Indian and British governments looked on aghast. Restitution comprised an ultimatum carried up-river by the paddle steamer *Ashley Eden*

under her master Captain Cooper and a volunteer crew – to a man her normal crew complement. The steamer *Dowoon* was dispatched to rescue expatriates from Mandalay who might otherwise suffer from King Thebaw's threat to massacre the British. The Flotilla Company subsequently carried all the men and munitions required for restitution, and peace again reigned.

The unification of Burma spelled well for the Irrawaddy Flotilla Company, which was set for a period of expansion. New mail paddle steamers were built, some 300ft long by 40ft breadth and of 900 tons gross, typified by *Mindone* and *Yomah*, delivered in 1886 for the new express service between Prome and Mandalay. Dorothy Laird, in her history of P Henderson & Company, describes the vessels:

> The vessels were designed by Denny, whose experience in constructing craft suitable for the difficult Irrawaddy conditions earned them their world-wide reputation for the design of shallow-draft vessels. The task of designing these ships presented a difficult problem. Powerful engines were required to give a good speed against the swift current, while structural strength was required to avoid breaking the ship's back if she stranded on one of the numerous shoals – a frequent occurrence on an unbuoyed river. At the same time, the weight had to be kept down.
>
> Denny made a careful study of the problem. To save weight, they early adopted steel instead of iron. They reduced hull resistance. They provided strength for the hulls by hogging the decks in an arch amidships.

The big steamers were designed in such a way that the European crew and clerical staff were accommodated on the main deck, along with some of the third-class Burmese passengers as well as light goods. The upper deck, which was shaded by an awning, accommodated the first-class cabins either side of the main saloon, with the second-class right aft. Amidships was given over to third class. Life in third class was described in a contemporary brochure:

A Burmese girl may be sitting there, doing up her wonderful hair with a tiny mirror before her, or grinding down her face powder from thanaka bark. A meal may be in progress with its accompaniment of many little dishes . . . and the children, eager to see each new thing, dart about in their curiosity from one group to anther . . .

Dorothy Laird summarised the company's operations towards the end of the nineteenth century:

The principal Rangoon to Mandalay service was maintained at that time twice weekly in both directions; from Rangoon to Henzada three times weekly in both directions; and from Mandalay to Bhamo fortnightly. From Prome to Thayetmyo there was a daily service. The run from Rangoon to Thayetmyo took six days, another six to Mandalay and six more to Bhamo. All the way up and down the river and on its tributaries on either side the short stages were covered by minor services, called ferry services. Each demanded tonnage of different characteristics − twin screw, paddle or sternwheel − and many different types according to the season and depth of water.

The company continued to expand, buoyed up at one stage by the export of oil aboard special flats on behalf of the Burmah Oil Company, until a pipeline was laid to Rangoon. The first triple-expansion engined paddle steamer was acquired in 1897, the 1,227-ton gross *Hindostan*, whose engines worked at an impressive 160psi. The paddle steamer *Beeloo* was used as the floating home for HRH The Duke of Clarence during his official visit to Burmah in 1889. Then in 1906 the new paddle steamer *Japan*, 1,320 tons gross, was put at the disposal of

the Prince and Princess of Wales, who had travelled by train from Rangoon to Mandalay but who returned to Rangoon on the steamer.

P Henderson & Company did make one serious error of judgement. Given the success of its associates on the Irrawaddy, it set out to replicate this success on the River Plate. The failed French company Compagnie La Platense of Paris had four fine paddle steamers built by Denny and one from a yard at Nantes. Two of the four Denny steamers had been built for the Buenos Ayres and Campana Railway, but on delivery came under the ownership of Lloyd Argentino. When that company failed to pay for the steamers Denny repossessed them and sold them to the Compagnie La Platense of Paris. In due course this company ordered a second pair of paddle steamers from Denny, the 1,255-ton gross paddlers *Apollo* and *Minerva*, but again payment was not forthcoming, so Peter Denny took a financial interest and with his son William, and directors from P Henderson & Company, formed the La Platense Flotilla Company in 1886.

There was a rival company on the Plate, Messageries Fluviales a Vapor, which operated a fine fleet of paddlers built by A & J Inglis that were shipped out from the Clyde. The newest ships were *Saturno* and *Olympo*, completed in 1884 and tested on trials at 15 knots. This company attempted to buy the ailing La Platense company before Denny and the Henderson Line stepped in. As it was, conditions were unknown to the newly formed Denny/Henderson enterprise and were quite unlike the political and physical constraints known so well on the Irrawaddy.

In 1886 William Denny and John Galloway, a director in the new company, went to Buenos Aires to see what could best be done. Their first decision was to buy out Lloyd Argentino, but acquisition of Messageries Fluviales a Vapor was not quite so easy. Meanwhile, John Galloway having returned to Scotland, William Denny, whose emotions were upset by illness, took his own life in March 1887 by shooting himself at his lodgings in Buenos Aires. Shortly afterwards Galloway returned and completed the purchase of Messageries Fluviales a Vapor, but he was too late to lift William Denny from his despair. Sadly the company, now of course a monopoly, failed in 1889 following the collapse of the Argentine economy and the subsequent revolution of July 1889. William's father, Peter Denny, survived his son and died peacefully at the age of 74.

In later years sixteen of the Irrawaddy paddle steamers and ten sternwheelers were requisitioned in the First World War for service on the Tigris and Euphrates in support of the Mesopotamian campaign. Three of the sternwheelers were lost in the tow across the Persian Gulf, but the remainder survived intact.

The Irrawaddy company owned forty-one paddle steamers at the outbreak of the Second World War. They were between 125 and 326ft long (up to 1,300 tons gross), and there were also twelve sternwheelers up to 132ft in length. The entire fleet numbered 650, vessels including barges pontoons and cargo flats.

Pearl Harbor was raided on 7 December 1941, and by Christmas Rangoon was under air attack. The Irrawaddy Flotilla Commodore, Captain Coutts, was killed in the first air raid along with his chief engineer while loading the big paddle steamer *Nepaul*

for Mandalay. Following the subsequent invasion by the Japanese, 550 of the fleet of 650 vessels were scuttled or blown up to prevent them falling into enemy hands. Major Eric Yarrow, RE, MBE, later Sir Eric, of the famous Clyde firm of warship builders, was responsible for scuttling many of his firm's products ahead of the Japanese invasion. Postwar the Irrawaddy company was reinstated with what few assets survived, but a mandate from the Governor was issued in January 1946 regarding compensation for losses and the need to get the inland waterways on the move again. Burma attained independence in May 1948 and the company was nationalised. Two and a half years later the nationalised company was found unworkable and dissolved.

The other British-owned river fleet was that on the Yangtze River in China, inaugurated by the newly formed China Navigation Company. John Swire formed the company to operate three large river paddle steamers, *Pekin* and *Shanghai* of 3,100 gross tons and the smaller *Inchang* of 1,780 gross tons, ostensibly as an inland extension to Alfred Holt's Blue Funnel Line service to the UK. The steamers were built in 1873 at Pointhouse, Glasgow, by A & J Inglis and were followed in 1874 by another 3,000 gross tons paddler, *Hankow,* from the same builder. They all made their own way to

The burnt-out steamer *Hankow* (1874) at Hong Kong on 14 October 1906. Note the walking beam protruding above the port paddle box.

China with many coaling stops on the way, and were unusual for Clyde-built ships as they were equipped with American-style walking-beam engines. This was a reflection of the available engineering skills on the China coast at that time. Subsequent paddle steamers for the company's river and coastal services were largely built by Inglis, which at that time was also exporting to Australia with paddle steamers destined for Bay Steamers of Melbourne and the like.

Two of the three original China Navigation Company paddlers were lost. *Shanghai* caught fire in 1890 and was beached near Mud River Fort on passage up river to Hankow from Shangai. About 200 of the deck passengers were drowned after they panicked and jumped into the river. The following year *Inchang* was wrecked on a coastal voyage from Shanghai to Ningpo with the loss of 43 lives. Only *Pekin* saw its career through to the end, when it was withdrawn from service in 1912. In the meantime the big steamer *Hankow* caught fire just after 3am on the morning of 14 October 1906 while alongside at Hong Kong. Within a space of just 45 minutes it was razed to main-deck level, with extensive damage below. So fierce was the blaze that 130 lives were lost and many of the bodies were never recovered.

Of the many other networks of river steamers that have evolved over the years, the great sternwheelers of North America certainly catch the eye. The stories of Steamboat Bill, the tales recounted by Mark Twain, the poetry and the music that have been written about these steamers and the people associated with them are legendary. The sternwheeler offered a number of advantages for river work. Tonnage for tonnage, it was narrower than its side-wheel counterpart, it had no sponsons and could berth alongside, which was useful for cargo handling, and above all its paddle wheel was better protected at the stern. The stern wheel was out of the way of fallen trees and other debris that rivers so often carry during the rains, and was less likely to suffer damage from the sandbanks that become a hazard at times of low water. The image always is of the Ohio-Mississippi steamer with its tiered decks and shallow flat-bottomed hull, twin stove-pipe funnels and large stern wheel churning the muddy waters. But the river steamer was equally important in the Great Lakes and on the Savannah and Hudson rivers.

The wonder of the Mississippi sternwheelers is no better encapsulated than in an article in *Harper's New Monthly Magazine*, June to November 1870, describing the big steamer *Thompson Dean*:

> Her actual carrying capacity is 3,200 tons. She is 290 feet in length and 56 in breadth. From her keel to the roof of the upper cabin she includes 40 feet. Above this is the 'Texas' which is an upper row of cabins, where the officers quarters are, and on top of which is imposed the pilot house. The main cabin is plainly but well furnished, with large state rooms on either side. Below it is the main deck, where the big boilers and furnaces and engines are . . . there is a deep spacious hold, where 1,500 tons of freight may be stowed away . . . Perhaps the most ornamental and most needful parts of this noble creature, as we see her from the outside, are the two big black smoke stacks.

The author of the article, George Nichols, explains:

> Steamboats of the largest size, such as the *Thompson Dean*, *Great Republic*, *Richmond* and others, do not go above St Louis, neither do they ascend the Ohio, except for a short distance, because of shoal water and rapids. On a full river, however, they can pass over all of these, and then these monster craft can appear at the levee at Cincinnati.
>
> St Louis is the greatest transfer depot on the river. Steamboats bring to this point freights from the upper Missouri and Mississippi and all the rivers which empty into these largest of the water

courses, and thus there is abundance of business for the great export mart of New Orleans.

Perhaps the most celebrated sternwheelers on the Mississippi-Ohio were *Delta Queen* and *Delta King*. Their gross tonnage was about 1,850. The two steel hulls were built by William Denny on the Clyde in 1924 and shipped out piecemeal to Los Angeles for final construction. The vessels were truly international: the cross-compound condensing engines were built by Denny at Dumbarton to American plans, while the wheel shafts and cranks were forged in Germany by Krupp and later machined in America. The Greene Line Steamer *Delta Queen* outlived *Delta King* and ended its days working river cruises alongside the older and smaller *Belle of Louisville*, which was built at Pittsburgh as *Idlewild* in 1914. Interestingly, nearly sixty sternwheelers were built on the Clyde over the years for export far and wide. The last three were delivered in 1950, of 350 tons gross and destined for the United Africa Company.

Of course, the romantic in us harks back to the great race between *Robert E Lee* and *Natchez* in 1870. The race took the steamers from New Orleans to St Louis. The victorious *Robert E Lee* won in just over 3 days and 18 hours, deciding once and for all the fate of the estimated $1 million dollars that had been waged on the contest.

The success of luxury river cruises elsewhere led to the building of the new *Mississippi Queen* in 1976 and *American Queen* in 1995 for the Delta Steamboat Company. The latter received the engines from the long abandoned dredger *Kennedy*, the cylinders were rebored and the cracks in the castings repaired. Babcock & Wilcox watertube boilers supply the steam, not fired by wood as tradition would have it, but by oil. Generators supply electricity for the ship and the extensive hotel facilities, while safety regulations insist on twin bow thruster units and steerable stern thrusters.

Robert E Lee (1866) from an oil painting by August Norieri, *c.*1876. (LOUISIANA STATE MUSEUM)

The river was also important for freight, and in the late nineteenth century all the cotton left the region for the coast by 'cotton packets'. The last of these was *America*, built in 1898 and originally configured as a wood burner. Its career was prematurely ended by the combined attacks of the Depression and depressed freight rates on the railways, although increased use of barge traffic also hurt the steamers (see Chapter 10).

The Hudson River was more the province of side-wheelers. The Delaware tended to accept secondhand tonnage from the Hudson operators in the early days, and was always a second best to the Hudson. Speed was all-important on the Hudson River, and some fine paddle steamers were developed for the run up from New York to Albany. By the early 1860s the Hudson River offered the world's fastest steamers, with *Daniel Drew* having 'attained the ex-

traordinary speed of 25 miles per hour (about 22 knots) without assistance from either wind or tide'. (Such speeds were possible with the bigger American hulls, whereas smaller paddlers in Europe could barely achieve such speeds.) *Daniel Drew* was owned and operated by Daniel Drew, and sold at auction to Alfred van Santvoord in 1863. It was converted to a day boat and became the nucleus of the newly formed Hudson River Day Line.

Typical also of this era was *New World*, built in 1850, 380ft long after lengthening by 62ft in 1855, 36ft breadth at the water line and 69ft across the sponsons. Its walking-beam engine, built by T Secor & Company of New York, had a stroke of 15ft and the cylinder was a massive 76in; the paddle wheels were 46ft in diameter. It had 347 state rooms and 680 berths. *The Illustrated London News* of 27 July 1861 described *New World*:

TABLE 6 Examples of paddle steamers built for use on the River Hudson between New York and Albany

Ship	Built	Hull	Length x breadth (feet)	Engine	Comments
Steam Boat	1807	Wood	133 x 13	Boulton & Watt 1 cylinder	Often referred to as *Clermont*, and later renamed *North River Steam Boat*
Fulton	1812	Wood	134 x 31	Crosshead	Designed by Fulton
Chancellor Livingston	1815	Wood	157 x 34	Crosshead	Designed by Fulton; first to receive a deck cabin; 11 knots
Albany	1826	Wood	212 x 26	Walking-beam	First with overhead hogging trusses; 1839 lengthened by 77ft
Empire	1843	Wood	308 x 31	Walking-beam	Drew only 4ft 6in
Hendrick Hudson	1845	Wood	330 x 40	Walking-beam	People's Line; first Hudson steamer over 1,000 tons gross
Isaac Newton	1846	Wood	338 x 40	Walking-beam	People's Line
New World	1850	Wood	353 x 36	Walking-beam	People's Line; first to have boilers outside on sponson guards; 1855 lengthened by 18ft and third deck added
Francis Skiddy	1852	Wood	312 x 38	Walking-beam	
Mary Powell	1861	Wood	286 x	Walking-beam	
St John	1864	Wood	420 x 51	Walking-beam	People's Line
New York	1887	Wood	341 x 74	Walking-beam	Hudson River Day Line
Adirondack	1896	Wood	440 x 50	Walking-beam	New Jersey Steamboat Company
Hendrick Hudson	1906	Steel	391 x 82	Compound	Hudson River Day Line; electric lighting
Robert Fulton	1909	Steel	356 x	Walking-beam	Hudson River Day Line; engine from *New York*, destroyed by fire
Alexander Hamilton	1924	Steel	350 x 72	Triple-expansion	Hudson River Day Line

The last of the cotton freighters was the *America* (1898), which had a 28-year career on the Lower Mississippi.

the immense stack of sleeping cabins, the projecting sponsons, or 'guards', the remarkable manner in which the rigidity of the hull is maintained by trussing with wooden beam, brace, iron tie rods etc., without which the vibration of the mass would be terrific, while with it the whole is so steady that a passenger cannot feel in the slightest degree either the beat of the engine or the revolution of the paddles. The boilers of this vessel are placed outside on the guards, a singular position for such great weights, but tending much to keep the vessel cool, as well as adding to her safety. This class of vessel, with more or less of top hamper in the way of cabins, is used on all the waters in the eastern and northern States.

What the story failed to report was that the flyer *New World* had sunk to the bottom of the Hudson River only four years earlier. An emergency stop caused its walking beam to collapse through the bottom of the ship when the supporting timber A-frame, which had become rotten, collapsed (see Chapter 4). It was only later in the 1880s that steel A-frames were introduced.

The Albany to New York route on the Hudson River was upgraded in 1880 when the 1,500-passenger paddle steamer *Albany* was delivered, and again in 1887 when its running mate, *New York*, came into service. From then on, a steamer left New York and Albany daily at eight o'clock in the morning and arrived at its destination at six o'clock in the afternoon. The pair was described in a contemporary guide:

> The spacious cabins are finished in highly polished woods, handsomely panelled, and are finished luxuriously and adorned in statuary and paintings by celebrated artists. The dining rooms are on the main deck, where the traveller can enjoy an excellent dinner and lose nothing of the view of this most charming of American rivers.

Another famous steamer was *Mary Powell*, built in 1861 for Captain Absalom. It was operated by him and later his son until it was sold in 1902 to the Hudson River Day

Line. Captain Absalom was disappointed with his steamer's speed, and at the end of its first season had the hull lengthened by 21ft, with the result that it became the fastest ship on the river.

Typical of the later Hudson River steamers were the *Hendrick Hudson* of 2,847 tons gross, built in 1906, and *Robert Fulton*, a 2,168-ton-gross paddler completed in 1909. The route down the Hudson, of course, followed Fulton's experimental *Steam Boat/Clermont* of so very long ago. The last paddler was the *Alexander Hamilton*, 2,367 tons gross, built for the Day Line in 1924 by the Bethlehem Shipbuilding Corporation at Sparrows Point. While the older *Hendrick Hudson* could manage 24 knots in its day, the newer steamer was designed for a service speed of 21 knots, being driven by a set of diagonal triple-expansion engines.

Big though the Hudson River steamers were, the Great Lakes steamers were even bigger. The Detroit overnight service to Buffalo on Lake Erie, for example, was maintained by 7,739-ton side-wheel paddlers such as *Greater Detroit* and *Greater Buffalo*, the largest paddle steamers ever built other than Brunel's *Great Eastern*. These massive seven-deck steamers offered all the amenities of the luxury liner, with cabins and state rooms available to suit, and a range of public rooms and restaurants, although bars were conspicuously absent aboard ship during the years of Prohibition (see Chapter 8).

The Murray and Darling rivers in Australia were home to more than 300 paddle steamers between 1835, when the 55ft-long *Mary Ann* arrived on station, and 1953, when the last cargo service ended. Captain Graeme Andrews, in an article first published in *Sea Breezes* in May 1984, described some of the problems with perennial navigation on Australian rivers:

> Voyages up the more distant rivers sometimes lasted more than a year as paddlers became marooned in the pools left as river levels fell. In many cases the crew left the steamer and went [to work] on the nearest property or in the nearest town but there is one well known story of a paddler carrying a load of seed potatoes whose crew planted them on the banks near the stranded steamer. When the rains came and the river gradually rose they harvested their 'cargo' and arrived in port with a load of new potatoes for sale.

More recently, a number of motor and steam paddle vessels have been introduced to cater for tourists on one-day and longer cruises.

The Hudson River Day Line's *Albany* (1880), showing its walking beam high up between the paddle boxes and partly hidden by flags.

The Köln Düsseldorf
steamer *Bismarck*
(1914), which enjoyed
a 60-year career on the
Rhine.

Paddle steamers have been synonymous with the River Rhine for many generations. In 1853 services were consolidated with the merger of the Preussisch-Rheinischen Dampfschiffahrtsgesellschaft of Köln with Dampfschiffahrtsgesellschaft fur de Neider-und-Mittelrhein of Düsseldorf to form what became known as the KD (Köln Düsseldorf). The merger was brought about by declining freight and passenger returns as the new German railway network became established. As time passed, the KD bought out various smaller companies and worked initially in competition, although from 1927 in collaboration, with the Dutch Steamboat Company. In due course the paddlers were successively withdrawn. The Düsseldorf company's magnificent *Bismarck* of 1914, for example, was withdrawn in 1974 and scrapped four years later, and the *Cecile*, built for the Köln company in 1910, last ran in 1983.

Today there are survivors on the Rhine. Despite being sunk in 1945, the paddle steamer *Goethe*, completed in 1913, was completely rebuilt and now runs in the summer between Koblenz and Rudesheim. The Dutch also have *Majestic*, likewise sunk in the Rhine in 1945 but later raised and rebuilt.

Paddle steamers were also an integral part of the scene on many other rivers, such as the Ganges in India and the numerous rivers of Russia. The Russian steamers typically offered four classes for passengers, although their main income was from the cargo they carried on trips that could be over a thousand miles long. Most of these river services have now been overtaken by road and rail, but not all, and those that do still run make the most of the tourist potential with modern diesel 'steamers'.

Even in the Congo Free State, the Belgian Congo from 1908, British shipbuilders supplied a number of small steamers for the mission societies. The Congo is navigable from Leopoldville, 800 miles inland to Stanleyville. The first steamer was built by Cockerill at Hoboken in 1879. Named *En Avant*, it had a draft of just one foot and a length of 40ft. It was soon joined by a small British-built sternwheeler operated by Livingstone's Inland Mission. From 1889 several big cargo sternwheelers were shipped out from Belgium and assembled at Leopoldville. Many of these operated successfully until the early 1950s. The first passenger sternwheelers were the 145ft-long trio *Brabant*, *Hainaut* and *Flandre*, all carrying their Flemish names from Cockerill, their builder, far into the Congo on the express Leopoldville to Stanleyville route. Today, tugs tow barges up and down the river but the air link has superseded the sternwheeler.

In Britain, the river, rather than estuarial, paddle steamer was essentially limited to the Thames, with regular services operated 'above bridge' from London, with onward connections by screw steamer to Windsor and beyond. The largest of the paddle steamers, a tiddler compared with her American relatives, was *Queen Elizabeth*, 141 tons gross, built for Edgar Shand in 1895. It carried up to 709 passengers from London Bridge to Kew, Richmond and Hampton Court until the First World War. Small paddle steamers also ran on rivers such as the Trent at Nottingham and the lower reaches of the Severn. A distinct breed of steamer was also developed for passenger carrying on the Caledonian Canal in Scotland. *Gondolier* operated the Caledonian Canal passenger service from 1866 for a total of 73 years. Rarely leaving its fresh-water province, it was ulti-

The largest of the Thames 'above bridge' steamers was *Queen Elizabeth* (1895).

Gondolier (1866) in the locks at Fort Augustus in the Caledonian Canal.

Maid of the Loch (1953) backs away from Balloch Pier on Loch Lomond on 24 August 1970. (AUTHOR)

mately taken by the Admiralty and sunk as a block ship at Scapa Flow in 1939.

Paddle steamers were also built for service on various inland Scottish lochs. One of the most famous Loch Lomond steamers was *Prince Edward*. Richard Coton described her delivery from the builders in 1911:

> The *Prince Edward* was built for the Dumbarton and Balloch Joint Lines Committee, and was in her time the largest vessel on Loch Lomond. This, indeed, had repercussions, for while proceeding up the River Leven from her builder's yard [A & J Inglis] to the Loch at Balloch, in the manner similar to her predecessors, she was stranded – and was

forced to lie where she was until the spring of the following year, 1912. As expected, the water level in the river rose and the *Prince* was floated off, but she then had to be packed with school children (given a holiday for the occasion) to make her low enough in the water to pass under a bridge farther upstream. She finally entered service on the loch in July 1912.

Prince Edward shared the Loch Lomond services with the *Prince George* and *Princess May*, the latter two paddlers also built by A & J Inglis in 1898. There had been a steamer service on the loch since the little steamer *Marion* in 1817. By the early 1950s *Princess*

May was past its prime, and consideration was given to replacing it with a pair of small motor ships. To everyone's delight the British Transport Commission decided to order a large paddle steamer, the last conventional large paddle steamer to be ordered in Britain. This was *Maid of the Loch*, built in sections by A & J Inglis at Pointhouse and brought to the loch for final assembly (no schoolchildren needed this time). It is equipped with an old-fashioned compound diagonal engine built by Rankin & Blackmore at Greenock with steam generated by oil-fired navy boilers. On trial on the loch it attained its design speed of 14 knots, and for its first two seasons ran alongside *Prince Edward*. Declining traffic sent *Prince Edward* up the Balloch slipway for the last time, where it was cut up for scrap in 1955.

Maid of the Loch continued to ply the waters of Loch Lomond each summer against a background of deteriorating patronage. Intense advertising brought some return and allowed the steamer to remain in service through the 1960s, despite its ownership being shared with a bus company during 1969. Twice it hosted Her Majesty Queen Elizabeth II, the first time in 1965 for a cruise, and the Royal Standard was again flown in 1971. Such royal patronage boosted ticket sales, and *Maid of the Loch* remained active until the end of the 1981 season. Since then it has lain at Balloch Pier under various owners, but it is now open to the public as a static exhibit, and future renovation work might one day see it in steam again.

Paddle steamers that plied the Swiss lakes tended to live to great ages in their fresh-water environments. The last to be built was in 1928, but fifty survived until 1950, although there were just twenty in 1970, reflecting the need to withdraw the older steamers, many of which were built in the nineteenth century. As boilers came up for renewal, some of the steamers were re-equipped with diesel-electric machinery while others were chosen for reboiling. Of the larger vessels, *La Suisse*, built in 1910, and *Simplon*, laid down in 1913 and delivered only in 1920 because of the intervention of the First World War, are still in steam on Lake Geneva. Owned by Compagnie Générale de Navigation, these steamers have become iconic reminders of the one-time

The Swiss steamers *La Suisse* (1910) and *Simplon* (1920) are still in steam on Lake Geneva.

heyday of the Swiss lakes paddlers. Also on the lake are the paddlers *Savoie* of 1914 and *Rhône*, completed in 1927.

Lake Lucerne was an important highway even before the first steamship, *Stadt Luzern*, was introduced in 1837. Access to the northern end of the important St Gotthard Pass was by boat, as the precipitous shores prevented pack mules continuing up to the pass. Boatmen did not take kindly to the steamer as they watched their business eroding away, but an agreement was reached and *St Gotthard* was introduced to the Lake in 1843. Both steamers were built locally by Escher Wyss. A rival company then ordered two paddle steamers from Ditchbourne & Mare in London to be brought overland to Lucerne. These were the *Waldstätter* and *Rigi* of 1847 and 1848 respectively. *Waldstätter* was damaged by stranding after 71 years' service, but *Rigi* is preserved at the Museum

of Transport in Lucerne. Business was good until the Gotthard Railway opened in 1882, when the steamers could easily have become redundant.

Happily, tourists had started to visit the area and the lake steamers were high on their itinerary. A number of paddlers were introduced subsequently, of which the *Uri*, built by Sulzer Brothers in 1901, is undoubtedly the best known. *Unterwalden* came from Escher Wyss in 1901, and Sulzer built the *Schiller* in 1906 and the *William Tell* in 1908. The fastest of them all is the 17-knot *Gallia* built by Escher Wyss in 1913, and the largest of them is a new *Stadt Luzern*, built in 1928. All five of these paddlers are still in service on the lake. Paddle steamers also ply other Swiss, Italian and German lakes to this day, while the *Blümlisalp*, on Lake Thun, is currently undergoing a programme of major renovation.

Maid of the Loch (1952) being assembled on the Bulloch ship in February 1952. The funnel was repainted all yellow prior to the launch date in March. (LINDA GOWANS COLLECTION)

8 PASSAGE WEST: ON THE GREAT LAKES

Side-wheel and propeller steamers were fundamental to westward expansion. They reached their zenith on the Great Lakes before railroad lines connected far-flung waterfront settlements in the states of New York, Pennsylvania, Ohio, Michigan, Indiana, Illinois, the Wisconsin Territory that eventually became the states of Wisconsin and Minnesota, and Ontario, Canada. By the early 1850s railroads were beginning to augment overland services with their own steamboat lines to carry passengers and freight between railheads, which broadened their reach well into middle America and Canada. This combination service gave steamers a new purpose, extending the useful lives of many into the early 1900s.

From an article by George Jepson in *Wooden Boat*, May/June 2011

The steamer had a pivotal role in America's expansion to the west during the 1830s and 1840s. The overland routes were served by stagecoaches suspended on leather straps placed between the axles and dragged by weary horses across rough-and-ready turnpikes. The early steamers might have been unreliable, but they offered incomparable comfort to those New Englanders and arriving immigrants who needed to travel westwards into middle America and Canada. There were risks on the Lakes, including floating ice and fog, along with occasional squalls, but these were small compared with the risks of an overland journey. Bob Whittier in his book on American paddle steamer engines quotes a visiting Frenchman's description of the comforts of the steamboat:

I must repeat again that the American stagecoaches are untrustworthy. It is impossible to conceive of the frightful inconvenience of these vehicles. One gets soaked crushed, shaken, thrown about and bumped every foot of the way. Coaches are shattered, horses killed, and passengers crippled by the many stagecoach accidents. To pass from the steamboat to the stagecoach, especially in bad weather, is to descend from paradise to hell!

The early steamers on the Great Lakes were sailing ships with auxiliary paddles, but as time went on the design evolved into vessels that were deeper-drafted and had higher freeboard than their counterparts on inland waters elsewhere in America. Timber was available in abundance and craftsmen were ready to work it, so a thriving wooden-ship industry soon emerged at a number of centres in the Great Lakes. The classic design of overhanging main deck in the form of an extended fore and aft sponson, deckhouse from stem to stern and white livery complete with the ship's name across the paddle box soon became standard.

The very first steamer on the Great Lakes was *Ontario*, built in 1816 for service on Lake Ontario. In quick succession it was followed by the British-owned *Frontenac*, built in Kingston, Ontario, in 1817, *Charlotte* in 1818 and *Dalhousie* in 1819, all for service on Lake Superior. The key structural issue was the provision of a strong and stable platform in the hull for the single-cylinder, vertical-crosshead engine and its associated supporting A-frame. Robert Fulton was the design engineer for both *Ontario* and *Frontenac*. Although essentially sailing ships with paddle wheels, they started to bring some semblance of timetabling to the otherwise haphazard schedules of the many sailing schooners and brigs on the Lakes.

Perhaps the most famous of the early

steamers on the Lakes was *Walk-on-the-Water*, a literal translation of the colloquial American Indian name given to the steamer. It was 135ft long by 32ft wide, again essentially a sailing ship with paddles, characterised by a billet-head bow and a transom stern. The engines were designed by Robert Fulton. *Walk-on-the-Water* was completed in August 1818 at Black Rock, for the Lake Erie Steam-Boat Company, and started its weekly run from Buffalo to Detroit and back, calling at Erie, Grand River, Cleveland and Sandusky. It was the first steamer to transit into Lake Michigan on a charter for the American Fur Company. *Walk-on-the-Water* was wrecked near Buffalo in November 1821.

The opening of the Erie Canal in 1825 prompted a new and important trade for the steamers. Barge traffic now had access from the Hudson River at Albany, with steamer connection to New York, all the way to Buffalo at the end of Lake Erie. Four years later the obstacle of the Niagara Falls was removed when the first Welland Canal opened, connecting Lake Ontario with Lake Erie. The canal was periodically upgraded, though it was many years before it was widened sufficiently for steamer traffic, and then the preference was for screw-propelled steamers, or propeller steamers as the Americans call them, rather than the broad-paddle steamers. The Lakes and the various canals enabled massive and rapid demographic growth in the west, providing communications to the coast and to New York via the Lake steamers, barge traffic on the Erie Canal and the Hudson River steamers (see Chapter 7).

It was not long before the crosshead engines, most of which had closed condensing systems, were superseded by the more efficient beam engine. The steamers had begun to evolve into two-deckers in parallel with those on Long Island Sound, the Hudson River and Chesapeake Bay. The first beam engines emerged on the Great Lakes in 1837, aboard the magnificent wooden steamers *Milwaukee* and *Cleveland*. By 1840 the standard arrangement of lower deck for freight and baggage and upper deck for passengers was adopted, initially by *Indiana*, an arrangement that was to stand the test of time. *Indiana* was built at Buffalo and spent its life commuting between there and Toledo. George Jepson writes in *Wooden Boat*, volume 26:

During the 1830s and 1840s steamboats rapidly shifted from hulls that resembled sailing ships to new and different hull shapes. In 1833 *Michigan* – 145 feet long with a 29 feet beam and 11 feet 2 inch depth – was launched in Detroit by shipbuilder Oliver Newberry. The hull featured a main deck that extended out over the paddle boxes but curved inward forward and aft to eventually meet the bow and stern. The additional width amidships allowed a cabin to be built on the main deck; this feature became a hallmark of Lakes side-wheelers. Before this breakthrough, most cabins were located below the main deck in the fashion of ocean-going steamers.

Michigan also had two engines and 28ft-diameter independently driven paddle wheels. The two big beam engines could power the ship along at more than 17 knots in calm water. But when the ship rolled, the different submergence of the paddle wheels made it yaw back and forth as one engine raced forward with reduced resistance from the paddle wheel while the other engine struggled to maintain speed with a paddle wheel choked with water. For this very reason the British Board of Trade insisted on a fixed shaft with same-direction wheel rotation.

The next development was the extension of the deckhouse from bow to stern. *Great Western*, completed at Huron, Ontario, in 1838, pioneered this concept with a deckhouse that ran from stern to foremast, while in successors the deckhouse was quickly extended right to the bows. *Great Western* ran on the Buffalo to Chicago service, and its innovative layout was so popular that it was copied in other steamers. The ladies' cabin and all the state rooms were on the main deck aft, while the deckhouse, with 'hurricane deck' above, contained the saloon, dining room and bar.

On Lake Erie there was the crack steamer *Erie*, delivered in 1837 and measuring 127ft by 27ft, although the paddle boxes added another 22ft to its breadth. Its engines provided 250hp and a speed of 14mph (roughly 12 knots) light ship with a draft of 5ft 6in, and a bit slower when loaded down to 7ft 6in. The paddle wheels were of 24ft diameter. The saloon was below the main deck aft, while cabins opened directly on to the main deck rather than into the lounge as was customary in those days.

The rapid increase in size of the steamers is illustrated by the Michigan fleet owned by A E Goodrich:

Huron, built 1852, 348 tons
Comet, built 1860, 350 tons
Seabird, built 1859, acquired 1863, 638 tons
Planet, built 1855, acquired 1863, 993 tons
Northwest, built 1867, 1,109 tons

The larger steamers ran from Buffalo to upper Lakes ports or from Niagara and Toronto to lower Lakes destinations. Some of the steamers had long careers in their fresh-water environment, while others succumbed to fire or storm. The Goodrich steamers *Chicago*, built in 1837, and *Sheboygan*, built in 1869, were disposed of only in 1915, their timber hulls and primitive beam engines having repaid their owners many times over. The attraction of the two ships was that their shallow draft enabled them to visit many of the smaller harbours that the deeper-draft, newfangled screw-propelled steamers could not access.

The Detroit and Milwaukee Railway needed a lake crossing between Milwaukee and Grand Harbour to complete the link to bring New York within two days' travel time of Milwaukee. Two steamers were designed by Captain F N Jones of Buffalo, based on the lines of the Collins and Cunard Line ships then running on the North Atlantic. Costing $200,000 each, the steamers were replicas indeed of their seagoing peers, ex-

cept for the tops of their beam engines rocking gently above the deckhouse. Christened *Detroit* and *Milwaukee*, they were constructed of wood with extensive use of iron bracing. All the public rooms, state rooms and other cabins were below the main deck, with only the pilot house above deck level, to minimise top hamper. Below decks there were two saloons, one forward and one aft of the machinery space, with stowage for freight and baggage either side of the boilers. They were fine-looking ships, known as the 'black ships', as they had black hulls with gold scroll work, two masts and red funnels with a black top.

However, it was not long before the New York Central & Pennsylvania Railroad was completed, allowing rail transport of grain to the coast. The new railroad system also gave the European immigrants a quicker ride into the Midwest. Sadly many of the smaller paddle steamers on the Lakes ended their lives and were not replaced, their business eroded both by the coming of the railroad and by the ingress into the Lake trade of the screw-propelled steamers, a rude invasion that had started in the 1840s. But, rather than reduce their overall tonnage, the shipowners on the Great Lakes were some of the first businesses to acknowledge that larger ships with greater payload and more passenger accommodation could offer cheaper unit costs. The economy of scale depended on a greater number of receipts, albeit at a reduced freight tariff and passenger fare, outweighing the increased cost of maintaining larger tonnage. This concept led to the building of the palace steamers.

The first of the palace steamers was *Empire*, built by George Jones in Cleveland and launched in June 1844. A mighty 253ft long by 33ft beam, it offered passenger comforts never before seen at sea, let alone on the Lakes. It featured grand cabins with arched ceilings complete with skylights and domed stained-glass features which by night contained illuminated chandeliers, panelled woodwork and white paint to provide a sense of space. The upholstery was the finest and the carpets the plushest. Most of the palace steamers ran from Buffalo to Detroit or Chicago, and only the smallest could fit through the Sault Locks when they were opened in 1855. A total of twenty-five large wooden steamers were built, the last, *City of Buffalo* being launched at Buffalo in 1857. An incredible 331ft long with a beam of 40ft, it offered accommodation that was as fine as any that Cunard and its rivals sported. Alas, just two months after *City of Buffalo* took up station on Lake Erie, the big ships were forced out of service one by one as the 1857 financial panic took hold, and their clientele stayed at home.

George Jepson describes the structure of these exceptionally large wooden ships:

> The great size of these vessels was made possible by iron fastenings and diagonal strapping, and the development of large, arch shaped hogging trusses that resembled today's suspension bridges and longitudinally stiffened the long and limber hulls. To support the heavy engines and boilers, holds were fitted with athwartship timbers. Tall A frames were fastened to the timbers to support and stabilise the exposed walking beam that sat above the hurricane decks and drove the monstrous paddle wheels.

Interest in Gothic architectural style was back in vogue during the palace steamer era, and shipwrights adopted and incorporated fine architectural details into wheelhouse designs. Gilded spheres or eagles graced the crowns of fancy domes, and pilothouse windows came in various shapes to provide an eye-pleasing flourish as well as a clear view for the helmsman.

The development of the paddle steamer on the Lakes was temporarily halted by the arrival of screw steamers better able to negotiate the various canal locks. The paddlers remained popular with passengers, tried, tested and accepted as they were by the travelling public, but they never again achieved the numbers of the mid-nineteenth century. But the paddle steamers had not yet reached their zenith, as the really big four-, five-, six- and even seven-deckers were yet to be created. Meanwhile, many of the small steamers were stripped of their engines and finery and converted into dumb barges. With the commissioning of the very large paddle steamers the total number of paddlers declined. There were only thirty-nine in operation in 1925, and the last ceased working in 1950, although the hulked *Trillium* was

Lady Elgin (1851), one of the famous palace steamers, was lost in a collision in 1860. (C PATRICK LABADIE COLLECTION/THUNDER BAY NATIONAL MARINE SANCTUARY, ALPENA, MISSOURI)

yet to return to the Toronto Isles tourist route in 1976.

Losses on the Lakes were considerable, and even the big palace steamers were at risk. *Alabama* was lost in the early hours of 30 August 1854, after springing a leak just two hours out of Buffalo while bound for Cleveland. Its master managed to bring it into shallow water so that the main deck remained dry, and there was no loss of life. Another palace steamer was lost under altogether more challenging conditions when *Lady Elgin* collided with a heavily laden sailing ship in Lake Michigan during passage from Chicago to Milwaukee. The collision occurred in the dark early hours of 7 September 1860, the sailing ship apparently not carrying any lights when the paddle steamer struck it. The damage destroyed the watertight integrity of the wooden-hulled steamer, which rapidly flooded and sank, taking over 300 passengers and crew with it. Completed only in 1851, *Lady Elgin* had previously survived being aground, partly damaged by fire and involved in an earlier collision.

But other members of the palace steamer class survived as they slowly re-emerged from the financial panic in a variety of different guises, some dependent solely on tourist traffic. Two, *Mississippi*, the biggest of them all at 335ft in length, and *St Lawrence*, managed to stay in business on the route for which they were designed, be-

tween Buffalo and Sandusky. But *Mississippi* soon joined the Detroit to Buffalo service of the Michigan Central Railroad and remained so employed until the end of the nineteenth century, a monument to American wooden paddle steamer construction and a veritable credit to its builder, Francis Jones of Buffalo.

In Detroit, the night of 20 June 1868 was keenly remembered by those who had cause to take the ferry across Lake Erie. In the days before weather forecasts, when navigational aids were inadequate, accidents were bound to happen. The Detroit & Cleveland Navigation Company operated a night service between the ports of its name with the wooden paddle steamers *Morning Star* and *R N Rice*. Built in Detroit in 1862 and 1866 respectively, complete with walking-beam engines, both were renowned for the quality of their passenger accommodation: 'cabins adorned with splendid paintings, got up in the most approved style of art'.

Morning Star left its berth at Cleveland behind schedule at 10.30pm on 20 June, its 38 passengers delayed by the loading of 20 tons of pig iron. The night was clear and the waves were small, but as *Morning Star* progressed towards Detroit the Lakes sailing ship *Courtland*, loaded with 890 tons of iron ore, was inbound to Cleveland. At the subsequent inquiry it was learnt that *Courtland* carried only a weak portside light at the time of the collision. Captain Edward Viger

City of Toledo (1891), a popular steamer on Lake Erie, made its name in 1893 ferrying passengers from downtown Chicago to the World Fair site.

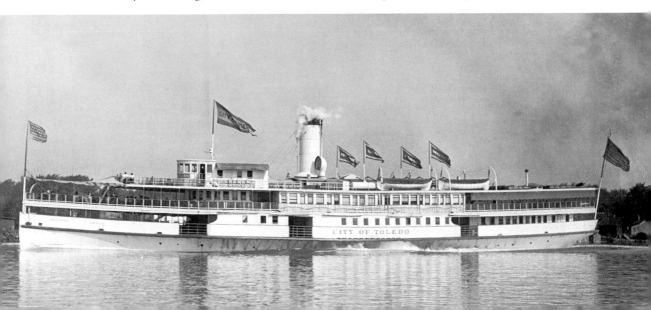

and his lookouts on the paddle steamer stood little chance of seeing *Courtland* in the black of night until it was too late. The impact occurred two hours out of Cleveland, when most of the passengers had settled for the night.

The initial impact was not itself catastrophic, as *Morning Star* was still buoyant. In attempting to back it away from the sailing ship, however, the two vessels came together, grinding away at each others' fabric. The two ships did finally part, both doomed with their heavy cargoes. At three in the morning the mate of *R N Rice*, on its way towards Cleveland, heard cries from the water. He turned his ship to give assistance, realising

only when he saw the mass of debris in the water that this was all that was left of *Morning Star*. Despite *R N Rice* staying in the vicinity until dawn, only a few survivors were found. Some 26 people lost their lives that night, but the company survived, despite *Morning Star* not carrying any insurance.

Among the paddle steamers built on the Lakes in the late nineteenth century was the famous *City of Toledo*, designed principally for tourist duties on Lake Erie. It was chosen to ferry passengers to the Chicago World Fair in 1893. *City of Toledo* was built in 1891 for the Toledo & Islands Steamship Company, to take holidaymakers in season out to Put-in-Bay. It was later

---

Frank E Kirby (1849-1929)

Ashley & Dustin's *Frank E Kirby* (1890) was named in honour of its designer.

Frank Kirby was born in Dover County, Ohio, son of Stephen and Martha Kirby. He followed an active career which was to influence shipbuilding profoundly throughout the Great Lakes. Best known for designing the many big steamers that extended the railroad services across the Lakes, Kirby is particularly remem-

bered for the grand and glamorous paddle steamers he designed to bring people and freight west across the inland seas of the Great Lakes.

Educated at Cleveland and later Saginaw, Frank Kirby went in the 1860s to the Cooper Institute Night School in New York. Here he switched from studying art to follow a passion for naval architecture. His first job was with the Delameter Iron Works of New York, where he was able to see shipbuilding at first hand. During a visit home Frank was introduced to leading industrialist Captain Eber B Ward. In 1864 Ward had introduced the Bessemer process of steel production to Wyandotte, Michigan, and his family also controlled a large line of lake steamers. Ward was good at recognising talent, and Frank Kirby clearly created the right impression. Ward took Frank to Wyandotte to build a large tug, *E B Ward Jr*, and Frank designed not only the boat, but also the engine and boiler.

The success of the tug, in terms of efficiency and power, launched Frank Kirby's career. His next project was the small paddle steamer *Queen of the Lakes*. Particular care was taken over the lines of the hull and the length-to-breadth ratio. Indeed, Frank Kirby made several trips to Europe to learn about iron ship-building and maritime technology, and he made copious sketches and drawings, not only of structural features but also of the scrollwork and other details. Upon Ward's death the Wyandotte yards were absorbed by the Detroit Dry Dock Company, one of the founders of which was Captain Stephen R Kirby, Frank's father. Frank's younger brother Joe then became the chief engineer and naval architect.

In October 1876 Frank Kirby married Mary Thorpe. The couple had one son.

The composite steamer *City of Detroit* of 1889 was the first of the sixteen large paddle steamers that Kirby was to design and build for the Detroit & Cleveland and Cleveland & Buffalo lines over a period of forty-six years. Equally notable were the graceful excursion steamers designed for the White Star, Ashley and Dustin, Detroit and Windsor and Hudson River Day Lines. But the Wyandotte and Detroit shipyards also built numerous ore carriers, package freighters and Detroit River and Lake Michigan railcar-ferries. By the 1880s competition hit hard among lakeside shipyards and Kirby was instrumental in the formation of the American Shipbuilding Company in 1898. This included both the Detroit and Wyandotte yards. Kirby helped draft the Steamboat Inspection Code and was involved in a host of projects, including a pioneer ice-breaking ferry.

One iron-hulled excursion paddle steamer, built in 1890 by the Detroit Dry Dock Company and launched in February 1890, honoured its designer with the name *Frank E Kirby*. It was commissioned by the Ashley & Dustin Steamer Line, Detroit, Michigan, and was 210ft long by 30ft breadth and had an 800ihp Fletcher-design walking-beam steam engine and two coal-fired box boilers. It operated between Detroit and Sandusky, Ohio, with stops at Put-in-Bay, Middle Bass Island and Kelleys Island. In 1925 it was renamed *Silver Spray*, and shortly afterwards renamed *Dover* for service between Detroit and other Lake Erie ports. Sadly, it was gutted by fire in February 1929 while laid up at Wyandotte, and was scrapped in the early 1930s.

One of Frank Kirby's best-known projects was the creation of the largest and grandest paddle steamers the world would ever see, *Greater Buffalo* and *Greater Detroit*. They were launched in 1923 and built at a cost of $3.5m each. Kirby lived to see his magnificent steamers thrive in the boom before the Depression took hold; he died in New York on 26 August 1929.

sold to the local White Star Line for service between Buffalo and Port Erie in Canada, and ended its days running from Toledo to Detroit and Toledo to Port Huron. It was scrapped in 1948.

Bigger and bigger steamers were being designed for the Lakes from the 1880s onwards (Table 6). As the traditional walking-beam engine could not satisfy the demand for ever-increased power, naval architects such as Frank E Kirby, long associated with the Detroit based shipbuilding industry, turned to the twin-cylinder compound engine, adopting an inclined principle to accommodate the massive weight of the machinery. The development of the really big paddle steamers, largely for use on overnight runs, was down to two relative newcomers on the Lakes. These were the Cleveland & Buffalo Transit Company (the C&B) and the Detroit & Cleveland Navigation Company (the D&C).

The C&B was established by Morris A Bradley in 1885 and incorporated in 1892, when Bradley became its president. The passenger and freight service between Cleveland and Buffalo was maintained by *State of Ohio* and *State of New York*.

The 203ft-long, 807-ton *State of New York* had been built in 1883 for the D&C as *City of Mackinac* (it was later sold back to

D&C in 1909 to run from Detroit to Saginaw and other nearby ports). Early in its first D&C life the ship had served the famous amusement park at Crystal Beach in Ontario, which was near Buffalo. It was here on Lake Erie that it was best known.

City of Buffalo was added to the C&B fleet in 1896 and near-sister *City of Erie* replaced *State of Ohio* in 1898, allowing a new overnight service to be developed to Toledo using the older steamers. *City of Buffalo* and *City of Erie* were state-of-the-art, big, fast and luxurious paddle steamers designed by Frank Kirby. They represented the zenith of the walking-beam engine and presented Lakes travel with a new concept in size and luxury spread across not two decks as had long been the norm, but three decks, save for the engine and boiler spaces.

The D&C Line was known for the largest and most palatial steamers on the Lakes and, as its name suggests, was the mainstay of the Detroit and Cleveland route. Various steamers were deployed on the route, including the celebrated paddle steamers *City of Cleveland* and *City of Detroit*, designed by Frank Kirby and built in 1886 and 1889 respectively. The first of the big three-deckers, they offered 120 luxurious state rooms. The *City of Cleveland* cost $300,000 to build, while *City of Detroit* is

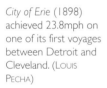

City of Erie (1898) achieved 23.8mph on one of its first voyages between Detroit and Cleveland. (LOUIS PECHA)

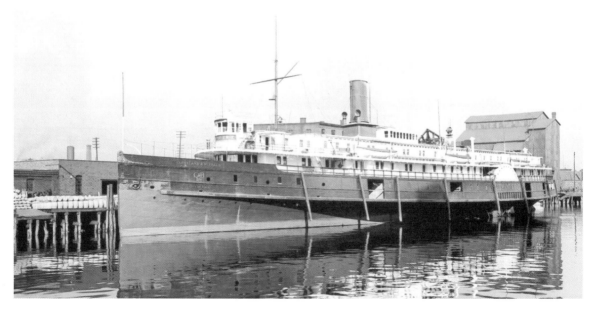

recorded as having completed an early crossing between Detroit and Cleveland at a steady 24.4mph (22 knots). This pair was superseded by mega-steamers that were intended to outclass, outsize and outrun even the big steamers of the C&B. These were *City of Cleveland* and *City of Detroit III*, built in 1907 and 1912 respectively. In 1909 the company took over the operations of the Detroit & Buffalo Steamboat Company and became owner of the two mega-sisters *Eastern States* and *Western States*. These dated from 1901 and 1902 and had been the first of the big paddle steamers to shun the walking-beam engine in favour of the inclined or diagonal compound engine. They were also the first four-deckers.

The triple-expansion engine was tried on a number of excursion steamers, the most famous of which was *Tashmoo*, designed by Kirby for the Detroit White Star Line and delivered in 1900. It had three decks and a comfortable turn of speed in excess of 22 knots. However, it was smaller than the new overnight paddle steamers and measured just 1,344 tons gross.

So convinced was the president of the White Star Line that his ship was the fastest on the Lakes that he laid down a challenge, saying he would give $1,000 to any ship that could beat his in a long-distance race. The challenge was inspired by media hype generated by an earlier race between two Lake steamers, and the White Star Line clearly saw the challenge as good advertising. Cleveland & Buffalo president J Wescott quickly accepted, and entered his crack paddler *City of Erie* against *Tashmoo* in a race along the *City of Erie*'s normal route, a voyage of 82 nautical miles in all. *Tashmoo* was badly hindered when the pilot of the excursion steamer had to navigate out of sight of land using compass courses alone (an unusual occurrence for any White Star Line steamer), and *Tashmoo* had to slow at one point to deal with an overheating condenser. Ultimately the *City of Erie* came in second to *Tashmoo*, the victor passing the 82-mile mark just 45 seconds before the loser.

But despite the obvious triumph of the triple-expansion engine, few other paddle steamers were so equipped, and all of the big Lakes steamers were subsequently given inclined compound engines. *City of Erie* did, however, show that the walking-beam engine was a match for any of these new technologies, save for its greater weight and volume.

The C&B added Cedar Point and Put-in-Bay to its ports of call in 1914. As passenger services became increasingly popular, the luxurious *Seeandbee* was commissioned in 1913 to work between Cleveland and Buffalo. One of the larger paddle steamers to grace the Lakes, the mighty coal-fired, steel-hulled *Seeandbee* was essentially a champion of its class and at one time the world's largest paddle steamer. I L Evanston described the *Seeandbee* in an article in *Lakeland Boating* for February 2001:

> She was 500 feet long with a 98 foot beam, housing six decks, 510 staterooms and 24 lounges. Her engines provided 12,000 hp, allowing her to cruise at 18mph [16 knots]. The ship was launched at Wyandotte, Michigan, in November 1912 and made her maiden voyage the following June. She was launched without a name, adorned instead with large question marks on each side of the bow. As part of a vast marketing campaign to drum up excitement for the maiden voyage, the company was holding a 'Name the Ship' contest. The winning name was submitted by a schoolgirl and *Seeandbee* was painted on the bow when the great steamer arrived in Buffalo for the first time on 19 June 1913.
>
> Thousands of people jammed the lakefront to watch the enormous vessel with its four great smokestacks manoeuvre up to the dock. Those lucky enough to be invited aboard found themselves in a huge Edwardian palace. Passengers entered through a lobby on the main deck. Here were the pursers' and stewards' offices, the ship's tele-

The D&C Line's *City of Cleveland* (1907), later renamed *City of Cleveland III*.

phone switchboard and the check-room. Aft was the huge main dining room. Above the main deck were three decks of staterooms and parlours and in the centre, the grand saloon – a huge room, three decks high. All the passenger areas were finished in mahogany and ivory.

The weekend traffic was the greatest; out from Cleveland on Friday night and back on Sunday night. The ship operated the night service until 1932, although it ran profitably only between May and Septem-

Engine manoeuvring platform, *City of Cleveland* (1907).

ber after legislation required additional crewing of the vessel.

By the 1920s the Detroit & Cleveland Navigation Company was the largest passenger and freight operator on the Lakes. It had been extremely profitable during the First World War and the 1920s, and it was able to order two new ships to support its night services. The steamers were designed by Frank Kirby and built in Lorain, Ohio. They were launched in 1924 as *Greater Buffalo* and *Greater Detroit*. I L Ivanston again:

Each steamer was 518 feet long with a beam of 100 feet. They were the largest passenger ships on the lakes and the largest true paddle steamers ever built ... The saloon rose though two decks and galleries on either side gave access to the staterooms. Each ship had more than 1,500 berths. The interior was designed by the New York firm of W & J Sloane & Company in an adaptation of the Renaissance style. Both ships went into service on the company's longest run between Detroit and Buffalo. Through 1929, the Detroit & Cleveland Navigation Company operated at a profit. That year, it carried more freight tonnage than ever before. Revenues exceeded all years prior. But at the beginning of

TABLE 7 Examples of the bigger steel-hulled steamers showing progressive increase in decks and tonnage

Ship	Built	Length x breadth (ft)	Gross tons	Decks	Engine	Career
City of Mackinac	1885	203 x 34	807	2	Vertical beam	Built for Detroit & Cleveland Steam Navigation Co; 1892 to Cleveland & Buffalo Transit Co; 1893 renamed *State of New York*; 1899 to Cleveland & Buffalo Line; 1906 to Detroit & Cleveland Steam Navigation Co; 1918 to Goodrich Transit Co; 1923 to Western Transportation, Chicago; 1936 scrapped
City of Cleveland	1886	272 x 40	1,923	3	Vertical beam	Built for Detroit &Cleveland Steam Navigation Co; *c.*1891 renamed *City of Cleveland II*; 1907 transferred to Lake Huron and renamed *City of St Ignace*; 1929 to Cleveland Canada Navigation Co and renamed *Keystone*; 1932 gutted and scrapped
City of Detroit	1889	287 x 41	1,919	3	Vertical beam	Built for Detroit & Cleveland Steam Navigation Co; 1912 renamed *City of Detroit II*; 1925 to Cleveland & Buffalo Transit Co rebuilt as day excursion steamer and renamed *Goodtime*; 1930 to Nicholson Erie-Dover Co, Detroit; 1941 scrapped
City of Chicago	1890	216 x 34	1,073	2	Vertical beam	Built for Graham & Morton Transportation Co; 1900 third deck added; 1905 lengthened; 1915 rebuilt and named *City of St Joseph*; 1935 hulked; 1942 sank in storm Lake Superior
City of Buffalo	1896	298 x 44	2,398	3	Vertical beam	Built for Cleveland & Buffalo Transit Co; 1937 gutted by fire
City of Erie	1898	316 x 44	2,498	3	Vertical beam	Built for Cleveland & Buffalo Transit Co; 1938 laid up; 1942 scrapped
Eastern States	1901	350 x 45	3,077	4	Inclined compound	Built for Detroit & Buffalo Steamboat Co; 1909 to Detroit & Cleveland Navigation Co; 1950 laid up and later scrapped
Western States	1902	350 x 45	3,077	4	Inclined compound	Built for Detroit & Buffalo Steamboat Co; 1909 to Detroit & Cleveland Navigation Co; 1959 scrapped
City of Cleveland	1907	402 x 54	4,568	5	Inclined compound	Built for Detroit & Cleveland Navigation Co; 1908 renamed *City of Cleveland III*; 1950 in collision on Lake Huron and laid up; 1954 scrapped
City of Detroit III	1912	455 x 55	6,061	6	Inclined compound	Built for Detroit & Cleveland Navigation Co; 1924 transferred from Detroit-Buffalo to Detroit-Cleveland service; 1951 laid up; 1956 scrapped
Seeandbee	1913	485 x 58	6,381	5	Inclined compound	Built for Cleveland & Buffalo Transit Co; 1939 to Cleveland & Buffalo Steam Ship Co (purchased in 1941); 1942 to US Navy renamed *Wolverine* and converted to aircraft carrier
Greater Detroit	1924	519 x 58	7,739	7	Inclined compound	Built for Detroit & Cleveland Navigation Co; scrapped 1956
Greater Buffalo	1924	519 x 58	7,739	7	Inclined compound	Built for Detroit & Cleveland Navigation Co; 1942 sold to US Navy renamed *Sable* and converted to aircraft carrier

Data based on Great Lakes Maritime Collection, www.alpenalibrary.org

Western States (1902) was built for the Detroit & Buffalo Steamboat Company and was the first steamer on the Lakes with an inclined compound engine.

1930, things began to change rapidly. By the end of the year, revenues had fallen by more than 25 per cent. This was repeated in 1931 and again in 1932.

The popularity of the passenger excursions in the 1920s prompted the C&B to buy *City of Detroit II* from the D&C line. It was rebuilt and renamed *Goodtime*, offering excursions and 'moonlight rides' on the Cleveland–Cedar Point and Put-in-Bay routes.

But all too soon the lorry and the passenger coach began to erode the profitability of lake passenger shipping. *Seeandbee* was withdrawn in 1932, a victim of the Depression, although it did undertake some Lake cruises over the next five years. The destruction of *City of Buffalo* by fire in 1938, along with the Depression, led to the bankruptcy and liquidation of the C&B, and both *Good-*

The Gothic Room aboard *City of Detroit III* (1912). Much of this interior is preserved at the Dossin Great Lakes Museum near Detroit.

The excursion steamer *Tashmoo* (1900), owned by the Detroit White Star Line, at Port Huron.

Greater Detroit (1924), clearly showing the arched roofs over the upper deck lounges. This and *Greater Buffalo* were the world's largest paddle steamers.

The *City of Buffalo* (1896) ablaze at Cleveland on 29 March 1938, with 'firemen playing water on the burning boat'. (ACME PHOTO, CLEVELAND BUREAU)

time and *City of Erie* were sold for scrap.

The Acme Photo, Cleveland Bureau, press release accompanying a photograph of *City of Buffalo* dated 29 March 1938 and depicting 'firemen playing water on the burning boat', under the banner 'Honeymoon special destroyed by fire', reads:

The *City of Buffalo*, which has carried thousands of newly married couples from Cleveland to visit the famous honeymoon spot, Niagara Falls, was destroyed by fire while anchored in the Ninth Street Slip in Cleveland. The boat, with her sister ship *City of Erie*, anchored just forward of the *City of Buffalo*, had been undergoing repairs all winter for the coming summer season. $25,000 had already been spent on repairs and she would have been completed this week. The boat, constructed of steel and wood in 1896, was believed a total loss. No estimate of the loss was given, but officials of the Cleveland & Buffalo Transit Company, owners of the two boats, said it could not be replaced for under $1 million.

Greater Buffalo and *Greater Detroit* were mothballed in 1938 but returned to service in 1939, *Greater Detroit* finally being withdrawn only in 1950. *Seeandbee* and *Greater Buffalo*, however, were bought by the US Navy in 1942 for conversion to aircraft carriers specifically for training navy pilots for service in the war. The two training carriers, renamed USS *Wolverine* and USS *Sable* respectively, had flight decks of similar length to the *Independence*-class light carriers. They worked throughout the year, seven days a week, out of Chicago on Lake Michigan, escorted by Coast Guard icebreakers as required. Together they helped prepare over 35,000 pilots for combatant service.

Greater Detroit and its surviving fleetmates, *City of Cleveland III*, *City of Detroit III*, *Western States* and *Eastern States*, all enjoyed an increase in passenger revenues during the war as fuel was rationed and overnight travel by steamboat again became attractive. But by the end of the war patronage once again fell. On 26 June 1950 *City of Cleveland III* was struck aft by the Norwegian freighter *Ravenfjell*. Five passengers were killed in the collision, and dozens injured. The two ships survived, but this incident sounded the end of the D&C, which was formally dissolved in 1951.

This left just one service operated by a paddle steamer, the Detroit to Windsor, Ontario, passenger and train ferry *Lansdowne*. It had been ordered by the Grand Trunk Railway to connect the Grand Trunk yard at Detroit with the Canadian National yard at Windsor. Named after the

USS *Wolverine* (1913), formerly the famous steamer *Seeandbee*, was converted into an aircraft carrier in 1942 for training purposes. (C PATRICK LABADIE COLLECTION/THUNDER BAY NATIONAL MARINE SANCTUARY, ALPENA, MISSOURI)

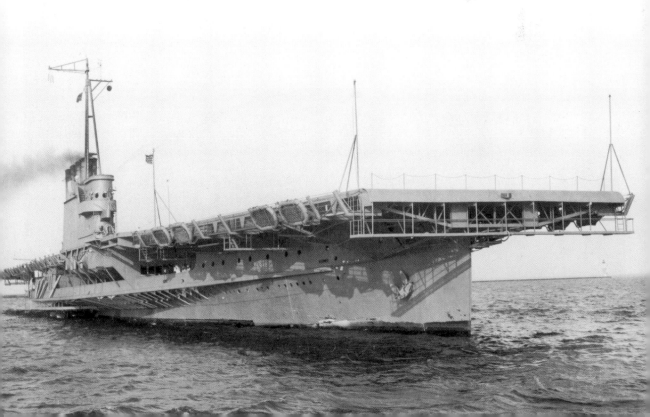

Marquis of Lansdowne, who was Governor General of Canada at the time, it was built in 1884 by the Detroit Dry Dock Company. It was 318ft long, with twin rail tracks from stem to stern. *Lansdowne* was equipped with two independent compound engines fed by four Scotch boilers at a pressure of 65psi. It was truly double-ended, having two pairs of 'stacks' and two pilot houses, one at each end of the ship.

Lansdowne's main role was to carry passenger railcars, a role it fulfilled for seventy years. This came to an end in 1955, when a road tunnel and bridge allowed direct access between Detroit and Windsor. *Lansdowne*, now with only two stacks and only one of its original pilot houses, carried on ferrying up to sixteen freight rail cars each crossing. In 1970 the port engine was condemned, and it was assumed that it would sail no more, but, cut down to a dumb barge, it continued the run until 1972, when the Detroit terminal was sold for redevelopment. Not done yet, the elderly *Lansdowne*, albeit almost unrecognisable, was used for a while on the short run across the Detroit river under the command of the pusher tug *Margaret Yorke*.

That would have been the end of the paddle steamer on the Great Lakes, but in 1906 a small double-ended excursion paddle steamer, *Bluebell*, had been built for the Toronto Isles service for the Toronto Ferry Company, and it was joined four years later by a consort named *Trillium*. Both were powered by compound horizontal engines with coal-fired Scotch boilers. By Great Lakes standards they were small, *Trillium* being 150ft long by 39ft broad (50ft across the paddle boxes). Nevertheless, they were initially licensed to carry 2,000 passengers in the sheltered waters of Toronto Harbour. For many years the two paddle steamers enjoyed considerable popularity. In 1919 *Trillium* took the Prince of Wales and his entourage out to the Isles, becoming the only Great Lakes steamer ever to receive royal patronage. The City of Toronto took over the operation of the Toronto Ferry Company in 1926, and management later passed to the Toronto Transit Commission. But by the late 1940s patronage had fallen away and the service was abandoned. *Bluebell* was stripped out and converted into a refuse barge in 1954, a role to which it objected by sinking under its load of garbage on more than one occasion. *Trillium* was withdrawn after the 1956 summer season and was abandoned in a quiet corner of Toronto Harbour, alongside its stinking former companion, where the pair were allowed to rot.

By 1973 there was renewed interest, as new holiday homes were being built on the Isles and there was a suggestion that *Trillium* might fit the requirement for a new ferry. Absurd though it might seem, a feasibility study demonstrated that repair of *Trillium*, now sunk into the mud of its shallow lagoon, was a cheaper option than building an entirely new ship. Massive public support for the old steamer prompted Toronto City Council to approve, in November 1973, expenditure of $950,000 on repair work. *Trillium* was duly raised and towed to a local yard for inspection and repair of the hull. The hull was found to be in reasonable condition, preserved in a fresh-water environment, and when deemed 'seaworthy' the vessel was towed from Lake Ontario through the Welland Canal to the Lake Erie port of Humberstone. It was reconstructed as closely as possible to its original state, although modern regulations demanded numerous structural changes. For example, the original boilers were replaced by an automatic oil-feed system, aluminium replaced wood for the superstructure, and it was equipped with modern navigational aids (the radar being concealed in a mock cabin structure when not required). Following two years of work *Trillium* was reinstated on its old route in May 1976. It remains in steam to this day, and is now owned by the Great Lakes Schooner Company operating out of Toronto.

9 THE SALOON STEAMER AND *PRINCESS ALICE*

While Britain was exporting paddle steamers and engineering know-how the world over, the paddle steamer was evolving to suit the leisure industry. The result was the saloon steamer, copied essentially from the inshore and river steamers plying the Hudson River in America and the Great Lakes, which had cabin accommodation on the main deck and, in some instances, also on a higher hurricane deck. The saloon steamer was encouraged in Britain by the concession made to Clyde steamer operators in the early 1860s that deckhouses and deck saloons be tonnage-exempt (well, until such time as the politicians of the day realised quite how much revenue Government was forfeiting). Needless to say, at most seaside resorts the saloon steamer became the hallmark of modern luxury, attracting the patronage of visitors and even conveying those visitors from Glasgow 'doon the watter' to the Lower Clyde resort towns, or from London Bridge down the Thames to seaside destinations such as Southend or Margate.

While the Americans favoured the land-type beam or walking-beam engine, the Europeans developed the side-lever engine, then the oscillating engine, and then the diagonal engine. There was one other significant difference between British and America architecture, and that was the quality and type of accommodation. The Americans had developed fast river and lake steamers and had no qualms about building accommodation blocks above the main deck. Top hamper in sheltered waters was not a particular issue, as described in an article discussing the differences in *The Illustrated London News* in 1861:

An examination of the construction of these vessels, and the innumerable details and contrivances necessary in them, give one a very high idea of the mechanical skill and inventive powers of the American people. From the colossal beam engine which propels her, down to the minutest fitting-up of the bed cabins, the barber's shop, or the lavatories, everything that ingenuity can devise for making things perfect has been done. We cannot say that we have observed the same attention to those details upon which the comforts of the passengers so depend on board English ships. It arises from this cause – that in America the building and fitting of the cabins is done by a class of people who devote themselves entirely to such work and study to attain perfection at it. In England the ship builder who designs the ship applies his whole ability to perfecting the hull, rigging and fittings of the deck, and doubtless builds a vessel better adapted to bear the rude handling of stormy, winter seas than is produced in any other part of the world. But cabin comfort he despises, and thinks lubbers only require them, so leaves it pretty much to ship joiners and inferior people, who do them all after one plan, whether the vessel be intended to navigate the Baltic in winter or the Red Sea and Indian Ocean in winter.

The basic design of the steamers in Europe had changed little other than increased size in keeping with more powerful engines. The main change was that the auxiliary steam sailing ships had evolved into auxiliary sail steam ships, with coastal and estuarial steamers reliant only on a stay-sail forward to help with steerage rather than to push the vessel forwards. The steamers were essentially flush-decked, with a platform between the tops of the paddle wheels for the master to keep his vigil, his view forward partly obscured by the ship's funnel. He could send orders by way of a relay boy sitting at the engine room skylight, ready to tap out instructions to the engineer below with a spanner, or shout instructions aft to the helmsman, positioned at his wheel more or less above the rudder.

Colin Fleetney wrote in *Paddle Wheels* for August 1969:

> The first forty years of steam on the high seas, from the mid-1820s to the mid-1860s, were years of fantastic progress. This progress was achieved mainly by the simple method of hard-earned experience gained in the handling of the many engine types at sea. The cost was terribly heavy, heavy both in terms of the expenditure of hard cash on many failures, in the many disastrous losses of ships, and in the appalling loss of human life in consequence of the latter.

The paddle steamer, even in the very early days of steam, made a significant impact on society. The summer steamer from Liverpool to Bagillt and Foryd (which soon developed into the resort town of Rhyl, but was originally described merely as an unenclosed common behind the dunes) started in 1822. Beaumaris was soon included on steamer runs from Liverpool, where boarding houses quickly began to appear on the green, Bangor and then Caernarvon, where the burghers built public baths and a ballroom to entice the travellers on the steamer to come ashore and spend their money in the town. The trip to Beaumaris or Bangor was a six-hour voyage which in steerage cost five shillings.

But it was not all sweetness and light, as the passengers aboard the little steam packet *Rothsay Castle* found on passage to Beaumaris on 18 August 1831. The vessel had left the Mersey in the morning with 130 aboard and a single carriage loaded on deck. The weather was increasingly heavy. By eight in the evening the steamer was only abreast the Little Orme, and took a further two hours

to put the Great Orme on the beam. Passengers demanded of the captain that he turn back or head for the shore, and they even offered to repay their passage monies. The captain knew better, or perhaps the drink inside him knew better, and he forced the ship on into the gathering storm. The vessel began leaking badly, and with a list developing the passengers were put to the pumps. By midnight the ship was wallowing severely, albeit not far from shelter, when it hit the Dutchman's Bank off the entrance to the Menai Strait. There were few survivors, but one passenger who did survive wrote:

> She struck again with tremendous force and her fragile shell-work, which had previously given way through the insufficiency of its fastenings, was torn asunder by the mightier shock, leaving ample space for the fierce gush of waters in every direction; and she soon lay a helpless wreck.

Rothsay Castle was of slight build, designed for service on the quiet waters of the upper Firth of Clyde. It was built in 1816, and when it came to Liverpool was already a tired and worn-out vessel. The tragedy did, however, promote regulations relating to seaworthiness and to the competence and sobriety of the captain in charge of a steamer; although not, it would seem, that of the engineer, the steward or any other member of a ship's complement.

With time the reliability of the steamers improved and the confidence of the travelling public was won over. The Victorian need to visit the seaside reflected both royal patronage of selected resorts and the very squalor and filth of the cities. However, the health benefits of 'marine excursions', as the Victorians fondly termed a short trip on the briny, were perhaps overstated when the steamer *Scarborough* entered service in 1866. Its owners, the Gainsborough United Steam Packet Company, operating short sea trips from Scarborough pier, proudly proclaimed that 'their passengers would be well cleansed with seasickness, in the hope of removing chronic diseases that medicine cannot reach'.

But there had been a clear design problem with the early paddle steamer. The first-class saloon and other premium facilities were all on the lower deck. The sea air and the fine views were on the upper deck and were enjoyed by lowly deck passengers, and not necessarily by the premium ticketed first-class passengers.

Two developments conspired to change this paradox. They were the introduction of the watertight bulkhead to main deck level, which meant the end of long lower-deck saloons, and the introduction of tonnage exemption, which promoted deckhouses or deck saloons on the main deck, dedicated for the sole use of passengers. During the 1860s the key operators on the Clyde ceased building flush-decked ships and started to order saloon steamers. One of the last of the old order was the Greenock and Ayrshire Railway's *Athole*, completed in 1866 by Barclay Curle with a steeple engine made by its builders. One of the first of the new order was the second of David Hutcheson's three *Iona*s. And what a difference: light airy saloons with views on three sides through large windows repaid the premium ticket holders, while the deck class was confined to accommodation on the lower deck, with a small allocation to promenade on the main deck forward.

The first *Iona* was built as a flush-decked vessel, the second, a year later, with a fabulous array of deck saloons, and the third re-ceived these same deckhouses and their interior fittings from the second as it was made ready for the Federal blockade (see Chapter 6). Of course, neither *Iona I* nor *Iona II* ever made it across the Atlantic, but this example sets the move to the main deck saloon firmly in the early 1860s. At that time, where the Clyde shipbuilders and shipowners led, others followed. The Thames received its first saloon steamer only in 1865. *Alexandra* was built on the Clyde as a Confederate blockade runner, but was completed too late to be of service with the cotton crops. It was redesigned as a saloon steamer and sold to the Saloon Steam Packet Company of London, to become the largest and finest steamer then on the river.

The saloon steamer had arrived. Among the hype was the following description of *Alexandra* which appeared in *The Illustrated London News* of 15 July 1865:

The length of the *Alexandra* is 240 feet and her breadth 22 feet and 9 inches. She is estimated at 140 horse power, nominal, and she is capable of travelling at the rate of 20 miles per hour [just over 17 knots]. Her burden is 157 tons, and, being flat bottomed, her draught of water is scarcely 4 feet. This is considered a great advantage, and one which forms a special feature in the vessel's construction as the steam ships at present on the Thames have sharp keels, and could not,

One of the last flush-decked paddlers was *Athole* (1866), built for the Greenock & Ayrshire Railway. It was equipped with a steeple engine.

Built too late as a Confederate blockade runner, *Alexandra* (1864) was converted into the first saloon steamer on the Thames. (*THE ILLUSTRATED LONDON NEWS*)

therefore, be rendered capable of carrying the weight of a deck saloon. This deck saloon, formed upon the plan of the 'hurricane decks' known in America, constitutes the great novelty which the Directors have sought to introduce into this country. In this case they have adapted a vessel, originally intended for a blockade runner, to the peaceful purpose of conveying passengers from London Bridge to Gravesend. The vessel is substantially built, and her 'fitments' and decorations are ingenious and tasteful, without being unnecessarily costly, while the general arrangements for her management are such as will secure the favour of the public. The vessel is constructed for carrying 1,048 passengers, and these can be distributed that there need be no apprehension of over-crowding. The builders of the vessel were Messrs Kirkpatrick & McIntyre of Port Glasgow and Messrs Smith & Company of Greenock constructed the engines which are on the diagonal oscillating principle.

When the famous Clyde steamer *Gael* was delivered to the Campeltown & Glasgow

Steam Packet Joint Stock Company in 1867 it was a flush-decked paddle steamer with a large 'lower cabin'. In 1879 the accommodation was reconfigured as a saloon steamer, the former lower cabin became the dining saloon and the new large deck saloon aft of the sponsons became the focal point of the ship. It was also reboilered, but this meant a reduction in speed and an increase in coal consumption, which was the reason for its sale to the Great Western Railway before coming north again into the MacBrayne fleet from 1891 onwards. Here it was again reboilered, more successfully this time, and awarded a full-width saloon across the whole of the after part of the ship, as the after hold and mainmast had been removed. In this guise it ploughed the waters of the Hebrides until 1924, when it was sold for demolition.

As design evolved, steamers were built with an aft saloon, but were still characterised by huge paddle wheels. On the Clyde, Captain Williamson's fleet of iron-hulled single cylinder steamers, *Viceroy*, *Marquis of Bute* and *Sultana*, which he sold to the Glasgow & South Western Railway in 1891, were typical. Although this type of steamer was almost the standard of the day, the engine had a distinctive surge at each cycle of the cylinder, and ship and passengers swayed back and forth as the vessel ploughed its way across the sea.

Both the single and compound diagonal engines had the distinctive fore-and-aft surge, and it was to avoid this discomfort that first the steeple engine, and later the oscillating engine, were developed. In both types the thrust of the piston was either vertical or near-vertical, and the regular reversal of the piston when running gave only a slight vertical vibration. The oscillator superseded the steeple because it had fewer fixed and moving parts. For example, each cylinder in the steeple engine had a complex and heavy steeple casting, four piston rods and a connecting rod, whereas the oscillator had only one piston rod or connecting rod.

The excitement of the saloon steamer heralded as an 'all-British' development ignores what our American friends had been up to. Not only had the river steamers begun to carry deckhouses on the main deck since the 1820s, but some even had cabins on a second deck above. Even the dedicated excursion paddlers tended to be saloon steamers. *Wilson G Hunt* was commissioned for excursion work out of New York in 1849, complete with a full-width deck saloon on the main deck and a promenade deck with a deckhouse above. It had an old-style crosshead engine. After two years as a trip boat this feisty little steamer set off for Cape Horn en route for the California Gold Rush, there to make its fortune.

Over the next twenty years the American excursion steamers got bigger and bolder. The Long Island Sound steamers that cruised between New York and Rhode Island were hugely impressive. The wooden-hulled *Bristol*, built in 1867, was 373ft long, complete with wooden trusses and had, of course, a walking-beam engine, this one with a massive 110in bore and a 12ft stroke, and 39ft-diameter paddle wheels. But, like other American excursion ships of that period, it had main-deck accommodation from just short of the bows right the way to the stern, and slightly shorter hurricane

The former Alexander Williamson steamer *Viceroy* (1875) on the Clyde in the colours of the Glasgow & South Western Railway. This was a typical single-cylinder diagonal-engined saloon steamer. (BOB DREWETT COLLECTION)

deck saloon accommodation complete with domed ceilings.

Two of the four steam-driven British Royal Yachts were paddlers, *Victoria and Albert* of 1843 and *Victoria and Albert* of 1855. The third *Victoria and Albert* and, of course, the *Britannia,* now preserved at Leith, were propeller driven. Launched at the Royal Dockyard at Pembroke Dock on 25 April 1843, the first *Victoria and Albert* was a conventional paddler built at the command of Her Majesty following her first voyage in a paddle steamer, GSN's *Trident,* on returning from Scotland the previous year (see Chapter 2). It was an unassuming vessel, finely appointed inside but nothing special outside: ornate scroll-work at bow and stern, solid bulwarks instead of railings, a mizzen mast for all the flags that might need to be hoisted and large square windows to the lower deck. Her Majesty delighted in several summer cruises along the coast of her realm in her new yacht, although something a bit more modern was soon going to be needed.

The next *Victoria and Albert* was a much grander affair, with a thick iron-plate hull 360ft long. It was much faster too, making 15 knots if it needed to, but the main difference was that this paddler was finely appointed and was truly fit for a monarch and royal patrons. It was not entirely flush-decked, as it had a couple of deckhouses, each with designated royal purposes, including one for Her Majesty to stand on and take the salute. The ship required a crew of 240 when royalty was aboard, so it was not the cheapest of royal vehicles. It was launched from the same yard at Pembroke Dock in January 1855, whereupon her earlier namesake adopted the name *Osborne*. Victoria was delighted with her new steamer. *Osborne* was demoted to serving the Prince of Wales and later scrapped in 1868 when a new *Osborne* was ordered. Delivered from the same Royal Dockyard in Pembroke Dock in 1870, the new paddle steamer *Osborne* was essentially a Royal Tender, despite its gross tonnage of 1,850 and all its attendant magnificence. Above all, it was a proper saloon paddle steamer. The new *Osborne*'s main claim to fame was that it brought the body of Victoria's son, Prince Leopold, back from Cannes in 1884.

Not only was Her Majesty pleased with the new *Victoria and Albert*, but so too was her one-time guest, Khedive Isma'il of Egypt. He commanded that the ship be cloned, and the outcome was the Egyptian Royal Yacht *Mahroussa*, constructed by Samuda Brothers on the Thames in 1865. Again, this new Royal Yacht was essentially a saloon paddle steamer, provided with over-large paddle boxes, a clipper bow, antique-galleried stern, slender masts and raking bell-topped funnels. Inside there was great richness; the furnishings were second to none, with marble sink tops, gold fittings and plush soft furnishings fit only for a Khedive.

The machinery fitted aboard the *Mahroussa* was the best available. Seven rectangular boilers provided steam at 15psi to two oscillating engines with jet condensers. The two cylinders were both of 100in diameter, and the stroke was 8ft. In 1875 it was lengthened by 40ft, and surface condensers were fitted to the engines. In 1892 it was re-boilered and a steam capstan and steam steering gear were added to its inventory.

Each cylinder had to be worked as a separate engine for the first two or three revolutions, and 20 men were required to man the four large reversing wheels. Once in motion, the engines were trouble-free and smooth-running. In 1906 the old ship was again taken in hand, gutted almost to its iron shell, which was found to be in first-class condition, rebuilt as a triple-screw direct-action turbine steamer with three decks, and sumptuously appointed. Why install a new type of propulsion in a 41-year-old iron hull? The naval architects Harvard Biles and William Gray believed it was better built, with its thick iron plate, than any modern steel hull could be. How right they were: not a single plate or rivet had to be renewed during the reconstruction. The *Mahroussa* remained in service as the Royal Yacht until the abduction of King Farouk in 1952. It was then converted into a training ship, and is today cared for by the Egyptian Navy, a fine memorial of British shipbuilding and naval architecture.

The ageing paddle steamer *Victoria and Albert* slowly fell out of favour, and as the Queen grew older she shunned the Royal Yacht in preference for Admiralty vessels such as the sloop *Enchantress*. When the new propeller-driven *Victoria and Albert* was commissioned in 1901, following two years' work to correct an instability problem, the old paddler was decommissioned and later scrapped.

In the excursion trade many ships were modestly built, with just an after saloon, but were designed to allow a forward saloon to be added at a later date should resources allow and demand require it. Two examples of this are *Clacton Belle* and *Woolwich Belle*, built for the famous Belle Steamers excursion fleet on the Thames in 1890 and 1891 respectively, which received forward deck saloons only in 1912. Belle Steamers was inaugurated by local merchants in 1888 as the London, Woolwich & Clacton-on-Sea Steamboat Company, its objective being simply to bring Londoners to Clacton in order to spend money. The town itself owed its very existence to the steamers. Peter Bruff, the engineer who had earlier built the Eastern Union

Railway, built a steamer pier on the site of what later became Clacton, entirely on an entrepreneurial basis. When his pier was completed he took the paddle steamer *Queen of the Orwell* to the new pier with an invited passenger list of developers and fellow entrepreneurs. Pointing above the pier to a gap in the cliff he said: 'That is the land on which you can build the town,' and they did.

The humble British saloon steamer soon developed so that a promenade deck became available above the fore and aft saloons. By 1890 the forward promenade deck was extended right to the bow, with an unplated area below for rope handling. The first steamer to be constructed in this way was *Duchess of Hamilton*, completed for the Caledonian Steam Packet Company and placed on the Ardrossan to Brodick service. The benefit was an extended passenger deck; the disadvantage was that the forward rope handlers could not see or be seen by the bridge, but this was easily overcome by the fitting of docking telegraphs forward and aft for transmitting the necessary rope-handling orders. Notwithstanding, virtually all subsequent Clyde paddle steamers conformed to this design for some time, as many did elsewhere in due course, and the lack of vision from the forecastle was later resolved

Woolwich Belle (1891) on the River Orwell as built . . .

. . . *Woolwich Belle* after the 1911 season, with a new forward saloon.

by bringing the rope handling up to the promenade deck and plating in the former forecastle area below. The first vessel built like this was the rival Ardrossan to Brodick paddle steamer *Glen Sannox*, delivered to the Glasgow & South Western Railway in 1892.

In this phase the paddle steamer was equipped with compound engines that were faster running than the older oscillating engines. The size of the paddle wheel could, therefore, be reduced without losing the efficiency of the coupling to the water. The only other change was the bridge, which tended to be moved forward of the paddles and the funnel as, for example, in P & A Campbell's *Westward Ho* of 1894 and *Cambria* of 1895. They also had fully plated main decks up to the bow and were truly modern steamers in every sense.

Noteworthy was the Caledonian Steam Packet Company's *Marchioness of Lorne*, delivered by Russell & Company of Port Glasgow in 1891. It had the tandem triple-expansion engine based on Rankin & Blackmore's tandem patent, whereby the high-pressure cylinder exhausted into the low-pressure cylinder, as in the compound engine, but in the triple-expansion arrangement it did so via an intermediate-pressure cylinder. But the engine was a hybrid, as it

comprised four cylinders; two high-pressure, one larger diameter intermediate and one even larger low-pressure cylinder. There were two cranks, one connected to one of the high-pressure cylinders and the intermediate-pressure cylinder, and the second crank to the other high-pressure cylinder and the low-pressure cylinder. It was a peculiar hybrid arrangement, yet it was a start towards the compound engine, which, as far as the paddlers were concerned, would reign supreme for the next forty years.

But the Victorian expansion of the seasonal excursion steamer (including the Thames 'butterfly boat', which came out only in the summer and then flitted about) was not without mishap. The tragedy which befell the Thames steamer *Princess Alice* on 3 September 1878 put the excursion trade back by a decade on the Thames, and by a good few years elsewhere in Britain. It also put the ship's owners out of business.

Princess Alice was built in 1865 as one of a pair, *Kyles* and *Bute*, for the Wemyss Bay Railway Company. They had been sold in 1867 to the Thames excursion operator, the Watermen's Steam Packet Company, and resold to the Woolwich Steam Packet Company. The Wemyss Bay Railway Company had been dissatisfied with their performance,

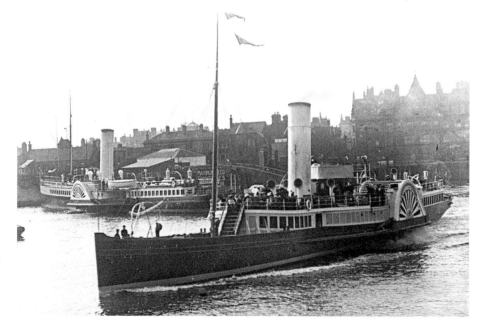

Cambria (1895) berthed at the stage at Cardiff, with *Waverley* (1885) in the foreground. Ten years advance in design: the bridge had been moved forward of the funnel, paddle diameters had shrunk and the main deck was plated up to the bows. In due course the large windows on the main deck were replaced by portholes (see page 150). (BOB DREWETT)

and was concerned with their weak construction, such as the thin iron plates, some of which were only ³⁄₁₆ in thick. The Watermen's company compounded the weakness by adding the now fashionable deck saloons with a new promenade deck above, to give the steamers a licensed passenger complement of nearly 1,000 down-river to Gravesend and just under 500 at sea. The vessels, which were big ships for the Thames excursion trade at that time, became popular with the public, and when taken over by the Woolwich company *Kyles* was renamed *Albert Edward* and *Bute* was named *Princess Alice*. It even fell to *Princess Alice* to convey the Shah of Persia around London Docks on his visit to the UK in 1873.

The tragedy occurred off Beckton on the return leg of a day trip to the coast. Children played on deck, a band was enter-

Marchioness of Lorne (1891) had a triple-expansion engine arranged over four cylinders with two cranks.

The moment of impact; *Princess Alice* (1865) and *Bywell Castle* (1870) at Beckton, from a contemporary painting by Dudley White.

taining passengers on the after deck and the ship had an air of contentment following a long warm day at the coast. *Princess Alice* left Sheerness with an estimated 487 passengers, and over 250 more excursionists embarked at Gravesend at 7pm for the journey back to London. Children under six years of age travelled free and those under twelve counted as half an adult, and it was never established just how many children were actually on board that evening.

Captain William Grinstead was in command, a popular master of a popular ship. The first mate, Lang, was also on the bridge, and helmsman John Eyres had substituted for the regular helmsman, who had left the ship at Gravesend with the master's consent. Unbeknown to Captain Grinstead, Eyres had never previously handled a ship of this size on the river. As *Princess Alice* approached Woolwich the steamer *Bywell Castle*, a hefty 1,376-ton collier owned by John Hall of Newcastle, was heading downstream in ballast, making the most of the ebb tide and about to take the bend below Woolwich.

The pilot of the big collier saw the port light of *Princess Alice* and assumed it was about to cross the river to take advantage of the slacker water near the north bank. But as *Princess Alice* felt the full force of the fast-ebbing tide it was swept towards the opposite south bank, and Captain Grinstead ordered Eyres to hold his starboard helm in an attempt to get the ship out of danger. Only when it reached the slacker water off the south bank did it answer its helm, and the crowded steamer then swung across the path of the collier, which had maintained its course throughout to pass the steamer port to port, with a devastating result. T E Hughes described what happened next in an article first published in *Sea Breezes* in October 1978:

> Within seconds, the collier towering some 20 feet above the doomed pleasure steamer, struck the *Princess Alice* just forward of her starboard paddle box cutting some 14 feet through her side and opening up her engine room which imme-

diately began to flood. Scores of passengers were hurled into the river by the force of the impact, whilst others hysterically jumped overboard in the vague hope of saving themselves.

Only 69 passengers were saved, and many of the dead were never recovered. Whether the weak construction of the ship contributed to the disaster remains unknown. The subsequent inquiry raised a number of questions about safety and the 'haphazard operation of ill-equipped steamers', while the excursion industry was taken to task as the target of a barrage of new regulatory controls. The passengers stayed away from the steamers in droves, and the newly regulated industry took a long time to rise off its knees again.

The industry did survive, but it was ten years before any new steamers were ordered for the Thames. Elsewhere, new tonnage was introduced, but to generally conservative designs using the traditional oscillating engine rather than the more modern compound engine. On the Clyde and Forth the paddle excursion and commuter steamer excelled, while in the south the post-*Princess Alice* recovery of the steamers was alluded to in E C B Thornton's book on Thames pleasure steamers:

> From 1897 … it was possible if you were prepared to pack a suitcase, or more likely a Gladstone bag, with the necessities for several nights, to board a pleasure steamer at Great Yarmouth and travel south and west as far as Plymouth or even possibly to Looe, with several changes of this fascinating type of vessel en route.

Part of this recovery was at the behest of the Fairfield Shipbuilding & Engineering Company. Much as it had done earlier with the Isle of Man Steam Packet Company, foisting new crack ships upon a successful operator, so it approached the Victoria Steamboat Association (VSA), this time with cheap mortgages. The VSA suddenly found itself being canvassed to manage two brand-new crack steamers to be paid for on long-term instal-

ments. The hire-purchase arrangement offered to the VSA was similar to the arrangement between Fairfield and the newly-formed Liverpool and North Wales Steamship Company, which had received the heavily mortgaged steamer *St Tudno* in 1891. The new steamers for the Thames were each developments of the *St Tudno*, respectively the *Koh-i-noor*, delivered to the VSA in 1892, and the *Royal Sovereign*, delivered to a financially separate company, the London & East Coast Express Steamship Service, in 1893, but managed by the VSA. In addition, the magnificent steamer *La Marguerite* followed in 1894 under another holding company, Palace Steamers.

The *Koh-i-noor* and *Royal Sovereign* were big, at 884 and 892 tons gross respectively, and were technically very advanced. Built entirely of steel, they were subdivided into watertight compartments, so that the first-class dining saloon had to be divided into

St Tudno (1891) was a fast steamer built by Fairfield Shipbuilding & Engineering for the Liverpool & North Wales Steamship Company.

La Marguerite (1894) started life on the Thames but operated for the Liverpool & North Wales Steamship Company from 1903 onwards. It is seen backing-off Garth Pier, Bangor. (BOB DREWETT COLLECTION)

GSN's *Swift* (1875) at Great Yarmouth. This ship and its compatriot *Swallow* were among the last conventional flush-decked passenger and cargo steamers. (JARROLDS OF NORWICH)

two parts, one either side of the dividing bulkhead. They had the two-cylinder diagonal-engine configuration, and the paddle floats were of the contemporary curved design. With engines providing 3,500ihp, they were fit for 19 knots. They also had bow rudders to facilitate steerage while going astern.

La Marguerite was found to be really too large and too fast for its Tilbury to the Continent day excursions, and in 1904 was placed on favourable terms with the Liverpool & North Wales Steamship Company to run alongside its *St Tudno*. In this arena, with slightly lower overheads and marginally reduced operating speeds, it became a huge success.

The late Victorian and Edwardian period witnessed the delivery of a host of fine saloon steamers. Many of these vessels became the mainstay of the British excursion industry well into the twentieth century, but as time went on the operating margins were insufficient to allow new tonnage to be built, and as ships were retired there were few replacements. The exceptions were the

commuter fleets of Red Funnel and the railway companies in the Solent and the Clyde, which went from strength to strength with all-year income boosted in summer by tourists. Meanwhile, the American excursion companies were in a different league with ships like *Tashmoo* offering grand and de luxe accommodation for excursionists on the Great Lakes (see Chapter 8).

Probably the last of the traditional passenger and cargo paddle steamers in the British registry were GSN's *Swallow* and *Swift*. They were also some of the last passenger paddlers to be built without any form of deck saloon. They served their owner's London to Ostend route, with occasional summer excursions from London to Great Yarmouth, from delivery in 1875 until withdrawn and replaced by a screw steamer in 1901. Passenger accommodation was below deck, and cargo was accommodated in small holds fore and aft, the main import being live rabbits to feed the poor of London and southeast England.

The unfortunate, but very successful, steamer without a saloon, *Lord Elgin*

John Kidd, an Edinburgh wine merchant, came into the Forth excursion trade to increase sales of his 'beverages' with the purchase, in January 1874, of the steamer *Lord Aberdour*. Kidd saw an opportunity when steamers were withdrawn from the Edinburgh up-river service to Stirling, and ordered two vessels from Richardson, Duck & Company at Stockton. These were named *Lord Mar* and *Lord Elgin* after owners of estates in the Forth Valley. Ian Brodie introduces the pair in his book on Forth steamers:

> They were the finest vessels built for service on the Forth to this time but sur-prisingly were not fitted with saloons, having instead a raised quarterdeck aft of the machinery giving a commodious main saloon, while a shade deck forward provided shelter for steerage passengers and adequate promenade facilities. At 160 feet long they were by far the largest vessels yet built for up river traffic and were certified to carry 715 passengers. Compound diagonal machinery was fitted for smoothness and economy, a type of engine then in its infancy and not used on the Clyde until 1889. It was the flaw in an otherwise perfect design. Though their speed was stated as 12 knots, it is doubtful if more than 10 was ever achieved in normal service.

Lord Elgin started in service running from Leith via Limekilns, Bo'ness, Alloa, Kincardine, Alloa to Stirling, before taking up its chief role of cruising, mainly in the lower Forth but sometimes as far afield as Dundee. Results were always disappointing, and on Kidd's death, in April 1880, it was agreed to dispose of 'the unfortunate steamer *Lord Elgin*'.

Lord Elgin's next career started in the 1881 season under the ownership of the newly formed Bournemouth & Swanage Steam Packet Company, which paid £5,000 for it. The company was formed by local interests, principally Bournemouth

Red Funnel's cargo steamer *Lord Elgin* (1875) bore little resemblance to the Forth excursion steamer it had once been.

Steam Packets, who were keen to stop Cosens & Company of Weymouth from creaming off the enhanced Bournemouth trade anticipated after the opening of the new pier in August 1880. *Lord Elgin*, still a modern steamer, did this admirably, and was joined for the 1884 season by the brand new *Bournemouth*. *Lord Elgin* then maintained the Swanage 'ferry' and *Bournemouth* took the longer trips. Sadly, in 1886 *Bournemouth* was wrecked in fog off Portland during a day trip to Torquay. *Lord Elgin*'s new companion became the former Clyde steamer *Brodick Castle*, while *Lord Elgin* added the new Southbourne Pier to its Swanage duties from 1888 onwards. Cosens finally acknowledged the competition in 1888 with the delivery of the prestigious steamer *Monarch*.

The Bournemouth & Swanage Steam Packet Company was reconstituted as the Bournemouth & South Coast Steam Packets in the winter of 1896/97. Competition with Cosens had become much fiercer, and it was no surprise when, in 1899, it was announced that the Swanage service would be shared by *Lord Elgin* and Cosens's *Empress*. By 1901 Cosens had bought *Brodick Castle*, leaving *Lord Elgin* the sole fleet member of the Bournemouth company. *Lord Elgin* continued to work in collaboration with Cosens until, in the spring of 1909, the Southampton Red Funnel company announced its purchase of the Bournemouth company, its assets and goodwill. Cosens was not best pleased, as it now had to find two steamers to work against Red Funnel, who left *Lord Elgin* on the Swanage service but also added *Stirling Castle*, which, like *Lord Elgin*, was a former Forth excursion steamer.

After the 1910 season *Lord Elgin* was transferred to the Southampton to Cowes cargo service. For this it was stripped of its saloons, the mainmast was replaced by a heavier structure with a large derrick, and the foremast removed. The fore deck and after deck were taken out to create a well deck for cargo and livestock, and increasingly, as time went on, for motor vehicles as well. In this role it was hugely successful and a most profitable unit for Red Funnel. It was only many years later, when the former Second World War tank landing craft *Norris Castle* was recommissioned for civilian duties with Red Funnel in August 1948, that the elderly *Lord Elgin* was reduced to second fiddle.

But in October 1952 *Lord Elgin* went right to the back row of the second fiddles. A new company freight-handling policy required all cargo, including livestock, to be handled by *Norris Castle* on lorries rather than crane loaded, as was the case with *Lord Elgin*. The livestock, of course, had previously embarked and disembarked on their own four hooves. For much of the time thereafter *Lord Elgin* was laid up, until in May 1955 it came out of retirement one last time to cover for the refit period for *Norris Castle*. Captain Joseph Sewley then took the 79-year-old veteran round to the breaker's yard on the Itchen. Captain Sewley had been in command of the steamer since 1923, a wonderful partnership which had brought livestock to market from the island while also keeping the island stocked with essential goods.

From unsuccessful excursion steamer on the Forth to highly successful steamer at Bournemouth, *Lord Elgin* ultimately became Britain's very last serving cargo paddle steamer. Its longevity is a tribute to its builders at Stockton. Its former running mate at Bournemouth for ten happy summers, Cosens's steamer *Empress*, also had a long and successful life, going to ship breakers just four months after *Lord Elgin* in 1955. *Empress*, the younger ship by just three years, had the very last oscillating engines operational in British waters. Amazingly, both ships had iron hulls and neither had any significant corrosion problems during their long lives.

10 OF TUGS, TENDERS AND TRAWLERS

The idea that a steamboat could be used profitably to tow sailing ships against adverse winds was realised on the Tyne, the Thames and the Mersey as early as 1815. On the Tyne to London coal trade the sailing colliers, which normally made only about eight voyages a year, were carrying out as many as thirteen round trips once the steam tug had become established. This not only brought about a degree of economy for the collier owners, but also avoided breaks in coal supply caused by ships holed up in port because of an onshore wind.

The first steamship on the Tyne was launched in 1814 from South Shore (Gateshead). It was built to a design not far removed from that of *Comet*, other than having one set of paddle wheels. Imaginatively named *Tyne Steamboat*, it set about earning a living as a passenger boat, running the ten-mile route down-river to Shields. Loading and unloading was carried out in mid-river, with boatmen acting as tenders. It was hardly surprising, therefore, that the whole endeavour lost money. Local industrialist Joseph Price bought the service in 1817, giving *Steamboat* the new name *Perseverance*. It was not long before he saw a more profitable use for his new acquisition, and he arranged a demonstration tow in July 1818 to take the sailing ship *Friends Adventure* to sea. The 13-mile tow began half an hour before high water and was completed just over two hours later. Any sceptics of the steam tug were soon silenced.

In 1822 the keelmen (a keel being a short plump barge) who carried the coal down-river to awaiting sailing ships went on strike, and coal shipments from the Tyne ceased. Coal was hauled down to the river by two steam engines named *Wylam Colly* and *Wylam Dilly*. As the engines were tem-porarily redundant it was proposed by the colliery owner to put *Wyliam Dilly*, minus its wheels, on to a wooden sledge aboard one of the keels and fit paddle wheels to the drive axle of the engine, which was suitably extended. With armed guards aboard 'tug' and a string of keels behind it, *Wylam Dilly* caught the pickets by surprise and success-fully broke the strike. So successful was the craft in its new role that *Wylam Dilly* (the water one, not the land one) stayed on the river towing its keels for several months. But purpose-built tugs soon arrived, and by the end of 1830 there were over thirty steam tugs on the Tyne earning their keep by towage and, when no jobs were in the offing, by carrying passengers up and down the river.

Over the decades the wooden paddle tugs did increase a little in power and size, becoming nearer 100ft long, rather than the 50ft of the early days. In the 1850s larger tows meant larger tugs. Manoeuvrability was also critical, and in due course tugs were equipped with two boilers and two engines that could drive the paddles independently. If a tug was at sea 'seeking' an inbound tow, it could bank one boiler right down and steam ahead slowly. Most tugs were owned by their masters, although some companies had acquired fleets of up to four vessels.

The wooden hulls of many of the tugs were not always up to the job, and the stresses and strains of towage caused many a vessel to spring a leak at sea and even to sink quietly at its moorings. As the wooden hulls aged so the losses increased; 13 per cent of all wooden tugs were lost in the period be-tween 1880 and 1889, and as many as 23 per cent of the dwindling fleet between 1900 and 1909 (the last British-built wooden paddle tugs were completed in 1885).

William Watkins's *Uncle Sam* (1849) was typical of the early wooden tugs with bowsprit and twin funnels abaft each other.

The raked bows and bowsprits of early tugs, typified, for example, by William Watkins's wooden Thames paddle tug *Uncle Sam*, soon changed to the more familiar straight stems which were better shaped for nosing into larger vessels to push them against a wharf. *Uncle Sam*, complete not only with bowsprit but figurehead as well, was built at West Ham in 1849 and equipped with an 80hp engine operating at 18psi. Unlike many other wooden tugs it enjoyed a long life, being re-engined in 1867 and reboilered in 1886, before it steamed to a Dutch breaker's yard in 1900.

In his book *British Steam Tugs* P N Thomas describes the attitude of the shipowner to the wooden paddle tugs:

Shipowners used the tugs but regarded them as a necessary evil and never ceased to complain about irregularities and excessive charges. In 1864 the Pilots were accused of being in the pockets of the tug men, accepting bribes to ensure that

Willam Watkins Limited

For over a century and a half the name of William Watkins was synonymous with towage on the Thames. The company was founded in 1833 by John Rogers Watkins and his 14-year-old son William, then fresh out of school. The previous year the dedicated steam tug *Lady Dundas* had arrived in the Thames from the Tyne, and this no doubt inspired father and son with a vision of steam towage on the Thames. *Lady Dundas* was so underpowered that it could not go against the tide, even without a tow, and it was back on the Tyne by 1835.

John Watkins went to H S Waite of North Shields to order his first wooden paddler, *Monarch*. It had a clinker-built hull 65ft long by 14ft broad, a raked stem and a counter stern. It had a simple flue boiler and its engine gave her 20 nominal horsepower, just enough to deal with the tidal currents on the river. In *British Steam Tugs* P N Thomas describes a model of *Monarch* that he found in Newcastle Museum:

There is a pole mast and a tall thin funnel aft of high paddle boxes. She has only a few structures on the deck, a companionway to the accommodation, a hatch to the bunkers and a cover over the crosshead slides of her side-lever engine. On the foredeck is a strange contraption; a wheeled bogie filled with scrap iron running on rails athwartships across the deck. The early tugs had a single engine and were difficult to manoeuvre using their rudder only. When the loaded bogie was run to one side the tug heeled over, dipping one paddle further into the water and enabling it to exert more thrust than the other which was barely touching the water. The idea worked but often resulted in a broken paddle shaft.

The little *Monarch* was a huge success, so much so that in 1845 it was given a new watertube boiler that greatly reduced fuel consumption. Then in 1856 it received 'patent' paddle wheels before again being reboiled in 1861. It is the *Monarch* that is seen towing the *Fighting Téméraire* to the scrapyard in J M W Turner's iconic painting. At the grand age of 43 the venerable *Monarch* was sold for scrap, realising the princely sum of £40.

In the early 1840s *Monarch* was joined by *Fiddler* and *Lord Warden*. *Punch* followed in 1846, but was quickly sold on to owners in Constantinople. A series of wooden paddle tugs followed, *Paul Pry* in 1847, *John Bull* in 1849 and *Uncle Sam* in 1849. *John Bull* was the first of the company's carvel-built steamers. In 1853 John Watkins's son, William, was encouraged to try his fortunes on the Mersey with *John Bull*. The enterprise was not a great success and the vessel was returned to the Thames in 1859, there to receive a new side-lever engine. *Uncle Sam*, on the other hand, was the biggest tug to date, being 102ft long, but was still built with clipper bow and bowsprit, a hindrance to any small vessel attendant upon others. Its main role was towing sailing ships out to sea, and sometimes down the Channel as far as the Isle of Wight if winds were unfavourable. It was joined in 1852 by *Britannia*, another wooden hulled seagoing tug, with bowsprit and figurehead, that was commonly seen in Channel ports until it went out to Constantinople alongside *Punch* in 1852.

The next two tugs to join the fleet were rather special, as Frank Burtt describes in his book *Steamers of the Thames and Medway*:

The *Victoria* was built in 1853, and was by far the largest and most powerful tug on the river for some years. She was built of teak and oak and had a gross tonnage

Watkins's *India* (1876) was a popular excursion steamer at Margate, but is seen here working at Weymouth in the summer of 1898.

of 152. She had a clipper bow and one of her improvements was a steam windlass which saved a great deal of time in hauling in the anchor. The *Victoria* was one of the few boats at the time to have two funnels athwart, but soon after the practice of having two boilers side by side became general.

In 1854 Money, Wigram of Blackwall launched the *Punch* – second of her name. She was a fine little iron paddler [the first in the fleet] of 115 tons gross drawing 6½ feet of water. At her bows she carried a fine carved wooden figurehead of Punch which was lost in a heavy sea in a gale in the Channel . . . The *Punch* was the first mercantile vessel to pass under Tower Bridge after the opening in June 1894 . . .

In 1857, the carvel-built paddler *Napoleon* was purchased, having been built at Southampton. It was the first tug on the Thames with two engines, each driving a paddle wheel independently. Its wooden hull was not quite the match for such power and required constant attention until the ship foundered at sea in 1881. The next major development was *Anglia*, completed in 1866 and known as 'Three-fingered Jack' because of its three funnels, one for each of three boilers, two abaft the paddle boxes and one ahead. *Anglia* had the largest bunkers of any seagoing tug at that time, but its tubular boilers and side-lever engines consumed coal rapidly to provide it with 700ihp. *Anglia* took the final leg of towing the steel cylinder containing Cleopatra's Needle to London in 1878. The tow had started from Egypt and was lost in the Bay of Biscay, then later salvaged and brought into Vigo, where *Anglia* took over.

Anglia was followed by an improved version, *Cambria* of 1870, again with a pair of side-lever engines, but only two athwart funnels. Burtt again:

The *Cambria* was distinguishable from other paddle tugs as she had side houses on the front of the paddle boxes. In 1876, the *Cambria* was chartered by the Duke of Bedford to visit the yachting regattas round the coast and for this purpose she was painted white and the funnels yellow. With her clipper bows she was a handsome craft, and in view of long seagoing trips was built with large cabins enabling the crew to sling hammocks. In 1887 the *Cambria* had the novel experience of being placed under arrest at Cherbourg . . . The *Cambria* had towed a vessel from Dunkirk, the law [in France] being that all coastal trade must be undertaken by French vessels.

The next major addition to the fleet was *India*, built by Westwood, Baillie & Company of Poplar in London. Designed for seagoing use, it had a gross tonnage of 218, but even with its two side-lever engines was underpowered. It found profitable summer employment running excursions out of Margate in the early 1890s, and later worked at Weymouth before being sold for use on the Tyne. So profitable was the excursion work that a dedicated excursion paddle steamer, *Cynthia*, was delivered in 1892 to work the summer trade at Margate. Idle during the winter months, it could not pay its way and was sold in 1894.

William Watkins Limited went from strength to strength, remaining one of the main independent tug companies throughout much of the twentieth century until it merged with other London tug owners in 1950. The distinctive funnel colours of a broad red band, low on a black funnel, were carried throughout, while in the early days the paddle tugs had black and green hulls and white paddle boxes.

Frenchman (1892), built as *Coquet* for service at Berwick, worked much of its life on the Humber in winter and at Bridlington as an excursion steamer in the summer.

Columbus (1865) ran seasonal trips from Liverpool to Llandudno and Menai. It is seen loading excursionists at Llandudno.

unfavourable. This required larger and more powerful tugs to be built, with greater bunker capacity.

Outwardly, the shape of the iron- and later the steel-hulled paddle tug did not alter much. The tugs nearly always had wooden bulwarks which were easy to replace if damaged, and as time went on the bulwarks had an increasing tumblehome, so keeping them out of harm's way. By the 1870s the screw tug was beginning to challenge the paddlers, and independent paddle wheels driven by separate boilers and engines came into their own, giving rise to numerous vessels with two funnels side by side, rather than fore and aft as in larger paddle steamers.

Many of the tugs tended to be used for passenger excursions when not required for towage duties. Although they were licensed for carrying a specified number of passengers, there are numerous examples of overloading and of unlicensed boats carrying out passenger work.

The tugs could not compete with the new saloon excursion steamers (see Chapter 9), and survived only in areas where the saloon steamer did not penetrate. Scarborough and Bridlingon were such resorts, and summer excursions by the paddle tugs *Cambria* and *Coquet*, later renamed *Frenchman*, are perhaps some of the best remembered, while the wooden hulled *United Service* and *King Edward VII* also continued to entertain excursionists at Great Yarmouth throughout the Edwardian era. The Hercules Steam Tug Company of Liverpool maintained the *Hercules* and *Columbus* on seasonal trips between Llandudno and Menai, and also from Liverpool on Sundays, until the company commissioned a saloon steamer in 1892. Famous London tug owner William Watkins stationed his seagoing paddle tug *India* at Margate for the summer months in the early 1890s. For this work the master was on a wage of 35 shillings per week (the equivalent of £158 today, based on the retail price index) but he also got a percentage of the passenger receipts as an incentive. In a letter to *Sea Breezes* in November 1950, F Bracey recalled:

one owner's tugs were used in preference to another's, or insisting on 'taking steam' when it was not really necessary. In some areas local harbour regulations forbade any pilot to have any interest in a tug in an effort to ensure that such accusations might be unjustified.

. . . In these early days there was no distinction between harbour, river or coastal tugs. Regardless of size they would undertake any kind of tow. All around the coast the local tugs were prepared to go to the assistance of vessels in distress, frequently with the lifeboat in tow. Indeed in Liverpool there was considerable rivalry between the tug companies for the honour of performing this service.

The first iron tug in service was probably *Defiance*, which was completed in 1841 and spent a large part of its career in the Mersey. By 1854 there were only 25 iron tugs in service. At that time demands on tugs increased, as ships now served the needs of the Crimean War as well as the ordinary domestic trade. Shipowners were now keen on longer-distance tows, perhaps all the way down the English Channel if the wind was

I wonder if there are any who can recall the [passenger] yachts that used to work from Margate Jetty. One was the *Moss Rose* and I think the other was called *Sunbeam*. I remember that if the slant of the wind was right, the yachts and Watkins' tug *India* would do the trip out to the Tongue Lightship and back, and the yachts would be first home.

The steam trawler was first tried successfully off Dunbar, using a small paddle steamer converted with a beam trawl. Paddle propulsion was preferred, as it was feared that the trawl net could foul a propeller. The first dedicated paddle trawler was built in 1870 for F Rushworth of Grimsby, but sailing smacks with fish wells were still popular. In 1877, during a slump in towage on the Tyne, the 34-year-old tug *Messenger* was equipped by owner William Purdy with a beam trawl and a derrick for just £19 10s. The 'new' trawler made £7 10s at the fish market at South Shields on its first trip, plus £5 for towing in a sailing ship. The sceptics had been confounded, and soon five more paddle tug/trawlers were seen alongside the fish quay.

The wooden paddle trawler was a distinctly northeast England phenomenon, as W Featherston recorded in *Sea Breezes* for January 1964:

Soon, larger paddlers, built of wood and iron were specially constructed for trawling and great hefty brutes they were. . . . As trawlers they were not attractive to look at, dirty, rusty and festooned with nets. However, when the screw trawlers finally ousted these 'toughs' the Tyne got some very attractive tugs when they were refitted for towing only . . . The last paddle trawler on the north east coast was the *Hartland* of Scarborough.

In 1882 the ex-Dublin tug *Toiler* was converted for trawling at Aberdeen. Within just six months the investment was paid for, and the steamer went on to reward its owners proudly. But at the end of the year the hard work had all but destroyed the fabric of the nine-year-old wooden vessel and it was set aside. The casualty rate of the wooden paddle trawlers was high, eight being lost during

The paddle tug *Dunrobin* (1876) was converted from a tug into a paddle trawler in 1895 and based at Scarborough. Note the heavy beam trawl and derrick aft.

autumn 1880 alone. This episode prompted the iron-ribbed, wooden-clad paddle trawler to be constructed, while some iron-hulled tugs were equipped with a beam trawl, such as the 1876-built *Dunrobin*, wrecked in 1894 and rebuilt as a trawler in 1895. It served out of Scarborough until 1908, when it was again driven ashore, later to be demolished where it lay. By 1881 the first screw trawler had been commissioned, spelling the end for the paddle trawlers, many of which forsook their fishing gear for a towing hook.

Small paddle steamers were also deployed to dredge oysters in the Essex rivers. They were short, stubby vessels which drew between 3ft and 4½ft of water and were ideally suited to their work in the Crouch, Blackwater or Colne estuaries. The first of the paddlers were two little wooden steamers built in Maldon in 1882 for the Roach River Oyster Fishery Company and named *Alice* and *Victoria*. The latter was still in service after the Second World War, although it was then earning its keep as a yacht. The best-known of the paddle oyster dredgers was the wooden-hulled *Pyefleet*, built for the Colne Oyster Fishery Board in 1895 and sold in the 1920s. Its successor was *Pyefleet II*, completed in 1930, the only paddle dredger with a steel hull, albeit with a

diminutive gross tonnage of just 31. *Pyefleet* was equipped with a compound surface-condensing engine, and *Pyefleet II* also had a compound engine. Both vessels had a registered breadth of 16ft, the older ship having a length of 50ft and the younger just 46ft. They were effectively self-propelled floating platforms with oval hulls built out over the sponsons. There was also the motor-powered Crouch paddle dredger *Speedwell*, built at Burnham in 1908 for Smith Brothers of Burnham-on-Crouch, and the Burnham Oyster Company also had a small steamer called *Shield*.

A variety of paddle passenger and baggage tenders were built. As early as 1848 the Cunard Steamship Company had *Satellite* on duty on the Mersey to attend to its liners anchored in the river. This little tug tender delivered 54 years' faithful duty to its owners. Passenger paddle tenders were also important on the Clyde, to attend ships at the Tail of the Bank off Greenock. The first was the Clyde Shipping Company's *Flying Foam* of 1865, which was joined by the Anchor Line's *Dispatch* in 1870 and the Clyde company's *Conqueror* in 1871. It was not long before paddle tenders were deployed on the Foyle, in the north of Ireland, to service the Atlantic liners calling off Moville and supply them with Irish emigrants destined for the

Walney (1904) famously overcrowded on the occasion of Barrow Football Club playing away to Blackpool in September 1913.

New World. At Plymouth the paddle tenders *Sir Francis Drake* and *Sir Walter Raleigh* started duties in 1873 and 1876 respectively, while dedicated tenders were working at Queenstown in the south of Ireland from the early 1880s.

It was at Queenstown that the ultimate paddle tenders, *Ireland* and *America*, were commissioned for the Clyde Shipping Company. Robins writes in *Passenger Tugs and Tenders*:

The Clyde Shipping Company, whose Irish connection was cemented though its coastal liner services, received two passenger tenders from J P Rennoldson & Sons' yard at South Shields in 1891. These were the famous iron-hulled paddle tenders *Ireland* and *America* designed for use in the south of Ireland at Queenstown. Although capable of towage they were primarily designed for the carriage of passengers and mail between the jetty at Queenstown and the emigrant ship waiting in the harbour. These vessels were the last contact with Ireland that many emigrants had before setting off for the unknown to try their luck in the New World. The *Ireland* and *America* each had a deck saloon from the paddle boxes almost to the stern and a separate saloon beneath the bridge which offered segregated accommodation in three classes, although steerage was by far the largest of the saloons (and the most austere). Immediately aft of the bridge was a small space for baggage and mail that could be accessed at main deck level from the quay at Queenstown, but discharged overhead through a hatch in the boat deck to the derricks on the big passenger ships.

Ireland and *America* were the very last contact with the ill-fated White Star liner *Titanic* as it lay off Queenstown before sailing for New York on 11 April 1912. Its passenger complement included a very large Irish contingent in third class who had boarded via the paddle tenders.

But technology was moving on, and screw tenders and tugs began to appear at a number of ports during the latter decades of the nineteenth century. Early screw tugs suffered from shallow draft, and it was only when the deeper-draft, wider-beam steam screw tugs were introduced that their worth was realised. A screw steam tug needs a deeper draft because the steam engine requires a fairly large diameter, coarse-pitch propeller because of its low speed. The change from paddle to screw is illustrated in Morecambe Bay, where the Furness Railway commissioned the magnificent passenger-carrying paddle tug *Walney* in 1904 for service out of Barrow-in-Furness. Its counterpart with the Midland Railway at the newly opened packet port at Heysham was the screw tug *Wyvern*, commissioned the following year. But the real difference between the two was that the paddle tug was still equipped with the outdated side-lever engine, whereas the screw tug had a compound engine.

Walney was one of the last passenger paddle tugs to be constructed in the UK. It was the second passenger tug so named to be stationed at Barrow. The first, of 200 gross tons, had been delivered by McNab & Company of Greenock to the Furness Railway back in 1868. The new *Walney* was destined for a 47-year career, the latter part of it spent with the London, Midland and Scottish Railway at Troon and Ayr. It was designed for towing duties based at Barrow, but was given a passenger saloon on the main deck and a certificate for 100 passengers, to support excursion work between Barrow and Fleetwood, work that was principally carried out by the company's excursion steamer *Lady Moyra*.

A key attraction was the manoeuvrability of the paddle tugs, a point not overlooked by tug owners such as the Manchester Ship Canal Company. The Ship Canal, being confined in width and with its long and thin terminal docks, needed tugs that could make their charges react quickly and accurately. The paddle tug, with a short crossed double-bridle arrangement to the

Manchester Ship Canal Company's *Rixton* (1907), showing the distinctive short-crossed bridle to Harrison Line's *Senator* (1917) on leaving Mode Wheel Lock.

tow at bow and stern, was the ideal machine for the Canal. The paddle tug also remained popular at ports in northeast England, where abundant cheap coal supplies also meant that the lower efficiency of the paddle tug compared with the screw tug could be overlooked.

The Manchester Ship Canal Company inherited a number of paddle tugs from the Bridgwater Navigation Company. These were generally small and ranged in age from *Bridgwater*, built at Liverpool in 1857, to *Queen of the Mersey*, which had been built in 1877, originally for cross-Mersey ferry duties. The company added a number of new and secondhand screw steamers before turning back to paddle propulsion. Six large purpose-built paddle tugs were ordered in the 1900s: *Barton* and *Irlam* came from J P Rennoldson & Sons in 1903, with independent

Malta (1875), built as *Benachie* for service on the Thames, spent 63 of its 76 years working in northeast England, latterly under the ownership of France, Fenwick Tyne & Wear Company.

sets of surface-condensing side-lever engines; *Eccles* and *Rixton* from J T Eltringham in 1905 and, in 1907, *Acton Grange* and *Old Trafford* from the same builder. The Eltringham tugs all had side-lever engines made by Hepple & Company, also of South Shields.

The six new Manchester tugs were distinctive in that their sponsons extended almost the full length of the tug to give maximum protection to the paddle wheels when working in the canal locks. The paddles were 7ft in diameter, with wooden feathering floats 2½ft wide by nearly 6ft long. They required a crew of just five men. The six tugs worked on the Canal until sold, one by one, between 1950 and 1953, having more than earned their keep.

Several veterans on the rivers Tyne and Wear were scrapped in the early 1950s. These included *Malta*, which had been built by J P Rennoldson at South Shields in 1875 for service on the Thames, originally with the name *Benachie*. Renamed *Malta* in 1876, when William Watkins bought it, the vessel moved back to the Tyne in 1888 when it was bought by Robert Stephenson Allen of Newcastle for £1,350. It worked on the rivers Tyne and Wear until sold for demolition in Scotland in 1951.

By the mid 1950s there was just one paddle tug left on the Clyde, *George Brown* at Irvine, dating from 1887, and one on the Forth, *Elie*, dating from 1912. The *Elie* was a bit of an oddity, built as the tug/tender *Pen Cw* for service at Fishguard for the Great Western Railway. Its builder, J T Eltringham & Company, equipped it with two single-cylinder diagonal engines. Paddle tugs remained popular on the northeast coast, but by 1956 there were just three Victorian paddlers left at Blyth, and a remarkable eleven on the Tyne and Wear, including the *Reliant*. Formerly the Manchester tug *Old Trafford*, it was subsequently bought by the Seaham Harbour Dock Company and remained with them until acquired by the National Maritime Museum in 1969. There were two more paddlers at Seaham and two on the Tees.

The younger of the two on the Tees was *John H Amos*. Built in 1931 for £18,500 for the Tees Conservancy Commissioners, it was the last steam paddle tug constructed for service in the UK. It had two compound-diagonal engines, one for each paddle, and was operated with the clutch between the two paddle shafts permanently disengaged to increase mobility in the confined waters of the Tees. A product of Bow, McLachlan & Company, Paisley, its design was not unlike that of the earlier series of paddle tugs built by that company for the Admiralty before the First World War. However, the builder went bankrupt during the construction of *John H Amos*, and any suitable material available in the yard was used to finish the job. Largely because of this it never achieved its design speed, and it was not until two years after its completion that the Commissioners finally accepted the vessel from the builder.

Most of the iron and steel paddle tugs, in fact some 90 per cent of them, came from three builders at South Shields on the lower Tyne. Richard Coton described these yards in his book on paddle steamers:

J T Eltringham & Company: The name of Eltringham had been associated with Stone Quay at South Shields since the first half of the nineteenth century. The family business was developed by Joseph Eltringham, partners being added in the 1880s. The yard specialised in building paddle steamers and tugs, later also trawlers. Business was transferred upstream to Willington Quay . . . the new premises opened in February 1914. The company was reconstituted as Eltringham's Limited in 1919, but was wound up during the 1922 slump.

Hepple & Company: This firm was originally based in North Shields. It specialised in tugs, but not only paddle tugs; orders came from as far afield as Trieste, Turkey and China. The business later became Hepple & Company (1919) Limited and carried on mainly with repair work until 1924 when it went into voluntary liquidation.

Camel (1914), namesake of the Admiralty *Camel* class of harbour tug, at Portsmouth in the early 1950s.

First of class: the launch of HM Tug *Director* by Mrs C H Mace at Yarrow & Company, Glasgow, 11 June 1956. (YARROW & CO)

J P Rennoldson & Sons: James Rennoldson established a shipyard at South Shields in 1863; the business passed to his son in 1878 . . . Large-scale expansion continued right up until the Great War, by which time there were four berths catering for vessels up to 240 feet long. The business eventually succumbed to the recession in 1929.

Ironically, one of the main champions of the paddle tug in the twentieth century in Britain was the Admiralty, Their Lordships

having earlier tried to discredit the paddle wheel for so very long. The attraction was that the paddlers, being of shallow draft, were lower-lying in the water than the screw tugs and could deal with the various overhangs of the naval ships they were to attend. But the work did not go to the normal tug builders, and Bow, McLachlan & Company at Paisley, J I Thorneycroft at Southampton, John Brown at Clydebank, and the Admiralty shipyard at Chatham were instrumental in delivering the new *Camel* class of paddle tug between 1907 and

The diesel-electric paddle tug *Griper* (1958) attends the Royal Fleet Auxiliary tanker *Brown Ranger* (1941) at Portsmouth in February 1969. (AUTHOR)

1915. Unlike their Admiralty predecessors, which were equipped with the old oscillating engines, the *Camel* class had twin compound machinery and were highly manoeuvrable. The last of the class was *Pert*, completed by Thorneycroft in 1916, which was essentially an enlarged version of the rest of the class, with a length of 170ft as opposed to the 144ft of the earlier fleet members. Its paddle wheels were 14ft in diameter and each revolution of the wheel displaced 60 tons of water, giving it the power (equivalent to 2,000hp) to move even the largest of battleships on its own. It had its own distilling plant to generate boiler feed water, and there were 17 auxiliary steam engines about the ship. The officers' cabins were comparatively large and grand aboard *Pert*, and it was always affectionately known to the tug-men as 'Crystal Palace'.

Pert survived until 1962, when, surprisingly, a new class of paddle tug was built to replace it and the other survivors of the *Camel* class. This was the *Director* class, designed by Yarrow & Company, neat and compact harbour tugs powered by diesel-

The stern-wheeler 'Big Mama', *Sprague* (1901), on the Mississippi with fuel oil flats above Baton Rouge in January 1948, just two months before it was decommissioned. Note the overhead hogging tension wires intended to prevent the hull breaking if the vessel were to go aground amidships.

electric machinery that allowed instant and independent reactions from the paddle wheels. Chain reduction drive connected two electric motors to the paddle shaft, which was split so that the paddle wheels could work independently. The tugs had a very low profile and were designed for working under overhanging flight decks and other protrusions from various types of naval ships. Seven ships were built by three separate builders on the Clyde, and commissioned from 1956 onwards, the final pair being *Griper* and *Grinder*, delivered in 1958. They were variously stationed at Malta and Gibraltar, *Dextrous* spending much of its career there, but the main occupation for the *Director* class was harbour work at Portsmouth and Devonport. The class was decommissioned in the 1970s.

The decline of the paddle tug was much the same in Europe. However, there was one breed of paddle tug distinctive to Europe, the river tug, typically a longer and slimmer version of the harbour tug, up to 250ft long by 80ft across the sponsons. They were used for hauling barges long distances, and although their paddles could not operate independently, the vessels' shallow draft allowed them to operate in reaches which prevented safe access for the deeper draft of a screw tug. Only about 40 paddle tugs survived the Second World War on the Rhine, and these were successively withdrawn and replaced by 'pusher'-type tugs, the last steam paddler, *Raab Kaarcher XIV*, leaving the river in 1967. That same year the last three paddle tugs were withdrawn from the Danube and scrapped, although steam paddlers were still active for a number of years on various Russian rivers.

In the Americas, north and south, in Africa and Australia, the sternwheel tug was preferred for pushing cargo flats and bundles of lumber. These vessels have now been replaced by motor tugs, although river trade has universally declined against competition from road and rail.

The mother of all the river tugs, the 'Big Mama' as it was affectionately called, was the Mississippi sternwheeler *Sprague*. Built by the Iowa Iron Works in 1901 for the Monongahela River Consolidated Coal and Coke Company, it was designed to push 56 loaded flats each carrying 1,100 tons of coal, and in 1907 broke all records by pushing 60 flats carrying a total 67,000 tons of coal. To do this its six fuel-hungry boilers fed enough steam to generate 2,000hp, equivalent to the towing power of the British Admiralty tug *Pert*. The power was slightly increased when its 40ft-diameter stern wheel was replaced by a 38ft-diameter wheel. Manoeuvrability was enhanced, as it not only had the normal rudder before the stern wheel but an additional rudder aft of the wheel as well.

But *Sprague* was no ordinary tug. It was 276ft long with a draft of just 7½ft, and when it was pushing a spread of loaded flats everything had to get out of the way. It ended its career working for the Standard Oil Company (Esso), pushing oil fuel flats up river, against the stream, from the Baton Rouge Refinery. Decommissioned in March 1948, the Big Mama spent the next 26 years happily entertaining visitors as a static exhibit at Vicksburg, complete with museum, restaurant and theatre. The ship was destroyed by fire in 1974 as it lay at its moorings; nobody was aboard.

11 MILITARY DUTIES FOR BRAVE LITTLE SHIPS

Europe still dominated the world at the start of the twentieth century, although the wealth and industry of the USA was a serious challenge, and countries such as Japan were to be taken seriously after her defeat of Russia in 1904. The halcyon Edwardian days came to an abrupt end with the accession of King George V and the increasing friction between the two established European factions; Britain, of course, was allied with France and Russia. Following the German assault on Liège on 5 August 1914 it was widely believed that war (the First World War) would be a quick and decisive affair. Four years later the world emerged a new and better-informed place, but with a whole generation of young men removed from its society.

The First World War necessitated the immediate call-up of a large contingent of British paddle tugs. They were used not only for towage, but also as messenger ships, inspection ships and for a host of other duties. Demand for harbour tugs was high owing to the increased shipping movements required to support the various overseas military ob-

jectives. But the excursion steamers, shallow-draft, fleet of foot and manoeuvrable, were also in demand by the Admiralty.

The First World War was the last infantry war. It was also a war that was fought at sea. Britain lost nine million tons of shipping during the four years of conflict, in which several deadly weapons were deployed for the first time, not least the submarine and various types of mines. It was the latter that immediately put the paddle steamer in great demand, its shallow draft providing an ideal platform for minesweeping operations. One by one the excursion and estuarine steamers were taken up for military service, hoisting the white ensign over a drab grey livery and adopting the grand title His Majesty's Paddle Minesweeper. The sweep wires were dragged astern of the vessel (see the photograph of *Yarmouth Belle*) at a depth that cut the anchor lines to the mines to make them break surface so that they could be destroyed. The little ships were hugely successful at their new task, and when HMPM 579, otherwise known as Belle Steamers' *Walton Belle*, fished up a new type of German mine in the

The minesweeper *Yarmouth Belle* (1898) equipped with a minesweeping trawl boom.

The hull design of P & A Campbell's *Glen Usk* (1914) was incorporated within the *Ascot*-class paddle minesweeper designed by the Ailsa Shipbuilding Company.

Thames estuary, these mines were known thereafter as '*Walton Belle* Mines'.

So successful were the paddle minesweepers that the Admiralty ordered a fleet of 37 new ones to be built, based on the hull design of P & A Campbell's Bristol Channel excursion steamer *Glen Usk*, newly completed by the Ailsa Shipbuilding Company at Troon. Ailsa was asked to complete the design of the first batch of 16 paddle minesweepers to be delivered in 1916, a design that was only slightly modified when orders for the second lot of 16 ships were placed. They were about 246ft long and had distinctive cruiser sterns. The ships were delivered between 1916 and 1918, the last five orders being cancelled as hostilities ended in 1918. The steam minesweepers had distinctive widely spaced funnels taking the exhausts from two separate boiler rooms, one

forward and one aft of the engine room. The *Ascot* class of paddle minesweeper, as the fleet was known, were all named after racecourses. Of the 27 vessels commissioned, five were lost in the war, one was sold and the remaining 21 were laid up after the war. Of these only two, HMS *Melton* and HMS *Atherton*, were later sold for commercial service and converted for use as Thames excursion steamers for the New Medway Steam Packet Company. The rest were scrapped.

Some of the bigger paddlers were used as troop transports. Frank Thornley described the role of *La Marguerite* in his book on North Wales steamers:

She was requisitioned in March 1915 and released in April 1919, thus completing over four years' service. With all lights out (the voyages were undertaken for the most part at night) gun at bow and stern and with hardly a sound on board except the throb of the engines, she made the Channel crossing between Southampton and various French ports under all conditions. Captain John Young, her regular commander on the North Wales service, was in charge. During this period the vessel steamed over 52,000 miles and carried 360,000 troops, the only mishap she had being a boiler explosion in which, unfortunately, four lives were lost.

HMS *Pontefract* (1916), one of the *Ascot*-class Admiralty minesweepers, on duty in July 1918.

St Tudno (see Chapter 9) was sold before the First World War to become a tender at Southampton for the Hamburg-Amerika Line. It too spent much of the war as a transport, ending its days working specifically for the US Government. The Clyde steamers *Duchess of Hamilton* and *Duchess of Montrose* were both initially deployed as troop carriers but later converted for minesweeping duties, and both were lost to mines while carrying out this work in the North Sea.

Even so, the paddle steamer was deployed only in a non-combatant role, the Admiralty having been wary of paddles on front-line duties since the early days of the nineteenth century. Some paddlers did, however, see action, while others sadly were lost to the mines they sought to destroy. Grahame Farr in his book on West Country steamers describes an encounter with a U-Boat:

on 15 August 1915 the [excursion steamers] *Brighton Queen*, *Westward Ho*, *Glen Avon* and *Cambridge* [P & A Campbell's *Cambria* in peacetime], sweeping near Smith's Knoll sighted a U-Boat making for some fishing craft. They promptly slipped their sweeps and made for the intruder, firing their puny armament as they went. The *Brighton Queen* claimed a hit with her third round, but it could not be positively observed. However, the submarine captain decided that discretion was the better part of valour and made off.

The submarine was sunk later that day, while *Brighton Queen* was lost to a mine nearly two months later. But action or no, there are some incredible stories of bravery and heroism, such as that of the man who swam through a minefield to rescue a shipmate on a life raft which was in danger of setting off mines floating on the surface.

The Barry Railway's paddler *Barry* was used initially as a transport, taking prisoners of war to various camps in Ireland and the Isle of Man. But in August 1915 it sailed from Bristol via Ilfracombe to Mudros in the eastern Mediterranean on a voyage that

lasted 24 days. There it was used as a troop transport to Sulva and Anzac, often unloading ammunition on its twice-daily trip under enemy fire. In 1916 it was employed on the shuttle between Mudros and Imbros and later around Salonika. Its Bristol crew were then relieved by Marine Reservists and the ship's name changed to *Barryfield* to avoid confusion with a US destroyer also named *Barry*.

Several other paddlers were sent to the Mediterranean, mainly on minesweeping, patrol and transport duties. The Red Funnel Steamers *Duchess of York*, *Queen*, *Stirling Castle* (formerly of the Galloway fleet on the Forth) and *Princess Mary* sailed in convoy to the Mediterranean in May 1916. *Stirling Castle* was mined off Malta and the *Princess Mary* was wrecked in the Dardanelles after the Armistice when it ran over the submerged wreck of HMS *Majestic*. Pockett's Bristol Channel Steam Packet Company's excursion steamer *Brighton* was sent to the Dardanelles as a water carrier, while the Devon Dock, Pier & Steamship Company's *Duke of Devonshire* and the Clyde steamer *Minerva* were also deployed in the Mediterranean but fitted out for minesweeping duties. The two Fairfield-built Isle of Man paddlers *Queen Victoria* and *Prince of Wales* (see Chapter 6), were also in the eastern Mediterranean, deployed on net-laying anti-submarine work designed to protect the troop carriers. On one occasion the pair escorted the Isle of Man company's screw steamer *Snaefell* to the beaches at Sulva during the Gallipoli Campaign.

The Isle of Man company paddlers *Empress Queen* and *Mona's Isle* were also requisitioned. *Empress Queen*, at one time the largest fast cross-Channel paddle steamer, came to a very unfortunate end. While on trooping duties to Le Havre it was returning to Southampton with 1,300 troops due for leave when it ran on to the Bembridge Ledge in thick fog in the early hours of 1 February 1916. The troops were safely transferred to attendant warships while the crew waited in vain for the tide to lift the ship off the rocks. As so often happens in these circumstances,

Ascot-class HMPS *Melton* (1916) was converted for commercial use in 1929 to become *Queen of Thanet*, and is seen here in its final guise between 1949 and 1951 as Red Funnel's *Solent Queen*.

the fog was later blown away and the ensuing wind and seas destroyed the ship.

Mona's Isle was initially used for trooping and later converted for submarine net-laying work off Harwich. At one stage it helped recover gold bullion from a wreck before the Germans could get it. On trooping duties it found a German submarine lying dead ahead at close range. Although the ship was about one hour's steaming from Le Havre with over 1,000 troops aboard, the captain headed straight for the sub, which managed to get one wild torpedo away. The portside steel paddle floats stabbed into the shell of the submarine, ripping at the conning tower and destroying its integrity. The victorious *Mona's Isle*, with its battalion of jubilant soldiers, steamed slowly on to France to discharge the men. It was later able to return to England under its own steam for repairs.

At the end of the war the paddle minesweepers were not immediately demobbed and returned to their owners, as the urgent task of cleaning up the remaining minefields had first to be completed. Nevertheless, the surviving *Ascot*-class vessels were soon laid up, one group being sold for scrap in 1922 and the second and last group in 1927, when two were resold and converted for use in the excursion trade as *Queen of Thanet* and *Queen of Kent*. Both ships were destined to return to minesweeping duties in the next world war. Their consorts would have been welcomed to that duty had they survived the ship-breakers' torches in the 1920s. Both *Queen of Thanet* and *Queen of Kent* again survived, and in the

late 1940s took up duties with Red Funnel Steamers, which had suffered heavy losses in the Second World War.

Perhaps the most unfortunate loss occurred on 18 November 1917 off Harwich Harbour. The Glasgow & South Western Railway steamer *Mars*, one-time favourite with excursionists on the Clyde (see Chapter 12), was run down after dark by a British destroyer while minesweeping. *Mars*, under the wartime name HMS *Marsa*, was run on to a sand shoal, where it settled in shallow water. High hopes of salvaging the vessel were quickly lost when it broke its back in deteriorating weather conditions – an unnecessary end to a fine steamer.

Immediately after the First World War, several paddle hospital ships were deployed to the White Sea in 1919. *London Belle* and *Walton Belle* were dispatched via Norway's North Cape as hospital carriers *HC2* and *HC3*. They assisted in the expedition against the Bolsheviks in North Russia, intended to halt the spread of Communism. The two little paddle steamers demonstrated admirable seagoing qualities but were not much used on arrival, other than for deploying landing parties, when snipers' bullets pock-marked their funnels and ventilators. Although *HC3* was captured by the Bolshevik army, it was retaken by an engineer officer from a British merchant ship who rallied the steamer's crew and regained possession. Both *HC2* and *HC3* later returned to the Thames, a voyage that took three weeks, and were released by the Admiralty only in May 1920. Two former Forth excursion steamers, *Ed-*

inburgh *Castle* and *Lord Morton* (*HC8* and *HC7*), were also sent to the White Sea but were blown up in September 1919 to avoid capture by the Bolsheviks.

The Clyde paddle steamer *Queen-Empress*, used in the First World War as a minesweeper, was also nearly abandoned in the White Sea when it ran aground. Recovered and safely brought home, it saw service again as a minesweeper in the Second World War.

One outcome of the First World War was the ending of paddle-steamer services on the Forth. In 1915 the four-ship fleet of the Galloway Saloon Steam Packet Company comprised *Redgauntlet*, formerly of the North British Railway fleet on the Clyde, *Edinburgh Castle* and *Lord Morton*, while D & J Nicol deployed the former Belfast Lough steamer *Slieve Bearnagh* on sailings between Kirkcaldy and Leith. Galloway also had the paddle steamer *Duchess of Buccleugh* completing at A & J Inglis's yard on the Clyde, but it was acquired by the Admiralty and reconfigured as a minesweeper, only to be sold and broken up in 1921. The three existing vessels in the Galloway fleet were purchased by the Admiralty, *Edinburgh Castle* and *Lord Morton* ending their days in the White Sea, while *Redgauntlet* was later sold to Algerian owners. *Slieve Bearnagh* survived service as hospital carrier *HC5*, but was fit for nothing but demolition after the war. The Galloway fleet was remembered in Southampton by its former steamer *Lord Elgin*, which ultimately survived in the Red Funnel fleet until 1955, when it was 79 years old (see Chapter 9).

Despite international restrictions on the rebuilding of Hitler's navy in the 1920s and 1930s, the German pocket battleship was commissioned and every effort was made for renewed hostilities. When war became inevitable, the evacuation of 20,000 London children was begun on 1 September 1939 by train and by sea, the threat of German air raids being immediate and real. Four Thames paddle excursion steamers, *Royal Eagle*, *Crested Eagle*, *Laguna Belle* and *Medway Queen*, were detailed along with the motor ships *Royal Daffodil*, *Royal Sovereign* and *Queen of the Channel* to board the children

either at Dagenham or Greenwich. Each child had a luggage label giving just name, school and likely destination. The children were taken to Ipswich, Lowestoft and Yarmouth as staging posts for onward transport to their new surrogate families. So smooth was the operation that the dispatch of the children was completed by 3 September. Hours later the Anchor-Donaldson liner *Athenia* was torpedoed and sunk 250 miles off the Irish coast with the loss of 112 lives. Its precious cargo consisted of 1,103 passengers, mainly women and children, mostly returning American citizens, all bent on distancing themselves from the potential war zone. The Second World War had begun.

An evacuation of children also took place from Glasgow and surrounding towns to Lower Clyde resorts and dormitory towns, and a number of steamers, including the LNER paddler *Jeanie Deans*, assisted. Later in the month *Waverly* went up-river to the Inglis yard for conversion, for the second time in its career, to a minesweeper.

Once again the paddle steamers were called up for official duty, and many of them formed into six minesweeping battalions:

7th   Flotilla based at Granton, near Leith, with five steamers
8th   Flotilla based at North Shields with five steamers
10th Flotilla based at Dover with eight steamers (the Dover Patrol)
11th Flotilla based at Grimsby with five steamers
12th Flotilla at Harwich with five steamers.

But this time there were even more deadly weapons facing the paddle minesweepers, of which the magnetic mine was a very serious hazard to anybody engaged in cutting mines free preparatory to their destruction. Paravanes were towed aft to cut the mine anchor cables. But there was another new threat, as the aeroplane had developed such that German bombers could pick targets at will, be they on land or sea, and more paddlers were deployed as anti-aircraft, or ack-ack, ships to

Part of the 7th Flotilla based at Granton was HMPM *Plinlimmon* (1895), seen here undergoing conversion for wartime duties at the GSN yard at Deptford Creek in 1939. In peacetime it was better known as P & A Campbell's *Cambria*, and in the First World War it served as the minesweeper HMPM *Cambridge*.

Royal Eagle (1932) on ack-ack duties, but not quite as fast as its wartime colleague *Jeanie Deans*.

combat this threat. The prototype for this role was the Thames excursion steamer *Royal Eagle*, and henceforth the ack-ack flotilla on the Thames became known as the Eagles. One old score was settled by the ack-ack ships *Jeanie Deans* of the LNER Clyde fleet and the Thames steamer *Royal Eagle*, both of which were claimed to be the fastest steamer in the universe. It appears *Royal Eagle* was no match for the Scot, and nothing more was heard of the challenge!

The effectiveness of anti-aircraft deployments were described by D D Hutchings from his experience aboard *Thames Queen* in the winter of 1942, in an article first published in *Paddle Wheels* for Summer 1972:

I am afraid that if we did shoot it was when anything came near, as we had no means of identifying any aircraft, but we apparently never hit anything. Anchored with any swell, the sponsons were hit from underneath by waves and the whole ship shook. About 100 of us lived aboard, and in 24 hours our fresh water was all used. I can still remember that our captain was Captain Horsham. He knew all the channels between the sandbanks off the East Coast without having to refer to charts. When loaded with water and ammunition the *Thames Queen* waddled out of harbour with a considerable list.

Of all the daring Second World War exploits of the paddle steamers, none will be remembered better than their role in the evacuation of the British Expeditionary Force from

the beaches at Dunkirk and La Panne in June 1940. Every vessel that could be mustered, including the fishing bawleys at Leigh-on-Sea, the river boats on the Thames and every conceivable craft in the vicinity, set sail for the Dunkirk beaches, there to face an aerial bombardment from the Luftwaffe. Perhaps the worst atrocity on the beaches was the loss of the big steamer *Crested Eagle* of the Thames excursion fleet. Its boilers were fired by oil, not a particularly flammable substance with a low flash point, but when its fuel tanks received a direct hit the explosion was enough to ignite its bunkers and instantly turn the crowded and partly loaded steamer into a fireball. There was sufficient steam in the boilers to ease the

ship quickly on to the beach, but even so only 150 men got away from the inferno.

Several other paddlers were lost at Dunkirk, including Campbell's *Brighton Queen*, which had so often been rostered on the long-day Brighton to Boulogne excursion service in peacetime. P & A Campbell also lost *Devonia* and *Brighton Belle* at Dunkirk. *Devonia* was off La Panne on 31 May when it was bombed and repeatedly shelled, causing extensive damage to the ship's hull. Any idea of scuttling the vessel in the shallow water might not have prevented the Germans from repairing *Devonia* and putting it to service again. As the boilers were on standby there was enough steam available to point *Devonia* straight towards

Ack-ack ship *Jeanie Deans* (1931) on the Thames.

Two contrasting descriptions of the Dunkirk evacuation:

From a transcript of a BBC broadcast by J B Priestley, 1940

And to my mind what was characteristically English about it was the part played in the difficult and dangerous embarkation not by the warships but by the little pleasure steamers. We have known them and laughed at them, these fussy little steamers, and called them 'shilling sicks'. We have watched them load and unload their crowds of holidaymakers – the gents full of high spirits and bottled beer, the ladies eating pork pies, the children sticky with peppermint rock. They were usually paddle steamers, making a great deal more fuss with all their churning than they made speed; and they weren't proud, for they let you see their works going round. They liked to call themselves 'Queens' and 'Belles', and even if they were new there was something old-fashioned, Dickensian, Victorian, about them. They belonged to the same world as pierriots and piers, sand castles and high teas, palmists and crowded sweating promenades.

But they were called out of that world. These *Brighton Queens* and *Brighton Belles* left that innocent world of theirs to sail into the inferno, to defy bombs, shells, mines, torpedoes and machine gun fire to rescue our soldiers. Some of them alas will never return. Among those that will never return was one I knew well, the pride of our ferry service to the Isle of Wight, none other than the good ship *Gracie Fields*. And now never again will we board her at Cowes and go down into her dining saloon for a fine breakfast of bacon and eggs. She has paddled and churned away for ever, but this little steamer like all her brave and battered sisters is immortal. And yet our great-grandchildren, when they learn how we began this war by snatching glory out of defeat, and then swept on to victory, may also learn how the little holiday steamers made an excursion to hell and came back glorious.

From an article by Bruce Grice, describing the attendance of the *Princess Elizabeth* at the sinking of the *Gracie Fields*, which first appeared in *Sea Breezes* for September 1984:

It was on 27 May 1940 that minesweepers attached to the 10th Flotilla based at Dover left the Downs for the beaches. The paddle minesweeper *Sandown* from the railway fleet, familiar in peace time to the Portsmouth to Ryde service, slipped her mooring in company with the elegant Thames excursion vessel *Medway Queen* of the New Medway Steam Packet Company, the P & A Campbell steamer *Brighton Belle* and the Solent paddler *Gracie Fields*.

The *Princess Elizabeth* was unable to join this impressive convoy as she was in the Dover basin for boiler cleaning. However, on 29 May . . . the vessel left for La Panne. Arriving at 2015 the crew immediately lowered the ship's boats for beach work, her guns constantly engaging enemy aircraft until dark. At 2105 the *Princess Elizabeth* received the signal from the *Sandown* to proceed and assist the *Gracie Fields* which had been attacked off Middel Kerke Buoy. The *Gracie Fields*, with troops embarked, was homeward bound. As she forged 'on course' a Dornier dive-bomber came low, mercilessly machine-gunning the paddle steamer's crowded deck. Then with deadly accuracy two direct bomb hits were scored, one exploding on deck, the other penetrating down the funnel and exploding in the boiler room. While the boiler miraculously withstood the eruption, a steam pipe fractured. As it was not possible to stop engines and sufficient steam pressure remained, the damaged vessel continued under way until out of steam. It was an erratic course, with a jammed 15° rudder . . . hard to starboard.

To effect rescue work a Dutch 'skoot', that had been taken over by the Royal Navy, was manoeuvred inside the *Gracie Field's* turning circle. Her bow was so positioned between the angle formed by hull and sponson of the steamer, and keeping her engine running, she was able to maintain station to secure and start taking off the wounded . . . The *Princess Elizabeth* was informed and returned to the beaches. At 0130 hours a signal came from the *Gracie Fields* to report that she was sinking. The remaining troops and ship's company were taken off the ill-fated Solent steamer, which was abandoned.

the beach and ram it hard into the shore. The objective was twofold: to create a short pier for uplifting troops from the beach, and to damage the integrity of the vessel to an extent that it could not be repaired. Still under shellfire, the crew calmly removed all useful and portable apparatus and ditched the remaining ammunition into the water.

The fifth loss was the almost brand-new Southampton to Cowes ferry and excursion steamer *Gracie Fields*. Built locally for Red Funnel at the Thorneycroft works at Woolston, it was a pretty little steamer with an open foredeck, a curved bridge front and a full-width saloon almost to the rope-handling area at the stern. It was twice attacked by aircraft. On the first occasion it was going about its lawful peacetime duties as a ferry when a flying-boat coming into Calshot collided with the paddler. The aeroplane's starboard wing hit *Gracie Field*'s mast and the aircraft dived into the sea adjacent to the ship's bows. Amazingly neither aeroplane crew nor passengers aboard the paddler were hurt. But on return from its second trip to Dunkirk on 28 May 1940, carrying some 750 soldiers, it was bombed and left disabled and making water with a number of casual-

ties aboard. Attempts to tow the ship back to Dover failed and it sank early the following morning after it had been evacuated.

The Clyde's *Waverley* was also lost during the Dunkirk operation. It was able to maintain its zig-zag course on its way back from the beaches until the steering gear failed. Nevertheless, its gunners brought an enemy bomber down shortly before the vessel received a direct hit. It sank rapidly, but not before most of the passengers and crew were able to scramble to safety aboard other ships.

The bravery and heroism of the whole Dunkirk story are legend. Lieutenant Edwin Davies was in charge of HMS *Oriole*, more familiar in peacetime guise as the Clyde paddle steamer *Eagle III*. His famous signal sums up his actions, which allowed 2,500 men to walk across his ship to board others and to load another contingent of soldiers aboard his own ship as the tide rose: 'Deliberately grounded HMS *Oriole* Belgian coast dawn 29 May on own initiative. Objective speedy evacuation of troops, refloated dusk same day. No apparent damage'. The whole time HMS *Oriole* was under constant risk of enemy fire.

In the USA the two mighty Great Lakes

Devonia (1905) in happier days, on an excursion to Boulogne, not that far from La Panne, where it was beached with bomb damage on 31 May 1940.

HMS *Oriole* (1910) was beached at Dunkirk under enemy gunfire to speed up the evacuation of troops. It is seen here at Troon in September 1940.

Thames convoy protection vessel HMPM *Skiddaw* (1896) was better known in peacetime as P & A Campbell's *Britannia*. It had served as the minesweeper HMS *Britain* in the First World War.

paddle steamers *Seeandbee* and *Greater Buffalo* were laboriously cut down to main-deck level and converted into the aircraft carriers USS *Wolverine* and USS *Sable* (see Chapter 8). Although not designed for combatant duty, and based thereafter out of Chicago, they were instrumental in the training of many thousands of navy pilots and contributed significantly to the American wartime naval capacity.

As the war slowly turned against the German might, a number of British paddlers were involved in the Normandy Landings in June 1944. HMS *Scawfell*, otherwise known as the Caledonian Steam Packet

Company's *Jupiter* and dating only from 1937, was one that was in the fray. Initially carrying troops into the Mulberry Harbours, it ferried equipment in until the fall of Antwerp in 1945, where it was transferred to serve its final military duties. The Campbell steamers *Glen Usk* and *Glen Avon* were used as inspection vessels at the Normandy beaches, and the company's *Britannia* was used as a guard ship. *Britannia* was later deployed alongside one of the Mulberry Harbours as a canteen ship, providing hot meals for the troops before they set off inland. *Britannia*, as HMS *Skiddaw*, was used as a convoy protection vessel on the Thames and

was later moved to the Scheldt estuary to join HMS *Scawfell*, while yet another Campbell steamer, *Glen Gower*, was also detailed to join them there. Among the many Thames-based convoy protection vessels in the later period of the war were such well-known names as GSN's *Laguna Belle* and *Ryde* and *Sandown* of Southern Railway's Isle of Wight fleet.

Other wartime duties were a little less hazardous, and included store ships and messenger and inspection duties. Even the elderly Humber paddle ferry *Killingholme* was found a role, acting as depot ship for the Barrage Balloon Command. It remained on the Humber only because its replacement, the paddler *Lincoln Castle* (see Chapter 12), was held up on the Clyde at the builders until July 1941, having failed to make its first delivery voyage in 1940 owing to compass problems. Whatever their role, the steamers carried greatly enhanced

crew numbers, accommodated in cramped quarters converted from day-passenger use to mess and sleeping spaces. They were all at the mercy of the weather, their sponsons susceptible to broadside waves, and were not at all comfortable in a beam sea. With many of the steamers designed for the sheltered waters of the Clyde or the Thames, few were built with year-round sailing in mind, save for the long-distance commuter steamers of the Clyde. But great seamanship and careful watch of the weather meant that none of the steamers was lost other than to the enemy.

David MacBrayne's paddle steamer *Pioneer* was not called up for the First World War, and nor for a long while was it called up in the Second World War. Instead, it was kept on its owner's services, taking essential stores out to the Hebrides and bringing back island produce. It had been launched in 1905 for use on the West Loch Tarbert

Convoy protection vessel *Laguna Belle* (1896), formerly Belle Steamers' *Southend Belle*.

The Isle of Wight ferry *Ryde* (1937) saw wartime duty both as an ack-ack boat and a convoy protection vessel.

The MacBrayne steamer *Pioneer* (1905) on the peaceful waters of West Loch Tarbert in September 1937. It ended its days as a floating research laboratory under the Director of Submarine Warfare.

to Islay service, on which a shallow-draft paddle steamer was ideally suited to the shallow water off the pier at the head of the loch. But it did finally serve its nation, for in 1944 it was requisitioned and stationed off Fairlie on the Lower Clyde to be used as the nerve-centre for submarine deployment in the Atlantic. Towards the end of the war it was re-equipped for the Director of Submarine Warfare to assist research into very low frequency underwater communication systems. In 1945 the Admiralty bought the now elderly paddle steamer from MacBrayne and gave it the rather daunting name *Harbinger*. The following year its paddles were removed and it was towed south to Portland, where it spent a further twelve years employed in various research activities.

Although this chapter is by no means a detailed account of the valiant paddle steamer in two world wars, it illustrates the important contribution made by this class of steamer. In 1939 there were 63 excursion paddle steamers of 100 gross tons and more in operation, but it was an ageing fleet in which replacement tonnage had been hard to resource. Richard Coton, in his book *A Decline of the Paddle Steamer*, wrote:

The direct effect of the Second World War on the career of the paddle steamer in Britain is disputable. Many of the older vessels were indeed lost in action or returned in such a state as to be unfit for further service. Of the 21 paddlers built in the 1930s, only four were lost in action, and three of these left sister ships which did not have post-war careers of any outstanding length. On the other hand, the hard usage in war service received by especially these newer vessels cannot have increased their life span.

12 THE EXCURSION ROLE

The scope of Campbell's range of excursions at the turn of the [twentieth] century was, to anyone knowing the Bristol Channel, almost unbelievable and took into account small ports which have long since either silted into decline or simply been abandoned. This says nothing of those resorts that could only be served by transferring passengers by boat, often under oars and in choppy sea conditions.

B M Leek in *Sea Breezes*, March 1992

The Edwardian years were the heyday of the excursion steamer. In many areas around the British coasts there were too many steamers for the business on offer, and slashed ticket prices made the 1900s very much a consumer's market. But this did not stop many of the operators from investing in new steamers to upgrade their fleets. For the most part the steamers were equipped with compound engines, and although speed was important, more to impress the rival companies than speed the passenger to a destination, it was no longer the vital ingredient. The key to success was a silver-service dining saloon to serve high tea on the Thames, Clyde or Forth, entertainment for the children, a bar and smoking room for dad and somewhere quiet for the ladies to retreat for a chat.

But just as the turbine steamer had rudely muscled into the fast cross-Channel steamer market, ousting many a good paddle steamer, so too did the turbine appear in the excursion trades. Of course, the very first commercial role of the turbine was to power the Willamson Buchanan steamer *King Edward*, itself a Clyde commuter and excursion steamer on the long Campbeltown service from 1901 onwards. A companion vessel, *Queen Alexandra*, followed in 1902 and allowed *King Edward* to be put on the Ardrishaig run in competition with the well established paddle steamer *Lord of the Isles*. Over the next ten seasons *Lord of the Isles* vied with the turbine steamer, its passenger numbers declining year by year, until it was sold to the owner of the two turbine steam-

ers. On the Thames the turbine steamer *Kingfisher* took up the all-important French day trips from Tilbury in 1906, and in 1914 the Liverpool and North Wales Steamship Company ordered its first turbine steamer, the ill-fated *St Seiriol*, which was lost in the First World War. Was this the beginning of the turbine ousting the excursion paddle steamer?

In fact the threat from the turbine was only the first of many threats with which the paddle steamer had to contend in the twentieth century. The next was the arrival of the coastal passenger motor ship, first championed on the West Highland routes by David MacBrayne in 1907 and later refined in the MacBrayne diesel-electric ships *Lochfyne* and *Lochnevis* in the early 1930s. Their electric propulsion motors, supplied by diesel generators, drove the propellers without the need for a reversing gearbox and gave the officer on the bridge total and immediate control of the ships' movements. The New Medway Steam Packet Company's 'steamer' *Queen of the Channel*, a diesel-driven near-sister of the Clyde turbine steamer *Queen Mary*, was a huge success on the Thames following its delivery in May 1935, and was the first of a succession of motor excursion ships which evolved along broadly the same pattern for service on the Thames. Captain Shippick at New Medway had pondered long and hard on whether to build another traditional paddle steamer or go modern. In the end he was persuaded by shipbuilder William Denny to go modern by drawing on their experience of building *Lochfyne* and *Lochnevis* for MacBrayne.

Typical of the cross-river and estuary ferries was *Heather Bell* (1862). It was the crack steamer on the Wallasey run across the Mersey from Liverpool for about 15 years, and ended its days operating excursions from Dublin with the name *Erin's King*.

But there were other threats: the motor coach, the motor car and the package holiday. All these social developments conspired against the seaside trip on the paddle steamer. The combination of declining trade and increased operating costs of steamers due to ever-higher fuel bills and mounting crewing costs meant that the ageing fleet of paddlers must inevitably also decline. Despite a number of new builds in the late 1930s and the immediate post-war years, decline they certainly did.

The nineteenth century witnessed the development of four types of passenger paddle steamer in service around the British Isles. These were:

- the fast commuter steamer services that connected at railheads on the lower Clyde for express train services into Glasgow,
- ferry services from railheads to island communities,
- seasonal excursion services, and
- cross-river ferry services.

The steamers on the first three types of steamer routes tended to merge into one class. This was increasingly the case as the nineteenth century progressed, as owners realised the tourist potential of many of their services. Clyde and Western Isle operators had long realised the market for excursions 'doon the watter', and David MacBrayne had been marketing the Royal Route for decades after Queen Victoria had long forgotten that she ever visited that part of the Highlands. Both the railway operators on the Clyde and David MacBrayne in the Highlands had steamers that were refurbished in the spring for summer excursion use, only to be put back into some corner of Bowling Harbour or Greenock for the winter months. This seasonality became an increasing feature of the paddle steamer as time passed.

Cross-river ferry services required another breed of steamer altogether, typified by the paddle ferries used for vehicles and passengers at Queensferry on the Forth, between Hull and New Holland on the Humber, at Tilbury and Woolwich on the Thames, and even at Milford Haven and the Menai Strait in Wales. There was also the dedicated passenger paddle ferry to be found on the Tyne and elsewhere. Some of these steamers were of considerable size, notably on the Forth, Mersey and Humber, and many are still remembered with affection.

One of the significant developments in the last quarter of the nineteenth century was the introduction of the compound, or double-expansion, engine, which made its appearance on the Clyde with the introduction of the fleet of the Caledonian Steam Packet Company, a subsidiary of the Caledonian Railway Company. Its early ships

were a mix of two-crank compound engines and single-crank tandem compound
engines, all of the diagonal type. The next
generation of engine, installed in *Marchioness
of Lorne*, designed for winter service on the
Arran route where thermal efficiency with
relatively long steaming was sought, introduced the triple-expansion diagonal engine,
albeit in a four-cylinder tandem design. This
arrangement was so successful that it was repeated in 1902 with the building of *Duchess
of Montrose* by John Brown & Company, and
in 1903 with its near sister *Duchess of Fife,*
built by the Fairfield Company. Both ships
had a shorter engine stroke than *Marchioness
of Lorne*, resulting in reduced machinery
weight, and their engines ran at higher revolutions. The *Fife*'s contract speed of 16
knots under trial conditions was exceeded

by 1½ knots. A significant further development for paddle steamers during the twentieth century was the introduction of the
three-crank triple-expansion engine. The
first Clyde steamer to be so fitted was *Jeanie
Deans*, built at the Fairfield yard in 1931 for
the LNER. Its design speed of 18 knots,
which was faster than the subsequent LMS
twins *Mercury* and *Caledonia* of 1934 and *Juno*
and *Jupiter* of 1937, was necessary in order to
compete with the LMS turbine *Duchess of
Montrose* on long-distance cruising.

Not all operators favoured triple-expansion machinery. P & A Campbell and Red
Funnel at Southampton both preferred the
simpler compound machinery. Southern
Railway stayed with compound machinery
for the magnificent pair of Isle of Wight
steamers *Southsea* and *Whippingham*, com-

It was not all plain
sailing. The Clyde
steamer *Duchess of Fife*
(1903) drying its
bottom plates on the
rocks at Kirn in August
1936, while *Marmion*
(1906) stands by.

Former ack-ack boat
Ryde (1937)
approaches the Royal
Pier at Southampton
on a Paddle Steamer
Preservation Society
charter excursion in
June 1969. (AUTHOR)

missioned in 1930, only accepting triple-expansion machinery in the next pair, *Sandown* of 1934 and *Ryde* of 1937.

Belle Steamers on the Thames invested heavily in the triple-expansion engine. *Clacton Belle* and *Woolwich Belle* had compound diagonal engines, but their five younger fleet mates, commencing with *London Belle* of 1893 and ending with the *Southwold Belle* of 1900, all had triple-expansion machinery. GSN's *Golden Eagle*, delivered by John Brown & Company of Clydebank in 1909, was one of the first to have a triple-expansion three-crank engine. Thames steamers traditionally kept the navigation bridge aft of the funnel; the first to break this rule was the Medway Steam Packet Company's *City of Rochester*, built in 1904, with bridge forward of the funnel and both bridge and funnel forward of the paddle wheels.

The very first paddle steamer built with boilers fuelled not by coal but by fuel oil was GSN's *Crested Eagle*, delivered by J Samuel White at Cowes in time for the 1925 season. Other steamers were subsequently converted to burn oil.

The ultimate Thames steamer design was *Royal Eagle*, although owner GSN nearly opted for a motor ship instead of a paddle steamer. There was considerable investigation of motive power before the design of *Royal Eagle* was finalised. Consideration of screw propulsion and direct-drive diesel engines was in the end given up in favour of steam and paddles. This decision hinged on the confined seaways the ship used, and the known ability of the paddle steamer to cope with the difficult conditions at the exposed pier-head berths in the Thames estuary. *Royal Eagle* was the last of all the Thames paddlers to be built, the first to have observation lounges and a sun deck, and the only Thames pleasure steamer to be built by Cammell Laird at Birkenhead. The bridge was still behind the funnel, and this was intended to assist conning the ship astern through Tower Bridge into the congested waters of the Pool. She was otherwise innovative in that she had forced draught oil-fired Scotch boilers feeding triple-expansion engines.

Royal Eagle, with accommodation for 2,000 passengers, was the most luxurious vessel on the Thames. Its lounges and other public rooms were fitted-out to a very high

SUBJECT TO ALTERATION

1937 AUGUST & SEPTEMBER PROGRAMME

1937 No. 5

"EAGLE" STEAMERS

Excellent
BREAKFASTS
LUNCHEONS
& TEAS
(fully licensed)

Book at the Piers or
in advance at
Company's Offices or
at principal Travel or
Motor Coach Agencies

Office at—
15, TRINITY Sq., E.C.3
Open 7 a.m. to 10 p.m.

(left margin, vertical) Excellent BREAKFASTS leaving Tower Pier 2.30 p.m.

(left margin, vertical, lower) Afternoon Cruises through London's Docks on Weds., Thurs. and Sats. in August and also 1st, 2nd, 4th, 9th, 11th, 16th & 18th September leaving Tower Pier 2.30 p.m.

(right margin, vertical) For particulars of day return trips to Ostend, Calais or Boulogne, and afternoon trips to Gravesend on Suns., Mons., and Tues.—see special handbills

LONDON to—

SOUTHEND, HERNE BAY, MARGATE, RAMSGATE, CLACTON, WALTON, FELIXSTOWE, LOWESTOFT, GORLESTON & YARMOUTH

(WEATHER AND OTHER CIRCUMSTANCES PERMITTING.)

Passengers are only carried on the Terms and Conditions printed on the Company's Tickets—see overleaf.

DAILY SERVICES (Excepting Fridays)

Book to MARK LANE STATION (Underground) for TOWER PIER

SOUTHEND, CLACTON, WALTON, Etc.

Pier.	†"QUEEN OF SOUTHEND" Time.	†"LAGUNA BELLE" Time.	†"CRESTED EAGLE" Time.
TOWER		8.30 a.m.	9.20 a.m.
GREENWICH	8. 0 a.m.	9. 0 ,,	9.50 ,,
N. WOOLWICH	8.30 ,,	9.30 ,,	10.15 ,,
Gravesend (West)	10. 0 ,,		
Southend	11. 0 ,,		Noon
Clacton	1.15 p.m.	1.45 p.m.	2. 0 p.m.
Walton	2. 0 ,,	arr. 2.50 ,,	—
Felixstowe	arr. 2.45 ,,		
Clacton	3.50 p.m.		
Lowestoft	7.30 ,,		
Gorleston	8.15 ,,		
Yarmouth	8.30 ,,		
Yarmouth	9.40 a.m.		
Gorleston	9.55 ,,		
Lowestoft	10.45 ,,		
Clacton	2.50 p.m.		
Felixstowe	dep. 2.50 p.m.	—	—
Walton	3.30 ,,	dep. 2.50 p.m.	—
Clacton	4.15 ,,	3.30 ,,	4.30 p.m.
Southend	6.15 ,,	—	6.15 ,,
Gravesend	7.30 ,,		
N. WOOLWICH	8.45 ,,	7.30 ,,	8.15 ,,
GREENWICH	9.15 ,,	8. 0 ,,	8.45 ,,
TOWER		8.30 ,,	9.15 ,,

(note in table area) Lowestoft, Gorleston and Yarmouth Service by P/S "Essex Queen," until 5th Sept. Passengers to and from London change at Clacton.

SOUTHEND, HERNE BAY, MARGATE, RAMSGATE, Etc.

Pier.	†"GOLDEN EAGLE" Time	†"ROYAL EAGLE" Time
TOWER	8. 0 a.m.	9. 0 a.m.
GREENWICH	8.30 ,,	9.30 ,,
N. WOOLWICH	9. 0 ,,	10. 0 ,,
Tilbury		11. 5 ,,
Southend	10.45 ,,	12. 0 noon
Herne Bay (Change at Southend)	12.30 p.m.	
Felixstowe (,, ,, ,,) arr. 2.45 ,,		
Felixstowe (,, ,, ,,) dep. 2.50 ,,		
Margate	12.45 ,,	2. 0 p.m.
Ramsgate	* (arr.)	2.45 ,,
Ramsgate	* (dep.)	2.50 ,,
Margate	4.30* ,,	3.45 ,,
Herne Bay (Change at Southend)	4.30 ,,	
Southend	6.30* ,,	5.45 ,,
TILBURY		6.45 ,,
N. WOOLWICH	8.30 ,,	7.45 ,,
GREENWICH	9. 0 ,,	8.15 ,,
TOWER	9.30 ,,	8.45 ,,

*On and after 31st July the "Golden Eagle" will run to Ramsgate on Saturdays only, returning from there 2.30 p.m., Margate 3.30 p.m.
Southend 5.30 p.m.

† NOTE :— FOR AMENDED SEPTEMBER TIMETABLES AND DATES OF LAST SAILINGS SEE OVERLEAF.

Through Bookings (except Bank Holidays) from Fenchurch Street Station, St. Pancras Kentish Town and intermediate stations to join the Steamer at Tilbury Pier Obtain special handbills giving times of departure and through fares at L.M.S. Stations or the Company's Offices.

FARES FROM LONDON

Children under 3 years of age free
under 14 half price

	"QUEEN OF SOUTHEND"	"LAGUNA BELLE"	"CRESTED EAGLE"	"GOLDEN EAGLE"	"ROYAL EAGLE"
Day Return *Mon., Tues., Wed., Thurs.	SOUTHEND 3/- CLACTON 4/- WALTON 5/- FELIXSTOWE 5/6	CLACTON 4/- WALTON 5/-	SOUTHEND 4/- CLACTON 6/-	SOUTHEND 3/- HERNE BAY 4/- MARGATE 4/6 FELIXSTOWE 5/6	SOUTHEND 4/- MARGATE 8/- RAMSGATE 9/-
Day Return Saturday and Sunday	Sat. Sun. SOUTHEND 4/- 4/- CLACTON 4/- 5/- WALTON 5/- 6/6 FELIXSTOWE 5/6 7/-	Sat. Sun. CLACTON 4/- 5/- WALTON 5/- 6/6	SOUTHEND 5/- CLACTON Sat. 6/- ,, Sun. 8/-	SOUTHEND 4/- HERNE BAY Sat. 4/6; Sun. 6/- MARGATE Sat. 5/- Sun. 8/- RAMSGATE Sat. only 8/- FELIXSTOWE Sat.5/6, Sun.7/-	SOUTHEND 5/- MARGATE 10/- RAMSGATE 11/-
Period Return	SOUTHEND 5/- CLACTON 7/6 WALTON 9/- FELIXSTOWE 9/6	CLACTON 7/6 WALTON 9/- LOWESTOFT 12/6 GORLESTON or YARMOUTH 14/-	SOUTHEND 5/- CLACTON 9/-	SOUTHEND 4/- HERNE BAY 6/- MARGATE 9/- Sat. 7/6 FELIXSTOWE 9/6 RAMSGATE 8/- Sat. only	SOUTHEND 5/- MARGATE 10/- RAMSGATE 11/-
Single	SOUTHEND 3/- CLACTON 5/6 WALTON 6/- FELIXSTOWE 6/6	CLACTON 5/6 WALTON 6/- LOWESTOFT 8/6 GORLESTON or YARMOUTH 9/6	SOUTHEND 3/- CLACTON 5/6	SOUTHEND 3/- HERNE BAY 5/- MARGATE 6/- FELIXSTOWE or RAMSGATE 6/6	SOUTHEND 3/- MARGATE 6/- RAMSGATE 6/6

FOR CIRCULAR BOAT AND RAIL ISSUES—SEE OVER.

DAY PASSENGERS TO FELIXSTOWE AND RAMSGATE DO NOT LAND, NOR DAY PASSENGERS TO WALTON PER "LAGUNA BELLE."
No Luggage allowed to Day-Trip Passengers. * All Bank Holiday Day-Return fares at Saturday Day-Return fares.
The Supplementary charge for use of Sun Deck on "Royal Eagle" 1/- for the single journey, 1/6 return; payable on board.
A varied Musical Programme is provided on all Steamers by Special Band Repeater Equipment.

THE GENERAL STEAM NAVIGATION CO., LTD., 15, TRINITY SQUARE, LONDON, E.C.3. Tel. Royal 3200. Ext. 128.

The concealed paddle boxes of the Clyde steamer *Caledonia* (1934) reflect the contemporary Art Deco mood. (AUTHOR)

The LNER's Clyde 'steamer' *Talisman* (1935) was the first of the diesel-electric paddlers. (DONALD B MACCULLOCH)

standard, and the dining rooms, which could seat 300, were serviced by a catering staff of 70. Eagle Steamers (GSN) themed its vessels to suit family tastes. *Royal Eagle* was marketed as 'London's Own Luxury Liner', *Crested Eagle* was the 'Greyhound of the River' and *Golden Eagle* was always 'The Happy Ship'. It was not uncommon for King Neptune to hold his Court on the afterdeck of *Golden Eagle*.

In the late 1930s GSN had an identity problem, with its mix of black hulled paddle steamers and all-white-liveried motor excursion vessels. *Royal Eagle* went through seasonal changes, having a corn-coloured hull for the 1935 season and being all white in 1939 in an attempt to give it a modern 'motor steamer'-type appearance.

A similar design feature, also relating to identity, started to creep in during the 1930s in the form of the concealed paddle box. The Denny-built *Caledonia* and the Fairfield-built *Mercury* were first to be so equipped, and also had cruiser sterns instead

of the customary counter stern. This was all part of the streamlining theme of the period Art Deco movement, and gave the steamers the appearance of screw vessels when viewed from the beam. On deck was a rectangular box and, below, the choke water escapes from the paddle boxes were shaped like saloon windows. Gone were the offline curves of the traditional paddle box and the symmetrical vents; gone, too, were any ornamental embellishments.

The motor paddle 'steamer' also appeared. This was represented singularly by DEPV *Talisman* (DEPV standing for diesel electric paddle vessel), built for the Caigendoran based LNER Clyde fleet at Pointhouse by Inglis and launched in April 1935 by Evelyn Whitelaw, the daughter of the LNER chairman. The LNER relied on shallow-draft paddlers to access the pier at the Craigendoran railhead, and the move to diesel power was probably a statement of modernity by the LNER directors.

Talisman had four diesel engines, each driving a direct-current generator that produced propulsive power coupled in tandem with an auxiliary service generator. These sets had been specially developed for propelling the LMS Railway's first diesel shunting locomotives. *Talisman* was totally unique in that its main propulsion motor was rigidly fixed to the paddle shaft without the introduction of gearing or chain drive, and produced around 1,300bhp at 50rpm. Derived from a steelworks' plate-rolling-mill drive, the motor was usually referred to as a twin-armature, but was in effect two motors contained in a single housing. They were rigidly connected to each other and to the paddle shaft. The paddles could not be rotated independently as the then Board of Trade Marine Survey Department would not permit independent rotation on passenger carrying ships unless under very particular and controlled circumstances. The diesel generator sets were connected in series such that the motor could take power from one, two, three or all four sets. The vessel's speed was 17 knots with all four sets in supply. Everything on board – lighting, heating and

cooking – was electric; there were no coal-fired stoves in this 'steamer'. Traditionalists were not pleased, and dubbed the new ship the 'clockwork mouse'. A rather disgruntled George Stromier wrote in *Scottish Field* magazine:

> Happily the designers did not resort to the disguised paddle box cult which had crept into the fleet the previous year, but the *Talisman* was given a none too graceful hull and an ugly cruiser stern, while the customary rail forward was replaced by a solid bulwark. The single funnel was flat-sided and had a quaint gadget, for all the world like a giant tiddlywink, on top, 'to cut out the noise of the diesels', it was said. Unfortunately it did not.

The ineffective tiddlywink, in truth a navy cowl, was removed in 1936. And when *Talisman* went to war in 1940 one of the LNER superintendents was heard to say: 'And let you no come back home again', but it did, and remained in service on the Clyde until the end of the 1966 season.

The main instrument board was situated next to the motor room and, as in the steamers, passengers could observe what was going on, only in this case it was in terms of the revolutions, electric current and power that were being produced. The fuel consumption of *Talisman*, compared with the conventional paddle steamer of the same name, which the diesel-electric ship replaced, was about one-eighth of the equivalent calorific value of the fuel required by the steamer on a like-for-like voyage. *Talisman* of 1896 was a vessel of the same length, but of slightly less displacement than the new ship.

A rather nice renaming of an elderly paddler steamer was instigated by the Cunard Line when its transatlantic liner *Mauretania* was withdrawn in 1935 and sold for demolition. As names cannot be protected by an owner other than by a current registration, Cunard approached Red Funnel Steamers to ask if it might rename one of its lesser units to protect the name *Mauretania*.

Red Funnel was delighted, and duly re-named its venerable excursion steamer *Queen*, dating from 1902, with the new Cunard affiliation. When the new *Mauretania* was under construction at Cammell Laird's yard at Birkenhead in 1937, the paddler relinquished its Cunard title and adopted the name *Corfe Castle* for its last year of service before it was sold for demolition.

With the paddle steamer under threat from turbine steamers, notably on the Clyde, and now also from the motor ship, one new technological development appeared towards the end of the 1930s. This was the German Voith-Schneider propeller system, which bears a certain resemblance to a feathering paddle wheel placed on its side and fully immersed beneath the ship. The propulsor is a cycloidal drive and consists of a large horizontal rotating disk (like a small paddle wheel) mounted on a vertical shaft, to which are attached a circular array of vertical stainless steel blades or vanes (a bit like paddle floats) of aerofoil section, and each blade can itself rotate around its vertical axis. The speed of rotation of the disk, along with the area of the blades, determines the propulsive thrust and the resultant speed of the ship. This is accomplished by very complex epicyclic gearing that alters the angle of attack of the blades in synchronisation with the rotation of the disk. A ship can be stopped and go either forward, backward or sideways and, indeed, in any direction through 360 degrees by the almost instantaneous change of thrust direction. By judicious small changes in the angle of thrust, when a ship is in full forward mode, steering and course keeping are effected.

Three ships were built with Voith-Schneider equipment for British owners in the lead up to the Second World War. The first was the Red Funnel Isle of Wight ferry *Vecta* commissioned in 1938, the second was *Lymington* for the Southern Railway, and the third was *Abercraig* for the Tay ferry crossing. All three could accommodate cars and light vehicles as well as passengers. All three suffered repeated mechanical failure in the war through lack of spares, so much so that *Vecta*

was laid up in 1942 and re-engined with diesel-electric drive in 1946.

These pioneers were nevertheless the start of yet another technical change. In due course, as parts became available during the 1950s, they proved highly successful, providing vessels with even greater manoeuvrability than conventional paddles ever could. In the immediate post-war period Southern Railway needed new tonnage on the Isle of Wight routes, and would have repeated Voith-Schneider equipment had it been possible to maintain the units aboard *Lymington* properly during the war years, and had units been available. The consequence was another diesel-electric paddler, *Farringford*, a product of Denny at Dumbarton and launched in March 1947. *Farringford* had twin diesels, generators and motors driving the paddles independently. The new ferry had concealed paddle boxes set within sponsons extending along the full length of the ship, almost making the statement, 'Look at me, I'm not really a paddle steamer at all!'

Operator P & A Campbell had come out of the war with a vastly depleted fleet. Five of its eleven paddle steamers had been lost in action, and two more were scrapped in 1946 as unfit for repair. It had ordered the big turbine steamer *Empress Queen* before the war to service the no-passport cross-Channel trips, and as these were not allowed after the war until the mid 1950s it became something of a red herring. Indeed, it spent so long laid up alongside the print works of one Bristol-based newspaper that the image of the ship alongside the works was incorporated into the newspaper's masthead!

Replacement tonnage was ordered as soon as wartime restrictions were lifted, and an order was placed with the local Bristol yard of Charles Hill & Sons for a fast triple-expansion-engined paddle steamer to be named *Bristol Queen*. It was engined by Rankin & Blackmore of Greenock, who also engined the current *Waverley*. This was the first of an ambitious four-ship order, the second contract being awarded to Fairfield

Shipbuilding & Engineering on the Clyde, who started work on the slightly smaller *Cardiff Queen*. *Bristol Queen* emerged in time to start the final sailings of the 1946 season on the Bristol Channel, and was joined by *Cardiff Queen* in time for the start of the 1947 season. They were handsome steamers, despite being adorned with concealed paddle boxes. Each carried two well-proportioned white funnels, and the deck saloons were picked out in French grey paint against the pure white paint of the hulls to sponson level. Once they were in operation the company announced the cancellation of plans to complete the proposed building of a quartet of steamers.

The Bristol Channel steamers were essentially conservative in design. This reflected a conviction that only a paddle steamer could operate successfully in the confines of the Bristol Channel and its various piers, some with shallow approaches. In truth, the two 'Queens' were to become an operator's nightmare, with expensive maintenance bills and hiked fuel-oil costs exacerbated by the fact that the boilers, unlike those of the diesel-electric paddler, could not be switched off overnight. Nevertheless, as time went on and fewer and fewer paddle steamers remained in service, the Bristol twins became an enthusiast's paradise and acquired a considerable following.

One more big paddle steamer was built after the war. This was the coal-fired triple-expansion-engined steamer *Waverley*, built by A & J Inglis for the LNER for summer excursions and ferry duties as a replacement for its namesake, lost at Dunkirk. It was built to a traditional, almost conservative, pre-war design. Its completion as a coal-burner simply reflected the lack of availability of suitable equipment, and it was converted to burn oil fuel during the winter of 1956/7. Like *Cardiff Queen* and *Bristol Queen*, the new *Waverley* soon became increasingly attractive as its peers were withdrawn. It was considerably disfigured in 1961 and 1962 when replacement funnels were installed in consecutive winters, sadly fitted with a different rake to

each other and giving the old vessel an eccentric look.

That was that. Apart from *Maid of the Loch*, completed for service on Loch Lomond in 1953, and a small car and passenger ferry, *Cleddau Queen*, built for the Pembroke Dock crossing in 1956, the paddle steamer, be it on ferry, commuter or excursion duties, fell into decline in UK waters. One by one the older steamers became uneconomic and too expensive to get through surveys, and one by one they were withdrawn and scrapped. Some operators took on discarded vessels. Cosens in Dorset built its last steamer in 1901, and with its low margins the seasonal excursion operator relied solely on the secondhand market thereafter. For example, the Red Funnel steamer *Princess Royal* was completed in 1906 by Thorneycroft but failed to meet the contract specifications on trials, and in service worked for its owner for only two weeks. Returned to the builder for modifications, specifically lengthening of the hull to increase deadweight and draft as well as speed, it was again put through its paces. At this stage Red Funnel demanded its money back, and the ship was resold to Cosens & Company and renamed *Emperor of India*.

The Cosens post-Second World War fleet thus comprised three elderly purpose-built steamers and three ageing secondhand purchases:

Monarch, built 1888, scrapped 1949
Victoria, built 1884, scrapped 1952
Empress, built 1879, scrapped 1955
Emperor of India, built 1906, acquired 1908, scrapped 1956
Consul, built 1896, acquired 1938, sold 1962 (scrapped 1968)
Embassy, built 1911, acquired 1937, scrapped 1966

Cosens also acquired a 'new' *Monarch* in 1951, after Red Funnel bought a significant financial interest in Cosens in 1946 to generate income in the excursion traffic, without unnecessary competition in a depressed

post-war market. *Monarch* had been built for the Southern Railway as the Isle of Wight ferry *Shanklin* in 1924, and Cosens eventually sold it for scrap in 1960. Each post-war disposal was the result of an ageing ship that could no longer pay its way in maintenance and statutory upgrades. In every case the business plan was one of inevitable and terminal decline, with no prospect of capital for investment in new ships. But it was also a sound business plan, as the disposal of the fleet, little by little, paralleled the declining demand for excursion services as recreational needs turned to new and more exciting activities focussed largely on the family car and the decline of the traditional seaside holiday.

After the post-war rush of building P & A Campbell's two 'Queens', the LNER steamer *Waverley* and the diesel-electric paddle ferry *Farringford*, news of any more new orders dried up. No more major paddle units were built thereafter for seagoing service in UK waters, although *Maid of the Loch* graced Loch Lomond from 1953 onwards (see Chapter 7). The key issue now was that the paddle steamers were ageing as time passed, and in each and every case it was

harder and more expensive to satisfy the Board of Trade that the ships actually deserved a passenger certificate. The owners parted with significant cash during each maintenance and survey, but there were insufficient funds to deal with major work as it arose. The economic savings from diesel and screw propulsion became increasingly compelling and, with declining patronage, the writing was on the wall for the paddlers.

The decade up to 1956 saw the withdrawal of 24 British passenger paddle steamers, all of which were sold for scrap. Although most of these were ageing vessels for which money was not available to keep them afloat, one or two big and modern steamers went under the ship breakers' torches. GSN withdrew and eventually scrapped the big and relatively modern *Royal Eagle* simply because its post-war replacement programme of motor ships had given the company an embarrassing over-capacity on its Thames services. The British Transport Commission similarly found that its relatively small but modern paddle steamer *Marchioness of Lorne,* known affectionately as wee *Lorne,* was no longer required when the much more economical *Maid*-class motor vessels entered service from 1953. When tried on the Wemyss Bay

to Millport service it was found to be too slow and was withdrawn from service. Sadly, no buyers were willing to take on these fine ships and extend their careers.

The decade to 1966 was even more critical, a further 28 paddle steamers being withdrawn and scrapped. One of these was the third of a three-ship act that was the mainstay of the River Dart Steamboat Company's Dartmouth and Totnes excursion fleet. The first retirement was the oldest of the three, *Compton Castle,* which went in 1962, next was *Totnes Castle* in 1963 and finally *Kingswear Castle* went in 1966.

While the first two were sold for static use, *Kingswear Castle* was sold to the Waverley Steam Navigation Company for £600 and lovingly renovated by enthusiasts from the associated Paddle Steamer Preservation Society. This little steamer remains in excursion use to this day, working in the Medway and lower Thames area during the summer months. It is the very last coal-fired compound-engined paddler in service in UK waters, its engines predating the ship by some twenty years, having been transferred from an earlier *Kingswear Castle* of 1904.

Bristol Queen retired in 1967, following the earlier withdrawal of running mate *Cardiff Queen.* Also in 1967 the old Clyde

The river steamer *Compton Castle* (1914) stood down for static use on tea-shop duties at Kingsbridge in July 1965.

The former LNER Clyde steamer *Jeanie Deans* (1931) ended its commercial life running excursions from London as *Queen of the South*, and is seen here at Southend; a great idea but a financial nightmare. (AUTHOR)

Wingfield Castle (1934) off Hull Victoria Pier in January 1969. (AUTHOR)

favourite *Jeanie Deans* gave up work on the Thames in its final role as the excursion steamer *Queen of the South*. In 1969 it was the turn of the Portsmouth to Ryde ferry *Ryde* and the Clyde steamer with the concealed paddle boxes, *Caledonia*, to retire. Neither went quietly; one rotted away in a backwater, the other burnt out alongside the Embankment in London while in use as a floating restaurant. Thus by 1970 there remained *Waverley*, the sole surviving paddle steamer on the Clyde; three coal-fired car and passenger ferries on the Humber dating

from the 1930s, the *Wingfield, Tattershall* and *Lincoln Castles*; the diesel-electric Isle of Wight ferry *Farringford*; plus *Maid of the Loch* and *Kingswear Castle*.

The Humber ferry paddlers were designed to cope with the muddy shallows of the 20-minute crossing between Hull and New Holland Pier. It was just long enough to allow passengers to go down to the small wood-panelled tea room, a cosy warm and often smoky contrast to the chill air out on deck. In the early days the steamers used to carry Lincolnshire produce to market in

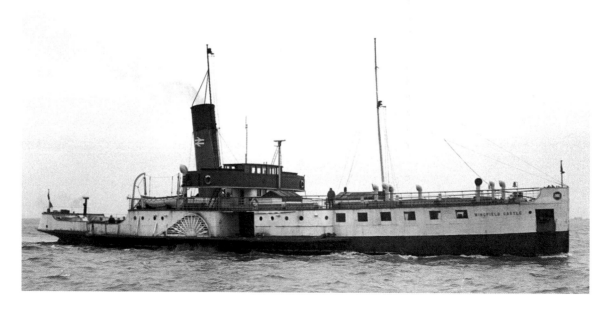

Hull. There was consternation one day in the late 1930s when a cow fell down the steep companionway to the crew's quarters in one of the ferries and the Kingston-upon-Hull Fire Brigade had to be summoned to assist in removing her.

The final strategy was to keep the three cross-Humber paddlers going until the planned completion of the New Humber Road Bridge, in the event much-delayed and eventually opened in 1981. But this was not to be. *Tattershall Castle* suffered boiler problems that were not worthy of repair, and *Lincoln Castle* failed a boiler inspection in 1973. The boiler aboard *Wingfield Castle* was also a concern, and it was withdrawn and the service 'dieselised' in 1974 when the Isle of Wight paddle ferry *Farringford* was brought round to the Humber. The diesel-electric paddler had its end ramps replaced by side ramps to serve the last few years of the Humber crossing. It was eventually scrapped where it lay in Hull in 1984.

So far, the story of *Waverley* is a happier one. Sold by Caledonian MacBrayne to the Paddle Steamer Preservation Society in 1974 for a token £1, it has since been care-fully renovated and upgraded to satisfy increasingly demanding statutory requirements to qualify for its passenger cert-ificate. Like *Kingswear Castle*, *Waverley*, now the UK's last seagoing paddle steamer, operates a seasonal programme of day cruises and excursions. Unlike the smaller river steamer, which stays near the River Med-way, *Waverley* operates a complex summer schedule that encompasses the Western Isles, Firth of Clyde, Bristol Channel, South Coast and the Thames. Sadly, it is no longer allowed to go either to the Republic of Ireland or the Isle of Man, as these are now considered to be 'foreign' voyages. To-gether, *Waverley* and *Kingswear Castle* main-tain an important link with the maritime heritage of Great Britain. Renovation is also ongoing on the former Thames steamer and Dunkirk veteran *Medway Queen*, but so much of the fabric of this ship is being reconstructed that it may only be a replica of a once-proud steamer. Be that as it may, it is important that these steamers are patronised as their upkeep is by no means trivial; their future is very much a case of 'use it or lose it'.

The former Isle of Wight ferry *Farringford* (1947) with end ramps removed and new side-loading ramps added while serving on the Hull-to-New Holland ferry in August 1974. (AUTHOR)

Eulogy of the Glasgow & South Western Railway steamer *Mars* of 1902

Song of a River Steamer by J J Bell, first published in *The Evening Times* and reprinted in J J Bell's *Clyde Songs and Other Verses* in 1910

I know the Clyde in its summer pride
And eke in its winter gloom;
I know what it is to carry good biz
And nothing but plenty of room;
I know the thousands who sail for fun,
The hundreds depending on me –
And in black o' the night or in blaze o' the sun
I'm as handsome a craft as you'll see!

Travellers watching my engines go,
Folk in my fine saloon,
Passengers pale in a Januar' gale
Or under an August moon,
Ladies sunning themselves on deck,
Gents with their choice cigars –
They all can feel they are quite genteel
Aboard the magnificent *Mars*!

In summer's tide, as you watch me glide
So prettily through the Kyles,
You never would guess that I've felt the stress
Of weather in various styles,
But, bless your soul! You should see me roll
And heave in a sou'-west sea,
With squalls a-crying and spindrift flying
All over magnificent Me!

Watch me trying the pier at Strone,
All for a lady's sake –
Risking a smash for threepence in cash
And looks that would give you an ache.
Hear the creak of my ropes pulled taut –
Wrung and tuned with the strain!
'Ear them snap with a horrible slap!
And . . . *watch me trying again!*

But now are the days when the Firth displays
Its peace and its happiest hues;
And now are the nights for the mixed delights
Of the popular evening cruise.
My skipper and crew are often in blue,
And seldom in glistening black –
And you needn't grow pale at the thought of a sail
To Kames in the Kyles and back!

Capable stewards attend below,
A band performs above –
The former's food is uncommonly good,
The latter's may do for love.
But whether you sail with pleasure or woe,
Under the sun or the stars,
You always feel you are quite genteel
Aboard the magnificent *Mars*.

13 IN THE WAKE OF *COMET* AND *CLERMONT*

The coming of the *Comet*, and, for that matter, the coming of *Clermont/Steam Boat*, had an incredibly important impact on the western world. Just as the internet has revolutionised communication in our lives over the last twenty years, so the humble paddle steamer revolutionised communication in the 1820s and continued to do so unchallenged for the next thirty years. The paddle steamer provided more or less scheduled sea services between coastal ports, across the Atlantic and Pacific and along inland waterways, most notably in North America. This helped to maintain communications with Empire, develop trade and boost national economies. The arrival of the paddle steamer, unreliable and erratic as it was in those early days, was timely. It supported the demands of industrial growth in Britain and Europe during the peace that followed the war with France. The Industrial Revolution provided industry with its essential steam-driven machinery; the paddle steamer provided the potential for commerce.

The impact of the steamship before 1850, and its important role in expanding the shipping market, was described by Basil Greenhill in his book *The Ship: The Life and Death of the Merchant Sailing Ship, 1815-1965*. Greenhill says that, before 1850:

> the steamer provided entirely new services on short range, high density, passenger routes, assisted the sailing vessel as a tug, and as a subsidised mail and passenger carrier on the Atlantic and eastern routes, provided a service which did not exist before.

Sarah Palmer, in an article in *The Journal of Transport History*, September 1982, expanded this theme:

The early history of steam shipping has received little attention from maritime historians except by way of contrast with steam's later spectacular development or as a means of demonstrating the resilience of the sailing ship ... nineteenth century British shipping history puts most stress on distant trades, despite the fact that the near and coastal trades provided most employment for shipping. It also reflects a curious interpretative bias where the degree to which steam supplants sail is regarded as the test of its economic, rather than technological, importance. . . . the steamship is of . . . interest . . . because its introduction represented an extension of the market for shipping services.

The story of the early paddle steamer is uniquely Anglo-American. It starts with experimental steamers, of which Fulton's *Clermont* and Henry Bell's *Comet* were of the first to gain commercial success. The paddle steamer rose in status as the transport vehicle in the heady days following the Industrial Revolution. It soon became the key link with Empire, pushing the Honourable East India Company's wooden walls off the seas, and it was not long before it provided the all-important link with the Americas. These were the days when Britain led the world in maritime technology and naval engineering, followed ever closely by America, with its experimentation in paddle steamer design.

The paddle steamer quickly evolved to provide a quick and relatively comfortable alternative to the notorious bumpy ride of the stagecoach, both in Europe and America. In so doing it greatly improved communications, as well as the potential for travel and the exchange of goods between coastal towns. The emphasis in America was also on using the many broad and navigable waterways as highways, and specialist steamers, many with stern-wheel drive rather than side wheels, were developed to ply the Mississippi, the Hudson and many of the other great American rivers. The Great Lakes also provided an opportunity for a network of fast and prestigious services to be developed, many of which were overnight inter-city services. These, in turn, promoted rapid growth of lakeside towns and cities in the 1830s and 1840s. This same 'drive west' through the Lakes enabled the great western plains of America to be developed for both the arable potential and the rich mineral wealth they possessed. The Great Lakes story highlights the immense role played by the paddle steamer in the growth of the USA, bringing forward the development of the western states by at least 40 years.

The difference between European and American steamer development was highlighted in an article published in *The Illustrated London News* in July 1861:

> The American vessels are nearly all running long passages on an even keel and in comparatively smooth waters, their rivers, lakes, and great sounds and estuaries being of that character; while in England we have scarcely any long journeys to make by water unless we cross either of the Channels or the North Sea, in which case the vessel, though she start from London Bridge, must be in every respect such a sufficient sea boat that she could cross the great Atlantic itself, for none can tell but that, in her little voyage to Boulogne or Calais, Rotterdam or Hull, she may have to encounter weather as bad as, if not worse than, any she might fall in with in a passage to New York.

But the paddle steamers' pivotal role in wealth creation during the nineteenth century cannot be overstated. In Britain, as elsewhere, the new creaky and smoky machines were at first regarded as a threat to the jobs of the Thames watermen and others like them, but were soon seen as the way forward. Indeed, by the 1850s, when the early screw propeller was coming into transatlantic favour, many passengers preferred the tried and tested and the relative smoothness of the paddle wheel. Geoffrey Body wrote in his book about British paddle steamers:

> Paddle steamers, by offering cheaper and more convenient travel than stage coaches, stimulated commerce between our coastal towns and between Great Britain and other countries. Before the paddle steamer there was no sort of reliability to the overseas news or mail and importing and exporting were at the mercy of wind and tide. All the early ocean steamers were paddle vessels. They helped to bring down fares and reduce freight rates with beneficial effects upon the trade, and thus the prosperity and wellbeing, of the British people.

There were constraints on the paddlers' development. The greatest of these was the ultra-conservatism of the Admiralty and the total lack of support given to technical progress by Their Lordships in the early nineteenth century. Why should a navy so supreme bother with technical improvement? 'It is up to lesser navies to attend to that if they should so desire.' Another major constraint, of course, was the volume and pressure of steam available from the early boilers. A wheelbarrow of finest farmyard manure was prescribed for repairing cracks in the early boilers, placed inside the boiler before getting up steam. The organic mess was assured to seal any leak. But the remedy only held true until the 1850s, after which boiler engineering became a little more sophisticated.

The coming of the *Comet* was indeed the start of a revolution. Henry Bell's disciples are legion. The Burns brothers, Laird, Napier, Cunard, Denny and all the others could not have guessed that Bell's simple concept of providing transport to carry punters from Glasgow down the Clyde to the family-run hydropathic resort at Helens-

Well done Mr Henry Bell! Extract from the British Government White Paper dated 12 June 1822, prepared by the Select Committee appointed to investigate the carriage of His Majesty's Mail between London and Dublin

It was not till the year 1807, when the Americas began to use steamboats on their rivers, that their safety and utility was first proved. But the whole merit of constructing these boats is due to natives of Great Britain: Mr Henry Bell, of Glasgow, gave the first model of them to Mr Fulton . . . to assist him in establishing them; and Mr Fulton got the engines he used in his first steam boat on the Hudson River from Messrs Bolton and Watt.

Mr Bell continued to turn his talents to the improving of steam apparatus, and its application in various manufactures about Glasgow; and in 1811 constructed the *Comet* steam boat, of 25 tons, with an engine of 4 horse power, to navigate the Clyde between Glasgow and the Helensburgh Baths . . . The success of this experiment led to the construction of several steam boats, by other persons, of larger dimensions and of greater steaming power; these having superseded Mr Bell's small boat on the Clyde, it was enlarged, and established as a regular packet between Glasgow and the western end of the Caledonian Canal at Fort William, by way of the Crinan Canal in Argyleshire. Mr Bell about the same time constructed the *Stirling Castle* steam boat, and employed her on the River Forth, between Leith and Stirling. He afterwards took her to Inverness where she has been for two years plying between that town and Fort Augustus, going 7 miles by the Caledonian Canal and 23 miles along Loch Ness.

Many other boats were successfully established about this time on the Forth and Clyde, and several on the rivers Tay, Thames, Mersey and Humber, and between Southampton and the Isle of Wight. It was not till the year 1818 that a steam boat was made use of to perform regular voyages at sea. In this year the *Rob Roy*, of 90 tons, built by Denny of Dumbarton, and with an engine of 30 horse power, made by Mr Napier of Glasgow, plied regularly between Greenock and Belfast, and proved the practicability of extending the use of the steam engine to sea navigation.

One of Cunard's *Britannia*-class steamers, patronised by Charles Dickens and his young wife.

burgh would later develop into the mainline service to New York. Henry Bell's role as champion of marine engineering has to be put into the rightful context of his contemporaries in America and France. It is perhaps fairer to say that the various pioneers of the day, including Fulton and Bell, collectively turned the concept of mechanical propulsion at sea into reality, though we in Britain naturally favour the local man. Besides, a British Government White Paper dated 1822 gives sole credit to Bell 'for the first practical steamship'!

After Bell had lost his pioneer steamer at sea he still pursued his vision of the steamship. His efforts bankrupted him; indeed, he never repaid the mortgage on *Comet*'s boiler, and after his second steamship was sunk in collision, disillusioned and in poor health, Bell finally gave up. His efforts were rewarded by a Government gift of £100 and an annual stipend of £50 from the Clyde Navigation Trust. Bell had shown the determination to prove the commercial value of steam, but it was really Symington before him, with his various engine trials using *Charlotte Dundas*, who had the engineering skills that allowed Bell to progress. Needless to say, the Industrial Revolution now had the transport machine it needed, and industry was set to blossom.

And blossom it did. But Charles Dickens sums up the early long-distance sea traveller's fears. He was clearly nervous of 'Winter-North-Atlantic' when he boarded Cunard's wooden paddle steamer *Britannia* in Liverpool in January 1842. And well he might have been, as the following passage from his *American Notes* illustrates so aptly:

> God bless that stewardess for her piously fraudulent account of January voyages! God bless her for her clear recollection of the companion passage of last year, when nobody was ill, and everybody dancing from morning to night, and it was 'a run' of twelve days, and a piece of the purest frolic, and delight, and jollity! All happiness be with her for her bright face and her pleasant Scotch tongue, which had sounds of old Home in it for my fellow-traveller; and for her predictions of fair winds and fine weather (all wrong, or I shouldn't be half so fond of her); and for the ten thousand small fragments of genuine womanly tact, by which, without piecing them elaborately together, and patching them up into shape and form and case and pointed application, she nevertheless did plainly show that all young mothers on one side of the Atlantic were near and close at hand to their little children left upon the other.

The fear of the sea, pitching and rolling the little paddle steamers about, was not confined to the wooden paddle steamers on the Atlantic. It was also a problem for the small iron paddlers on the Dover Strait in later years, as people such as Bessemer made valiant attempts to design configurations that might provide a smooth crossing that even the most delicate of passenger might withstand. It was only with improved boiler design that larger volumes of steam at higher pressures could be generated, allowing more powerful engines to be built to drive ever larger and more stable hulls with greater displacement. Unhappily for the paddle steamer, that same development coincided with the ascendancy of screw propulsion.

Steam propulsion in the early days came at a heavy price, with regular boiler replacements and serious maintenance to engines. More efficient machinery that was easier to maintain was not available until the second half of the nineteenth century. The early economics are reflected in the *29th Report to the shareholders of GSN*, issued in August 1839:

> The expenses required to maintain steam ships in a proper state of efficiency and repair have been found to reach so large an annual amount that, of the numerous steam companies which have been formed, scarcely one has been found, upon a review of their operations for ten years, able to maintain for the average of that period, a dividend of 5%, consistently of a proper sum to the maintenance of their capital, while, in many instances, the operations have terminated in the sacrifice of almost the whole of the property embarked.

Sarah Palmer again:

> By the 1850s and 1860s improved technology [including screw propulsion] was to modify the enervating effects of cost on steamship development generally. But ... [before 1850] manifest improvements in the design of steamships, which increased in power and capacity, were not cost-reducing.
>
> Given the relative fixity of costs as a proportion of earnings, the success of

steamship enterprise depended on the ability to command a sufficient volume and value of trade [i.e. not bulk low-value goods such as coal or grain] to permit regular, frequent voyages with little spare capacity. This determined the routes on which steam vessels were put into service and the pace at which they supplemented or replaced the existing sailing connection.

The development of better, more thermally efficient, machinery finally increased the steamship margins so that operators could return a profit. That this turnaround in the economics of the steamship should only begin to occur in mid century was short-lived good news, for the long-distance paddle steamer was about to be financially undercut by the even more cost effective screw-propelled steamer.

But it was a long time before the screw steamer was literally able to overtake the paddler. The cross-Channel day services all retained paddle steamers until the end of the nineteenth century. Speeds of up to 21 knots were attained against William Denny's prophecy that 22 knots would always be un-obtainable (the engineering reason for his statement seems to have been lost in time, but had to do with turbulent water between the paddle floats possibly due to too close spacing). Denny perhaps forgot that 22 knots (or 25mph) was the standard then set for the big paddle steamers on the Great Lakes. Then, in 1893, the Belgians proved

him wrong, when the cross-Channel packet *Marie Henriette* recorded 22.2 knots on trials. The race for paddle speed came to an end when Charles Parsons's turbines took to the water, and a succession of direct-drive turbine steamers appeared on the Dover Strait and elsewhere from 1903 onwards.

In the days when land transport was still underdeveloped, transport along rivers and lakes was the only way to export the cotton crop from America's southern states or the oil from Burma's oilfields. For these duties the sternwheel paddle steamer was developed. The wheel was protected from damage by flotsam because it was situated behind the hull of the steamer. Sternwheel passenger and cargo steamers are synonymous with the Mississippi, where mighty sternwheel tugs also pushed arrays of barges up the stream. The sternwheeler progressed to the Murray and Darling rivers of Australia, the Congo and Nile rivers in Africa, the great rivers of the Russian empire and anywhere else where a river was navigable and the road and rail networks were poor.

The American coastal and river paddle steamers tended to be larger than their European counterparts. The Americans also favoured the walking-beam engine, in which the beam was above the cylinder, not below it as it was in the side-lever engine. Many photographs of American steamers show the top of the beam protruding above the deckhouse, a give-away that the ship was equipped with a walking-beam engine. The leaders in the nineteenth century were the

'The fastest steamer on the Hudson River'. *Mary Powell* (1861), from a contemporary engraving.

The Clyde favourite *Lucy Ashton* (1888) at Craigendoran Pier. It was originally a member of the North British Railway fleet, and its career spanned 60 years, including two world wars.

steamers on the Hudson River, such as '*Mary Powell*, the fastest on the river', and the steamers of the Fall River Line, although the big paddlers on the Great Lakes were not far behind.

The paddle steamer provided an easy way of communication on the Great Lakes between American and Canadian ports. The economics of the early Great Lakes steamers benefited hugely from the great land speculation of 1831 that encouraged a continual movement of people westwards. When *Hercules*, the first propeller steamer on the Lakes, was delivered in 1843 at Cleveland, it had to compete head-on with the established paddle steamers. The paddle steamers clearly gave a smoother ride than the early propeller-driven craft, but it was the sheer economy of the propeller ships that won the day. Although they were not as fast, they were cheaper to run with lower tariffs, which meant that little by little the propeller steamers eroded the traffic from the paddlers. The return match was the economy of scale thinking that led to the world's biggest and fastest paddle steamers being developed on the Lakes from the 1880s through to the 1920s. But the economic returns on these big and expensive ships slowly dwindled, many being converted for excursion use or retired prematurely. Of course, competition from railways was as ef-

fective on the Great Lakes as it was in all other parts of the world, and ultimately the cross-lake journey fell into decline, the end coming rapidly after the Second World War. Ironically, the war itself had boosted passenger traffic as gasoline rationing forced car owners to return to public transport, be it by land or water.

On the Italian and Swiss lakes, and even on Loch Lomond, paddle steamers were a popular option, albeit much smaller than their many American counterparts. The fresh-water environment of these steamers promoted longevity, and a life expectancy of fifty years and upwards was the norm. In virtually every case the steamer services were destabilised with the development of competition from newly opened railways, after which the salvation of the steamers was the arrival of tourists. Tourism, the great nineteenth-century curiosity for travel and sightseeing, saved the steamers on Lake Lucerne, the rivers Rhine and Nile and on just about every other inland waterway which still supports a paddle steamer, although nowadays many have anything other than a steam engine down below.

In the UK the Victorian delight of a sea cruise and back in time for tea had developed from local tugs taking passengers round the bay, to dedicated saloon steamers that offered passengers every luxury they

Red Funnel Steamers' *Bournemouth Queen* (1908) charmed holidaymakers on the South Coast, with a cross-subsidy from ferry ticket receipts and harbour tug operations, until finally withdrawn in 1958.

could want. Much of the running with this class of steamer took place on the Clyde, where numerous favourites such as *Lucy Ashton*, *Columba* or *Duchess of Fife* come to mind. But where the Clyde steamer fleets progressed today, so the Thames, South Coast and Bristol Channel operators followed tomorrow, with favourites such as Red Funnel's *Bournemouth Queen* and the

GSN *Eagles*. There was always a strong-secondhand market for Clyde steamers bent on a second career in the south, and ironically a second career for those canny Scots, Peter and Alex Campbell, as well. They moved from the competitive Clyde to the easier and more profitable excursion trade in the Bristol Channel in 1888, and sold the goodwill of the Glasgow to Holy Loch trade,

Meg Merrilies (1883) standing off the Broomielaw in Glasgow c. 1885, with *Benmore* (1876) centre, and alongside from right foreground to left distant *Chancellor* (1880), *Vivid* (1864) and *Eagle* (1864).

along with two of the paddle steamers, *Meg Merrilies* and *Madge Wildfire*, to the newly constituted Caledonian Steam Packet Company. The sale was conditional on Captain Peter Campbell staying with the new company for two years. But they never forgot their roots, even conjuring up charmed hybrid names for their Bristol Channel paddle steamers such as *Glen Avon*, *Glen Gower* and *Glen Usk*.

One of the social issues on a family day out was dad's comment sometime in the trip: 'I'm just going down to look at the engines.' The engine room and control platform were features that had been on display to passengers since the days when it was mandatory for the steam gauge and release valve to be on view and in reach. Dad might not loiter to watch the gleaming pistons and cranks, nor to smell the hot oil and steam, nor even to appreciate the rhythmic clatter of the engines for, sadly, dad was off to the bar. Drinking and rowdiness became an issue even on the little passenger tugs, and always remained so, particularly with works outings and other large social group excursions. One Scottish company coined in on this by introducing a teetotal ship, the paddler *Ivanhoe*, which sailed the waters of the Clyde without ever a dram passing the lips of her grateful passengers. The mums and the children were grateful, even if the dads were not quite so pleased. However, the first alteration when *Ivanhoe* was taken over by the Caledonian Company was the installation of a bar!

But the margins of the excursion ship operator were small even during the peak demand of the 1900s, when the Thames excursion trade was enjoying its halcyon years. This was the era of the famous 'husband's boat' which was timed to leave London or Gravesend with a train connection, allowing the husbands to finish work at midday on Saturday and arrive at Margate by steamer in time to join their families for tea. Although competition was fierce, with the magnificent Belle Steamers fleet and the New Palace Steamers' *Koh-i-noor* and *Royal Sovereign* all vying for trade, the pickings remained plentiful for all. However, GSN's passenger receipts for 1902 indicate how marginal an operation the summer excursion ships actually were with their extensive winter retirement and spring refurbishment; the Thames excursion steamers gross passenger takings were £25,200, but the annual expenditure on the fleet was £22,680, yielding a profit of just £2,520. This compared with a profit of £10,918 on the year-round passenger receipts of GSN's home and continental trade fleet.

Whereas the GSN home and near-Continental trades carried on throughout the year, the gross passenger takings were smaller than the summer season takings on the excursion fleet, but the expenses on the latter left comparatively little profit. GSN undoubtedly cross-subsidised its excursion paddle steamers. Dedicated excursion operators could not enjoy such subsidy. However, the commuter services on the Clyde and of Red Funnel at Southampton had year-round employment. The latter also had its tug fleet, and, therefore, year-round income, albeit reduced in the winter months when the tourists stayed at home. Cosens on the South Coast were always pleased for any off-season tendering duties at Portland, and especially pleased when appointed the Admiralty's term contractor there. The Medway Steam Packet Company on the Thames had the summer passenger receipts to balance against winter overhauls and upgrades, but it also owned a shipyard so that repairs could be carried out in-house as other outside jobs allowed. The crew in the summer months were the same men who worked in the yard in the winter. This was a simple win-win situation, providing year-round employment for the men and a giving them a vested interest in doing the best job they could, working, as they were, on their own ship.

But it was harder for the excursion companies that had no such alternative money stream. On the Bristol Channel (and the South Coast) P & A Campbell managed to keep its finances in order by having a large fleet operating on diverse routes, but just how some of the smaller operators survived defies belief.

The economics of the small passenger and cargo (luggage boat) type ferries on rivers and estuaries were those of demand and tariff plus any available subsidy. Of course, once a bridge or tunnel opened the ferry service was destabilised. The London river is a good example, with only one surviving (free) vehicle ferry and one passenger ferry supplementing numerous bridges and tunnels. River commuter ferries have long provided a pleasant commuting alternative to crowed trains and buses – and still do so on the Thames. However, the nonsense caused by the London County Council (LCC) in its reaction to the withdrawal in 1902 of the London Steamboat Company's cross-city and inter-bank services between Hammersmith and Greenwich was nothing short of incredible. It commissioned a fleet of thirty near-identical little paddle steamers, each with a compound diagonal engine, at a total cost of £180,000. The resulting service was excellent, with steamers calling at all piers every ten minutes.

The LCC had overlooked competition, in this case from its own newly inaugurated tram system and from its burgeoning underground railway network. Two years after the fanfare of introducing the 30 little steamers the LCC put them all up for sale, realising just £393 per vessel for the newly formed City Steamboat Company to maintain a reduced service. Others went to a variety of owners up and down the land. So what exactly had the LCC achieved, apart from poor vision and huge financial losses? It removed

all competition on the river by granting itself huge subsidies, which led to the cessation of all winter river services after the 1909 summer season.

Perhaps the pinnacle of the twentieth-century career of the British paddle steamer was its monumental service to the nation at war. This was exemplified not merely in its role as a minesweeper in the First World War, nor just in its role as minesweeper or anti-aircraft ship in the Second World War, but in its finest hours helping evacuate the British Expeditionary Force from the beaches at Dunkirk. Many brave men and feisty little ships were lost during this defiant action, as visitors to the former Red Funnel paddle steamer *Princess Elizabeth* are reminded at Dunkirk Harbour, where it is now preserved

Raleigh (1905) was one of 30 London County Council steamers put in service on the Thames.

The Red Funnel steamer *Princess Elizabeth* (1927) at Weymouth; now used in a static role as a museum ship dedicated to the Dunkirk evacuation. (AUTHOR)

New Medway Steam Packet's motor ship *Queen of the Channel* (1935) and its numerous companions ultimately spelled the death knell for the paddle steamer.

in a static role as a museum ship.

The decline in the number of paddle steamers in Britain, Europe, the Americas and elsewhere that occurred after the war and through to the 1970s was both dramatic and unstoppable. Many of the steamers were old, and repair and maintenance costs were a large drain on resources, income was essentially seasonal, fuel bills and staffing costs were rising, and the economics of alternative transport methods were compelling. Ever since the New Medway Steam Packet Company commissioned the first big passenger excursion motor vessel, *Queen of the Channel*, in the 1930s, the writing was on the wall for the paddle steamer, and even for the diesel-electric paddle 'steamer'.

One by one the coastal excursion paddle steamers, the big stern wheel river steamers on the Mississippi and other rivers, the large paddle steamers on the Hudson River above New York and on the Rhine in Germany, and those on the European lakes – in fact all the paddlers the world over – were faced with withdrawal due to spiralling costs. The era of the paddle wheel was over. The paddle steamer, in whatever form it took, became a maritime curiosity talked about with great fondness by the older generation. To the young the paddle steamer remains just a solid and immovable exhibit in a museum, of little interest to an 'iGeneration' brought up on computer games and a miscellany of electronic wizardry.

The Clyde steamer *Waverley* (1947) seen in July 1969, was built for the LNER to replace an earlier namesake lost at Dunkirk. (AUTHOR)

The preserved and operational river steamer *Kingswear Castle* (1924) at Tilbury in June 1989. (AUTHOR)

But for those of us older folk there are, around the world, a number of paddlers preserved either as static exhibits or maintained in service for the discerning traveller to enjoy. These can be identified readily on the Internet (youngsters can help with this task), and a search-engine enquiry such as 'preserved paddle steamers' will provide links to a number of worthwhile websites. One of these will be the site for the UK Paddle Steamer Preservation Society. This society has been instrumental in maintaining two paddle steamers operational in UK waters, the former Caledonian Steam Packet Company's *Waverley* and the smaller river steamer *Kingswear Castle* (see Chapter 12). All of these operational steamer services the world over rely on public patronage and charitable donation if they are to continue in service; these are your ships for you to enjoy.

So it seems the fondly remembered paddle steamer rarely turned a profit in its 200-year career. It bankrupted its famous champion Henry Bell, it required large Government mail contracts, effectively Government subsidies, to send paddlers across the Atlantic and to the Far East, and was not cost-effective once the propeller steamer arrived on the scene. Wealth creator it may have been in the early nineteenth century, wealth destroyer it certainly was in the mid-

twentieth century. But in between, during the heady days of 21-knot steamers on the English Channel and the big and fast steamers in America and Canada, some good money was made by the paddle steamer for its owner. But it was a short-lived window of profit-making, limited to the second half of Victoria's reign through to the First World War (which yielded favourable Government charter rates for shipowners) and up to the start of the Great Depression in the 1920s.

The paddle steamer made its entry when Britain was leading the world and desperately in need of mechanised sea transport and towage for the sailing ships into and out of port. The paddle steamer departed from a very different world, in which Britain was no longer a great industrial nation nor a great seafaring nation, but a nation dependent on the ubiquitous container ship for nearly all of its consumable requirements.

In a lighter vein, in memoriam, given that we do still enjoy some token survivors of the paddle steamer in its various shapes and configurations around the world, what ought to be written on the tombstone? Richard Coton in his nostalgic book *A Decline of the Paddle Steamer* offers the following epitaph:

But from where do people catch this lunatic affection for paddle steamers? I

think I probably contracted the ailment aboard those two magnificent ships the *Jeanie Deans* and *Bristol Queen*. The feeling of power as you watched those three large cranks of the *Jeanie* whirling round and round in her shadowy engine room! It was not only the sight which impressed, for who could forget the smell of hot oil and the warmth of rising steam? And you could peer through one of the portholes in the side of the paddle box and watch the floats whirling overhead and then plunging down into the water.

Americans and Canadians and the admirers of the Rhine steamers and those of the European lakes will have others. But perhaps the lasting image of Charles Dickens's fear of sailing the Atlantic in mid-winter in the small wooden paddle steamer *Britannia* should be the universal epitaph. After all, he and his wife did bottle out six months later when, in mid-summer, they took passage east, on their return from the New World, in a sailing ship.

In America, the mighty Disney Corporation has the ultimate memorial, as Bob Whittier describes:

At Disney World in Florida there are two reproduction walking-beam steamers, the *Ports o' Call* and *Southern Seas*, which are used to carry visitors on short sight-seeing trips around that establishment's waterways. They are 100 feet long and are powered by small but authentic walking-beam engines built in 1971 by the Disney organisation's technical division. These engines have cylindrical bores of 23 inches and piston strokes of 62 inches,

and run at 20 revolutions per minute. The hulls are of fibreglass. They are very much worth visiting by steamboat enthusiasts, who can get from them some idea of the appearance, operation, sounds and smells of this type of propulsion.

Canada has *Trillium*, Britain has *Waverley* and Egypt still has the venerable iron-hulled former paddle Royal Yacht *Mahroussa*. The memory of the paddle steamer will always be there, long after *Waverley* has ceased to trade, whenever that might be. The memory will be different and personal: some recall the smell of stale beer and freshly cooked food below decks, some the smell of hot oil and steam near the engine room skylight, while for others it is the distinctive sound of the paddles striking water. But let it not be overlooked that the tombstone must not just record nostalgia, and that it should also record that the paddle steamer was the vehicle of industry and the maker of commerce.

The Helensburgh Town Council archive contains the following certificate, a final epitaph, deposited by John Wood & Company, shipbuilders, in October 1826:

We certify that in the year 1811 we built for Mr Henry Bell, engineer, a small steam vessel of 40 feet keel, 10 feet 6 inch beam, called *The Comet*, she being the first vessel in Scotland, and that Mr Bell was the first person who projected and carried into effect in this kingdom the use of steam vessels, which followed immediately his steps, and have proved, and are likely much further to prove, of such amazing importance.

REFERENCES

Various relevant magazines and journals include *Sea Breezes*, *Shipping Today and Yesterday*, *The Illustrated London News* and *Wooden Boat*.

Bell, J J, *Clyde Songs and Other Verses* (Gowan & Gray, London & Glasgow, 1910)

Body, G, *British Paddle Steamers* (David & Charles, Newton Abbot, 1971)

Bowen, F C, *A Century of Atlantic Travel, 1830-1930* (Sampson Low, London, 1932)

Brodie, I, *Steamers of the Forth* (David & Charles, Newton Abbot, 1976)

Burtt, F, *Steamers of the Thames and Medway* (Richard Tilling, London, 1949)

Coton, R H, *A Decline of the Paddle Steamer* (Paddle Steamer Preservation Society, York, 1971)

Cox, B, *Paddle Steamers* (Blandford Press Ltd, Poole, 1979)

Dendy Marshall, C F, *A History of the Southern Railway* (The Southern Railway Company, London, 1936)

Dickens, C, *American Notes* (Chapman & Hall, London, 1842)

Duckworth, C L D, and Langmuir, G E, *Clyde and Other Coastal Steamers* (T Stephenson & Sons, Prescot, 1977)

Emmons, F, *Pacific Liners 1927-72* (David & Charles, Newton Abbot, 1973)

Greenhill, B, *The Ship: the Life and Death of the Merchant Sailing Ship, 1815-1965* (HMSO, London, 1980)

Henry, F, *Ships of the Isle of Man Steam Packet Company* (Brown, Son & Ferguson, Glasgow, 1962)

Hilton, G W, *Lake Michigan Steamers* (Stanford University Press, 2002)

Laird, D, *Paddy Henderson, the Story of P Henderson & Company* (P Henderson & Company, Glasgow, 1961)

Lawson, W, *Pacific Steamers* (Brown, Son & Ferguson, Glasgow, 1927)

Osborne, J C, *The Comet and Her Creators* (Private publication: J C Osborne, 2007)

Palmer, S, '"The most indefatigable activity", the General Steam Navigation Company 1824-1850', *The Journal of Transport History*, Vol. 3, pp.2-22

Robins, N S, *The Cruise Ship: A Very British Institution* (The History Press, Stroud, 2008)

——, *An Illustrated History of Thames Pleasure Steamers* (Silver Link Publishing, Kettering, 2009)

——, and Meek, D E, *The Kingdom of MacBrayne* (Birlinn, Edinburgh, 2006)

Still, W N, Watts, G P, and Rogers, B, 'Steam Navigation and the United States'. In Woodman, R, (Ed) *The History of the Ship, the Comprehensive Story of Seafaring from the Earliest Times to the Present* (Conway Maritime Press, London, 1997)

Thomas, P N, *British Steam Tugs* (Waine Research Publications, Albrighton, 1983)

——, *Steamships 1835-1875 in Contemporary Records* (book and CD) (Waine Research Publications, Albrighton, 2009)

Thornley, F C, *Past and Present Steamers of North Wales* (T Stephenson & Sons, Prescot, 1952)

Thornton, E C B, *Thames Coast Pleasure Steamers* (T Stephenson & Sons, Prescot, 1972)

Winton, J, *An Illustrated History of the Royal Navy* (Salamander Books, London, 2000)

INDEX

Index of ship's names (year built in brackets)

Aaron Manby (1821) 6
Abercraig (1939) 164
Acadia (1840) 9, 56
Achilles (1838) 27
Actæon (1837) 23, 69
Acton Grange (1907) 141
Adirondack (1896) 93
Adriatic (1856) 61-63, 65
Africa (1850) 59
Alaska (1867) 35, 41
Alaskan (1884) 36
Albany (1826) 93
Albany (1880) 94, 95
Albert Edward (1862) 74
Albert Edward (1865) 125
Albert Victor (1880) 74
Alecto, HMS (1839) 57
Alert, HMS (1840) 57
Alexander Hamilton (1924) 93, 95
Alexandra (1864) 74, 119, 120
Alice (1857) 84
Alice (1882) 138
Alliance (1855) 72, 73
Amazon (1851) 17, 24, 69
America (1863) 46
America (1869) 33, 41
America (1891) 139
America (1898) 93, 94
American Queen (1995) 92
Anglia (1847) 83
Anglia (1863) 65
Anglia (1866) 133
Antelope (1850) 31, 41
Arabia (1852) 16-18, 59
Arago (1855) 15
Arctic (1850) 14, 16, 61
Arica (1867) 40
Ariel (1846) 27
Ariel (1855) 61
Arizona (1865) 41
Arno (1865) 66, 69
Asia (1850) 59
Atalanta (1836) 6, 19, 73
Atherton, HMS (1916) 146
Athole (1866) 119
Atlantic (1849) 16
Atrato (1853) 66, 69
Avon (1842) 69
Ayr (1824) 7
Baltic (1849) 14
Banshee (1862) 84
Barry (1907) 147
Barryfield (1907) 147
Barton (1903) 140
Beaver (1836) 35
Belfast (1820) 70
Belle of Louisville (1914) 92
Ben Bolt (1854) 37
Benachie (1875) 141
Benmore (1876) 177
Bentinck (1843) 19-21, 27
Berenice (1836) 6, 19
Bismark (1914) 96
Bluebell (1906) 116
Blümlisalp (1928) 100

Bogata (1852) 40, 67
Bolivia (1849) 40, 66
Bournemouth (1884) 130
Bournemouth Queen (1908 177
Braganza (1836) 27
Bridgwater (1857) 140
Brighton (1878) 147
Brighton Belle (1900) 150, 152
Brighton Queen, HMPM (1897) 147, 152
Brisbane (1852) 37
Bristol (1867) 121
Bristol Queen (1946) 164, 165, 167, 182
Britannia (1816) 5, 42
Britannia (1840) 9, 11-13, 46, 174, 182
Britannia (1852) 133
Britannia (1896) 154
Britannia, HMY (1953) 121
British Queen (1839) 8, 50
Brodick Castle (1878) 1, 130
Brother Jonathan (1854) 36
Bute (1865) 124, 125
Bywell Castle (1865) 125, 126
Cairo (1845) 86
Calais (1896) 75
Calais-Douvres (1889) 75
Caledonia (1840) 9
Caledonia (1934) 159, 162, 168
California (1848) 30, 31, 41
Callao 1858) 40
Cambria (1870) 133
Cambria (1879) 136
Cambria (1895) 124
Cambria (1895) 147, 150
Cambridge, HMPM (1895) 147
Camel (1914) 142
Camilla (1853) 69
Canada (1866) 66
Canton (1848) 86
Cardiff Queen (1947) 165, 167, 182
Carolina (1849) 41
Carrier (1858) 86
Castalia (1874) 76, 77
Chancellor (1880) 177
Chancellor Livingston (1815) 93
Charleston (1818) 5
Charlotte (1818) 101
Charlotte Dundas (1801) 4, 174
Chicago (1837) 103
Chile (1840) 28, 29, 40
Chile (1863) 40
China (1862) 64
China (1866) 33, 35, 41
City of Brussels (1869) 14, 64
City of Buffalo (1857) 104
City of Buffalo (1896) 108, 111, 112, 114, 115
City of Chicago (1890) 111
City of Cleveland (1886) 108, 111
City of Cleveland (1907) 109-110
City of Cleveland II (1886) 111
City of Cleveland III (1907) 111, 115
City of Detroit (1889) 107, 108, 111
City of Detroit II (1889) 111, 112
City of Detroit III (1912) 109, 111, 115

City Of Edinburgh (1821) 70
City of Erie (1898) 108, 109, 111, 114
City of Glasgow (1840) 23, 69
City of Londonderry (1827) 18
City of Mackinac (1883) 108, 111
City of Pekin (1874) 35
City of Rochester (1904) 160
City of St Ignac (1886) 111
City of St Joseph (1890) 111
City of Tokio (1874) 35
City of Toledo (1891) 105, 106
Clacton Belle (1890) 122, 160
Cleddau Queen (1956) 165
Cleveland (1837) 102
Clyde (1841) 22, 23, 69
Colombia (1850) 41
Colonel Lamb (1865) 84
Colorado (1864) 31, 32, 41
Columba (1878) 177
Columbia (1840) 9
Columbia (1861) 65
Columbus (1850) 31, 41
Columbus (1865) 136
Comet (1812) 2-5, 9, 13, 50, 131, 171-173, 182
Comet (1860) 103
Commodore (1854) 36
Commonwealth (1908) 14
Compton Castle (1914) 167
Connaught (1860) 65, 78-80
Conqueror (1871) 138
Constitution (1861) 41
Consul (1896) 165, 166
Contra Costa (1914) 85
Conway (1846) 69
Coquet (1892) 135, 136
Corfe Castle (1902) 164
Cornubia (1862) 83
Costa Rica (1864) 41
Crescent City (1848) 31, 41
Crested Eagle (1925) 50, 149, 151, 162
Cynthia (1892) 133
Dakota (1865) 31, 35, 41
Dalhousie (1819) 101
Danube (1865) 69
Dee (1841) 69
Defiance (1841) 136
Delta (1859) 27
Delta King (1924) 92
Delta Queen (1924) 92
Demerara (1851) 24, 25, 69
Demologus (1812) 4
Derwent (1850) 69
Devonia (1905) 150, 153
Dextrous (1956) 144
Director (1956) 142
Dispatch (1870) 138
Don Juan (1837) 17, 27
Douglas (1858) 83
Dover (1890) 107
Dover (1896) 75
Duchess of Buccleugh (1915) 149
Duchess of Edinburgh (1880) 74
Duchess of Fife (1903) 159, 177
Duchess of Hamilton (1890) 123, 147
Duchess of Montrose (1902) 147, 159

Duchess of York (1895) 74, 75
Duchess of York (1896) 147
Duke of Devonshire (1896) 147
Dunrobin (1876) 137, 138
Eagle (1846) 69
Eagle (1864) 177
Eagle III (1910) 153
Earl of Liverpool (1824) 6
Eastern States (1901) 109, 111, 115
Eccles (1905) 141
Eclipse (1821) 70
Ecuador (1845) 40, 41, 66
Ecuador (1863) 40
Edinburgh Castle (1886) 149
Eider 91864) 66, 69
Elie (1912) 141
Embassy (1911) 165
Emperor of India (1906) 165
Empire (1843) 93
Empire (1844) 103
Empress (1879) 130, 165
Empress (1887) 75
Empress Queen (1897) 81, 147
Empress Queen (1940) 164
En Avant (1879) 96
Enchantress (1865) 122
Enterprise (1821) 6
Eppleton Hall (1914) 47
Erie (1837) 103
Erin (1846) 27
Erin's King (1862) 158
Eugénie (1862) 74, 83
Europe (1864) 65
Euxine (1847) 21, 22, 27
Express (1848) 85
Fannie (1859) 84
Farringford (1947) 164, 166, 168, 169
Favorita (1865) 40
Fiddler (1840) 133
Flying Foam (1865) 138
Forfarshire (1836) 26
Forth (1841) 22, 23, 24, 69
Francis Skiddy (1852) 93
Frank E Kirby (1890) 106, 107
Franklin (1850) 15
Frenchman (1892) 135, 136
Frontenac (1817) 101
Fulton (1855) 15
Fulton I (1812) 4, 93
Fusilier (1888) 51
Gael (1867) 120
Gallia (1913) 100
Ganges (1850) 27
Garryowen (1834) 79
General Urbstende (185 4) 37
George Brown (1860) 141
Giraffe (1860) 84
Glen Avon (1912) 147, 154, 178
Glen Gower (1922) 155, 178
Glen Sannox (1892) 124
Glen Usk (1914) 146, 154, 178
Glencoe (1846) 50, 51, 72
Goethe (1913) 96
Golden Age (1853) 33, 34, 41
Golden City (1863) 34, 41
Golden Eagle (1909) 160, 162
Golden Gate (1851) 34, 41
Gondolier (1866) 97

Goodtime (1889) 111, 112, 114
Governor General (1848) 37
Gracie Fields (1936) 152, 153
Great Britain (1843) 8, 58, 59
Great Eastern (1858) 18, 44, 59, 60, 95
Great Liverpool (1837) 19, 20, 27
Great Republic (1867) 33, 41
Great Western (1836) 8, 42, 50, 69
Great Western (1838) 102
Greater Buffalo (1924) 14, 95, 107, 110, 111, 113, 115, 155
Greater Detroit (1924) 14, 95, 107, 110, 111, 113, 115
Grenadier (1885) 51
Grinder (1958) 144
Griper (1958) 143, 144
Haddington (1846) 22, 27
Hankow (1875) 90, 91
Harbinger (1905) 156
HC 2 (1893) 148
HC 3 (1897) 148
Heather Bell (1862) 158
Hendrick Hudson (1845) 93
Hendrick Hudson (1906) 93, 95
Henry Chauncey (1864) 41
Hercules (1843) 176
Hercules (1861) 136
Hermann (1848) 15
Hibernia (1843) 14
Hibernia (1863) 65
Hilda (1862) 83
Hindostan (1842) 19-21, 27
Hindostan (1897) 89
HMPM 579 (1897) 145
Hugh Lindsey 19
Humbolt (1851) 15
Huron (1852) 103
Iberia (1836) 27
Idlewild (1914) 92
Illalong (1852) 37
Imperatrice Eugénie (1865) 65
Inca (1856) 40, 67
Inchang (1873) 90, 91
India (1839) 21, 27, 59
India (1876) 133, 136
Indiana (1840) 102
Indus (1847) 27
Invicta (1882) 74
Iona (1855) 49, 82, 83, 119
Iona (1863) 49, 83, 119
Iona (1864) 49, 83, 84
Ireland (1891) 139
Irlam (1903) 140
Isaac Newton (1846) 93
Isis (1841) 23, 69
Isthmus (1850) 31, 41
Ivanhoe (1820) 70
Ivanhoe (1880) 178
James Watt (1822) 70
Japan (1867) 33, 41
Japan (1906) 89
Jeanie Deans (1931) 44, 149-151, 159, 168, 182
John Bull (1849) 133
John H Amos (1931) 141
John L Stevens (1851) 36
Juno (1861) 84
Juno (1937) 159
Jupiter (1835) 27
Jupiter (1937) 154, 159
Karim (1917) 87
Keystone (1886) 111
Killingholme (1912) 155
King Edward (1901) 157

King Edward VII (1901) 136
Kingfisher (1906) 157
Kingswear Castle (1924) 167-169, 181
Koh-i-Noor (1892) 82, 127, 178
Korea (1902) 35
Kyles (1865) 124, 125
La Marguerite (1894) 82, 127, 128, 146
La Perlita (1853) 40, 67
La Plata (1852) 16, 24, 69
La Suisse (1910) 99
Labouchere (1858) 36
Labrador (1866) 66
Lady Mary Wood (1842) 27
Lady Moyra (1905) 139
Lafayette (1864) 65
Laguna Belle (1896) 149, 155
Lansdowne (1884) 115, 116
Laurel (1863) 84
Le Nord (1898) 75
Le Pas de Calais (1898) 75, 76
Leinster (1860) 78, 79
Leith (1837) 7
Leopard (1858) 84
Leopold III (1892) 80
Leviathan (1848) 86
Leviathan (1858) 60
Lily (1880) 54
Lima (1851) 40, 67
Limena (1865) 40, 68
Lincoln Castle (1940) 155, 168, 169
Liverpool (1837) 18, 19, 27
Liverpool (1838) 8
Lochfyne (1931) 51, 157
Lochnevis (1934) 157
London Belle (1893) 148, 160
Lord Aberdour (1866) 129
Lord Elgin (1851) 104, 105
Lord Elgin (1875) 129
Lord Mar (1876) 129
Lord Melville (1822) 70
Lord Morton (1883) 149
Lord of the Isles (1891) 157
Lord Warden (1841) 133
Lord Warden (1896) 75
Lotus (1845) 86
Louis Dagmar (1880) 74
Lucy Ashton (1888) 54, 176, 177
Lusitania (1907) 60
Lymington (1938) 164
Ma Roberts (1858) 79
Mabel Grace (1899) 74, 75
Madge Wildfire (1886) 178
Madrid (1845) 27
Magdalena (1851) 69
Magician (1844) 58
Mahroussa (1865) 122, 182
Maid of the Loch (1953) 98, 99, 165, 166, 168
Majestic (1901) 1, 70
Malta (1848) 27
Malta (1875) 140, 141
Manchuria (1904) 35
Marchioness of Lorne (1891) 124, 125, 159
Marchioness of Lorne (1935 167
Margaret & Jessie (1858) 83
Marie Henriette (1893) 81, 175
Marjory (1815) 5
Marmion (1906) 159
Marquis of Bute (1868) 120
Mars (1902) 148, 170
Marsa, HMS (1902) 148
Marsila (1860) 27

Mary Ann (1835) 95
Mary Jane (1846) 50
Mary Powell (1861) 93, 94, 175, 176
Mary Queen of Scots (1949) 55
Mauretania (1902) 164
Medina (1841) 23, 69
Medway (1841) 69
Medway Queen (1924) 2, 149, 169
Meg Merrilies (1883) 177, 178
Melton, HMS (1916) 146
Mercury (1934) 159, 162
Mersey (1858) 69
Messenger (1843) 137
Michigan (1833) 102
Milwaukee (1837) 102
Mindone (1886) 88
Minerva (1893) 147
Misr (1917) 87
Mississippi Queen (1976) 92
Monarch (1833) 26, 27, 132
Monarch (1888) 130, 165
Monarch (1924) 165, 166
Mona's Isle (1882) 81, 147, 148
Mona's Queen (1885) 81
Mongolia (1904) 35
Montana (1865) 41
Montrose (1837) 27
Monumental City (1850) 37
Moozoffer (1846) 57
Morning Star (1862) 105, 106
Mountaineer (1821) 70
Munster (1860) 78, 79
Napoleon III (1865) 74
Nebraska 1865) 31, 32, 35, 41
Nevada (1865) 31, 32, 35, 41
New Granada (1846) 40, 66
New Orleans (1848) 37
New World (1850) 48, 49, 93, 94
New York (1864) 41
New York (1887) 93, 94
Norris Castle (1942) 130
North Star (1853) 61
Northerner (1847) 31, 41
Northwest (1867) 103
Nouveau Monde (1866) 65
Nyanza (1864) 27, 65, 66
Oeanic (1899) 60
Old Trafford (1907) 47, 141
Olympo (1884) 89
Ontario (1816) 101
Oregon (1848) 30, 41
Oriental (1840) 19, 20, 27
Orinoco (1851) 69
Oriole, HMS (1910) 153, 154
Orion (1846) 71
Orizaba (1854) 36, 41
Osborne, HMY (1870) 122
Osborne, HMY, (1843) 122
Osprey (1852) 40, 67
Pacha (1842) 27
Pacific (1849) 14, 16, 61
Pacific (1859) 65
Pacific (1865) 40, 68
Panama (1848) 30, 41
Panama (1856) 67
Panama (1866) 40, 65, 68
Paramatta (1858) 69
Parana (1851) 69
Paul Pry (1847) 133
Payta (1864) 40, 67, 68
Pekin (1847) 27
Pekin (1873) 90, 91
Pen Cw (1912) 141
Pentano (1860) 40
Perseverance (1814) 131

Persia (1856) 14, 16, 61, 64
Pert (1916) 143, 144
Peru (1840 28, 29, 40
Phoenix (1808) 3, 5
Pioneer (1905) 155, 156
Planet (1855) 103
Plinlimmon, HMPM (1895) 150
Pontefract, HMS (1916) 146
Ports o' Call (1971) 182
Pottinger (1846) 27
Precursor (1841) 21, 27, 59
President (1840) 8
Prince (1851) 69
Prince Arthur (1851) 80
Prince Edward (1911) 98, 99
Prince George (1898) 98
Prince of Wales (1887) 81
Princess Alice (1865) 124-126
Princess Elizabeth (1927) 152, 179
Princess Mary (1911) 147
Princess Maud (1904) 75, 76
Princess May (1898) 98, 99
Princess of Wales (1897) 74, 75, 147
Princess Royal (1906) 165
Princesse Clementine (1896) 81
Princesse Henriette (1888) 80
Princesse Joséphine (1888) 80
Priscilla (1894) 14
Punch (1846) 133
Punch (1854) 133
Puritan (1889) 39
Pyefleet (1905) 138
Pyefleet II (1930) 138
Queen (1883) 147, 164
Queen Alexandra (1902) 157
Queen Elizabeth (1895) 97
Queen Margaret (1934) 55
Queen Mary (1933) 157
Queen of Kent (1916) 148
Queen of Thanet (1916) 148
Queen of the Channel (1935) 149, 157, 180
Queen of the Mersey (1877) 140
Queen of the North (1895) 53
Queen of the Orwell (1862) 123
Queen of the South (1931) 44, 168
Queen Victoria (1887) 81, 147
Quito (1852) 40, 67, 68
Quito (1863) 40
Quito (1867) 40
R N Rice (1866) 105, 106
Rainbow (1838) 58
Raleigh (1905) 179
Ramapura (1887) 88
Rapide (1895) 81
Rasmara (1890) 87, 88
Rattler, HMS (1843) 57
Redgauntlet (1895) 149
Reina del Mar (1956) 68
Reina del Pacifico (1931) 68
Reindeer (1840) 69
Reliant (1907) 47, 141
Republic (1850) 31, 41
Rhône (1927) 100
Richard Lander (1951) 55
Richmond (1814?) 5
Riga (1848) 100
Ripon (1846) 27
Rixton (1907) 140, 141
Rob Roy (1818) 173
Robert E Lee (1866) 92
Robert Bruce (1820) 70
Robert Fulton (1909) 93, 95
Robert Napier (1850) 86
Robert the Bruce (1934) 55

Rothsay Castle (1816) 118
Royal Daffodil (1939) 149
Royal Eagle (1932) 149, 150, 160, 162, 167
Royal Sovereign (1893) 82, 127, 178
Royal Sovereign (1937) 149
Royal Tar (1832) 18, 27
Royal William (1833) 8, 10, 50
Ryde (1937) 155, 159, 160, 168
Sable, USS (1924) 111, 115, 154
Saint George (1822) 70
Saint Laurent (1865) 65
Saint Patrick (1822) 70
Sandown (1934) 152, 155, 160
Santiago (1851) 40, 67
Santiago (1865) 40, 68
Santiago (1871) 40
Sarah Sands (1846) 41
Satellite (1848) 138
Saturno (1884) 89
Savannah (1819) 5, 6
Savoie (1914) 100
Scarborough (1866) 118
Scaufell, HMS (1937) 154, 155
Schiller (1906) 100
Scotia (1847) 83
Scotia (1862) 14, 46, 64
Sea Horse (1811) 48
Sea Horse (1837) 36, 37
Seabird (1859) 103
Seeandbee (1913) 109, 111, 115, 154
Seine (1860) 69
Severn (1842) 69
Shanghai (1873) 90, 91
Shanklin (1924) 166
Shannon (1859) 69
Sheboygan (1869) 103
Siberia (1902) 35
Silver Spray (1890) 107
Simplon (1920) 99
Singapore (1850) 27
Sir Francis Drake (1973) 139
Sir Walter Raleigh (1876) 139
Sir Walter Scott (1900) 42
Sirius (1837) 8
Skiddaw, HMS (1896) 154
Slieve Bearnagh (1894) 149
Solano (1878) 85
Solent (1853) 69
Solent Queen (1916) 148
Solway (1841) 23, 69
Sonora (1853) 41
Sophia Jane (1831) 37
Southern Seas (1971) 182
Southsea (1930) 159
Southwold Belle (1900) 160
Sovereign (1822) 70
Speedwell (1908) 138
Sprague (1901) 143, 144
St John (1864) 93
St Louis (1854) 41
St Tudno (1891) 127, 128, 147
Stadt Luzern (1837) 100
Stadt Luzern (1928) 100
Stag (1853) 84
State of New York (1883) 108, 111
Steam Boat (1807) 3, 93, 95, 171
Stirling Castle (1814) 173
Stirling Castle (1899) 147
Sudan (1921) 86
Sultan (1847) 27
Sultana (1868) 120
Superb (1821) 70
Swallow (1875) 128
Swift (1822) 70

Swift (1875) 128
Syria (1863) 27
Taiping (1876) 88
Talbot (1819) 44, 70
Talca (1862) 40
Talisman (1935) 55, 162, 163
Tamar (1854) 24, 69
Tartar (1853) 86
Tashmoo (1900) 109, 113, 128
Tattershall Castle (1934) 168, 169
Tay (1841) 22, 23, 69
Telegraph (1852) 37
Tennessee (1848) 41
Teviot (1841) 24, 69
Thames (1841) 22, 69
Thames Queen (1898) 150
The Queen (1903) 75
Thistle (1859) 84
Tiber (1846) 27
Titanic (1912) 139
Totnes Castle (1923) 167
Trent (1841) 66, 69
Trident (1841) 26, 27, 121
Trillium (1910) 104, 116, 182
Triton (1882) 58
Truxillo (1972) 40
Tweed (1841) 23, 69
Tyne (1854) 69
Tyne Steamboat (1814) 131
Ulster (1860) 78-80
Uncle Sam (1849) 132
Uncle Sam (1852) 41
Unicorn (1838) 41
Union (1822) 70
United Service (1871) 136
United States (1840) 18, 19, 27
Unterwalden (1901) 100
Valparaiso (1856) 40, 67
Vanderbilt (1855) 61, 64
Vecta (1938) 164
Vectis (1853) 27
Viceroy (1875) 120, 121
Victoria (1853) 133
Victoria (1861) 74
Victoria (1882) 138
Victoria (1884) 165, 166
Victoria and Albert, HMY (1843) 121
Victoria and Albert, HMY (1855) 121, 122
Victoria and Albert, HMY (1899) 121
Violet (1880) 54
Vivid (1864) 177
Waldstätter (1847) 100
Walk-on-the-Water (1818) 102
Walney (1904) 138, 139
Walton Belle (1897) 145, 148
Warrior, HMS (1861) 58
Washington (1847) 15
Washington (1864) 65
Waterloo (1816) 5, 70
Waverley (1885) 124
Waverley (1899) 153
Waverley (1947) 1, 2, 164-166, 168, 169, 180-182
Western States (1902) 109, 111, 112, 115
Westward Ho (1894) 124, 147
Whippingham (1930) 159
William Fawcett (1828) 17, 18
William IV (1831) 37
William Tell (1908) 100
Wilson G Hunt (1849) 121
Wingfield Castle (1934) 168, 169
Wolverine, USS (1913) 111, 115, 154
Woolwich Belle (1891) 122, 123, 150

Wyvern (1905) 139
Yarmouth Belle (1898) 145
Yoma (1886) 88

Index of proper names

Anderson, Arthur 17, 19
Aspinwall, William Henry 30
Atlantic Mail Steamship Co. 31
Atlantic Royal Mail Steam Navigation Co. 64
Australian Steam Navigation Co. 37
Bell, Henry 2-5, 7, 9, 12, 173, 181
Belle Steamers 122, 141
Bourne, Richard 17
British India Steam Navigation Co. 87, 88
Brunel, Isambard 8, 42, 44, 58-60
Burns, James 7, 172
Burns Line 7
Burns, G&J / J&G 71, 84
Burns, George 5, 7-10, 172
Caledonian Steam Packet Co. 123, 158
Cameron & Co., Thos. 5
Campbell, P&A 124, 146, 147, 164, 177, 178
Chappell, Capt. Edward 22, 23
China Navigation Co. 90, 91
City of Dublin Steam Packet Co. 80
Cleveland & Buffalo Transit Co. 108-112
Collins Line 14-16, 59, 61, 62
Collins, Israel 15
Cook, Thomas 86, 87
Cunard & Son, Abraham 9
Cunard Line 59, 61, 64
Cunard, Samuel 8-11, 15, 172
Denny, Peter 90, 172
Denny, William 88-90, 92, 175
Detroit & Cleveland Navigation Co. 14, 105, 108-112
Dickens, Charles 11, 12, 173, 174
Dublin & London Steam Packet Co. 17
Duncan, Robert 9
East India Co. 6, 19, 21, 57, 79
Eastern Rly. 74
Eastern Steam Navigation Co. 21, 59
Elder, David 5
Elder, John 5, 68
Eltringham, J T & Co. 141
Ericcson, Jon 26
Fairfield Shipbuilding & Engineering 5, 81, 82, 126, 127, 147, 162
Fall River Line 14, 38, 39
Fitch, John 3
French Line (CGT) 65
Fulton, Robert 3, 4, 101
Gainsborough United Steam Packet 118
Galloway, John 89
General Steam Navigation Co. 6, 7, 25, 26, 58, 83, 121, 128, 161, 178
Glasgow & South Western Rly. 120, 121, 124
Glasgow, Dublin & Londonderry Steam Packet 5
Glover, Capt. William 29
Great War 145-149, 181
Grinstead, Capt. William 126
Holliday, Ben 31
Hudson Bay Co. 36
Hutcheson, David 49, 50, 82-84

Inman Line 64
Irrawaddy Flotilla Co. 87-90
Isle of Man Steam Packet Co. 81, 83, 126, 147
Kirby, Frank E 106-108
Köln Düsseldorf 97
Laird & Sons, Alex A 5
Laird, John 58, 79, 172
Law, George 30, 31
Livingston, Mortimore 15
London, Chatham & Dover Rly. 74, 75
MacBrayne, David 50
MacLellan, Lewis 5
Mail Steamer Bill, US (1847) 30
Mathie & Theakstone 7
McConnell & Laird 5
McIver, David 8-10
McQueen, James 22, 23, 66
Napier, David 4, 9-11, 44
Napier, Robert 4, 70, 83, 85
New York & Havre Steam Packet Co. 15, 16
North American Royal Mail Steam Packet 8
North British Rly. 85, 86
Ocean Steam Navigation Co. 15
P&O 19-21, 59, 65, 66, 86
Pacific Coast Steamship Co. 36
Pacific Mail Steamship Co. 15, 28, 30-36, 41, 46
Pacific Steam Navigation Co. 28-30, 40, 66-68
Peacock, Capt. George 29
Peninsula Steam Navigation Co. 17-19
Pettit Smith, Francis 26
Quebec & Halifax Steam Navigation 10
Robertson, John 4
Rogers, Capt. Moses 5
Royal Mail Steam Packet Co. 17, 22-25, 27, 66, 69
Royal Mail Steam Packet Co. 69
Rumsey, James 3
Russell, John Scott 22
South Eastern & Continental Steam Packet Co. 74, 83
South Eastern Rly. 74, 75
Southern Pacific Co. 35
Steele, Robert 9, 16
Stevens, John 3, 4
Symington, William 4
Taylor, James 4
Toronto Ferry Co. 116
United States Mail Steamship Co. 30, 31
Vanderbilt Line 61, 64
Vanderbilt, Cornelius 61
Victoria Steamboat Association 82, 126, 127
Vulcan Foundry 9
Watkins, William Ltd. 132, 133
Webb, William 31
Wheelwright, William 28-30, 66
Willcox, Brodie 17
Wood, Charles 9, 10, 70
Wood, John 4, 7, 9
World War II 90, 149-156, 176